THE
THEOLOGY OF
THE EARLY
GREEK PHILOSOPHERS

Oxford University Press, Amen House, London E.C.4

GLASGOW NEW YORK TORONTO MELBOURNE WELLINGTON
BOMBAY CALCUTTA MADRAS KARACHI LAHORE DACCA
CAPE TOWN SALISBURY NAIROBI IBADAN ACCRA
KUALA LUMPUR HONG KONG

THE
THEOLOGY OF
THE EARLY
GREEK PHILOSOPHERS

THE GIFFORD LECTURES
1936

BY

WERNER JAEGER

OXFORD
AT THE CLARENDON PRESS

Translated for the Gifford Lectures,
from the German manuscript,
by EDWARD S. ROBINSON

FIRST EDITION 1947
REPRINTED 1948, 1952

REPRINTED LITHOGRAPHICALLY IN GREAT BRITAIN
AT THE UNIVERSITY PRESS, OXFORD
FROM SHEETS OF THE FIRST EDITION
1960, 1964

PREFACE

THIS book, which might be entitled *The Origin of Natural Theology and the Greeks*, represents the Gifford Lectures which I delivered at the University of St. Andrews, Scotland, in 1936. How this subject is related to the purpose of the Gifford Lectures has been stated in the first chapter. The publication of this book has been delayed by other books which I have had to finish during these past ten years. The lectures now appear in a greatly improved form and with numerous additions, most of all the extensive notes. Although these have been printed at the end of the volume, for the convenience of the general reader, they form an essential part of my inquiry.

It is perhaps not unnecessary to state that the present book does not pretend to give a complete history of the early period of Greek philosophy with which it is concerned. Rather, I have concentrated on one particular aspect of this much-discussed subject, an aspect which has been unduly neglected or minimized by scholars of the positivistic school because in the early Greek philosophy of nature they saw their own likeness. Reacting against this one-sided picture, the opponents of this school have represented all Greek cosmological thought as an outgrowth of mysticism and Orphism, something quite irrational. If we avoid these extremes, there remains the fact that the new and revolutionizing ideas which these early Greek thinkers developed about the nature of the universe had a direct impact upon their conception of what they—in a new sense—called 'God' or 'the Divine'. It goes without saying that the terms 'God', 'the Divine', and 'theology' must not be understood here in their later Christian but in the Greek sense. The history of the philosophical theology of the Greeks is the history of their rational approach to the nature of reality itself in its successive phases.

In the present book I have traced this development through the heroic age of Greek cosmological thought down to the time of the Sophists. In a second volume, against the pre-Socratic background, I should like to treat the period from Socrates and Plato down to the time when, under the influence of this tradition of Greek philosophical theology, the Jewish-Christian religion transformed itself into a theological system in the Greek manner, in order to force its admission to the Hellenistic world.

It is my pleasant duty to thank the Delegates of the Clarendon Press for their generous offer to publish this volume and for the meticulous care with which it has been printed. I am greatly indebted to my translator, Professor Edward S. Robinson, now of the University of Kansas, and to Messrs. James E. Walsh and Cedric Whitman of Harvard University for their kind assistance with the final revision of the manuscript. I owe many thanks to Mrs. Cedric Whitman for making the indexes to the book.

W. J.

HARVARD UNIVERSITY
CAMBRIDGE, MASSACHUSETTS
January, 1947

CONTENTS

Hesiod – 10 –

CONTENTS

CHAPTER I

THE THEOLOGY OF THE GREEK THINKERS

THE aim of the Gifford Lectures has been determined once and for all by their founder, who specified that they should deal with that group of problems which we designate by the name of natural theology. Hitherto most of the lecturers have been philosophers or theologians. If I, as classical philologist and student of the humanities, have any justification for ranging my own efforts in this field along with theirs, it lies solely in Lord Gifford's further stipulation that the lectures may also deal with the history of these problems.

The venerable chain of tradition by which this history is linked together spans two and a half millennia. Its value is by no means purely antiquarian. Philosophical thought is much more closely and indissolubly bound up with its history than are the special sciences with theirs. One might perhaps say that the relation between modern and ancient philosophy is more comparable to that between the works of the poets of our own time and the great classical poems of the past. For here again it is from the immortality of past greatness that the new creation draws its vital breath.

Whenever we speak of the beginnings of European philosophy we think of the Greeks; and any attempt to trace the origins of natural or philosophical theology must likewise begin with them. The idea of *theologia naturalis* has come to our world from a work that has long since become classical for the Christian occident—the *De civitate Dei* of St. Augustine. After attacking belief in heathen gods as an illusion throughout his first five books,[1] he proceeds in the sixth to expound the Christian doctrine of the One God and sets out to demonstrate its thorough accordance with the deepest insights of Greek philosophy. This view of Christian theology as confirming and rounding out the truths of pre-Christian thought expresses very well the positive side of the relations between the new religion and pagan antiquity. Now for St. Augustine, as for any typical Neoplatonist of his century, the one supreme representative of Greek philosophy was Plato; the other thinkers were merely minor figures around the base of Plato's mighty monument.[2]

During the Middle Ages this commanding position was gradually usurped by Aristotle, and it is only since the Renaissance that Plato has again been his serious competitor. But throughout this period Greek philosophy—whether Platonic or Aristotelian —together with a gradually increasing amount of Greek science in Latin translation, was all that was left of Greek culture in the West at a time when the knowledge of the Greek language had vanished in the general cultural decline. If the continuity of the ancient Greek tradition was never entirely broken in Europe, it is due to the fact that Greek philosophy kept it alive. But this would not have been possible had not that same philosophy, as *theologia naturalis*, served as the basis for the *theologia supernaturalis* of Christianity.

Originally, however, the concept of natural theology did not arise in opposition to supernatural theology, an idea which was unknown to the ancient world. If we want to understand what natural theology meant to those who first conceived the idea, we must see it in its genetic context. The concept of natural theology was, as St. Augustine himself states, one which he had taken from the *Antiquitates rerum humanarum et divinarum* of M. Terentius Varro,[3] the prolific Roman writer and learned encyclopaedist of the last days of the republic (116–27 B.C.). In the second part of this massive work, which was entitled *Antiquitates rerum divinarum*, Varro had built up a theory of the Roman gods with thoroughgoing consistency and striking antiquarian erudition. According to St. Augustine he distinguished three kinds of theology (*genera theologiae*): mythical, political, and natural.[4] Mythical theology had for its domain the world of the gods as described by the poets; political theology included the official State religion and its institutions and cults; natural theology was a field for the philosophers— the theory of the nature of the divine as revealed in the nature of reality. Only natural theology could be called religion in the true sense, since a real religion meant for St. Augustine a religion which is true; the poets' mythical theology presented merely a world of beautiful make-believe. By Varro's time the State religion was already beginning to decline; he hoped to save it by maintaining that religion derives its own validity from the authority of the State as the earlier of the two institutions. Religion is to him primarily one of the basic forms in the

social life of the human community.[5] This thesis is one which
St. Augustine stoutly opposes. He looks upon Varro's State
gods as not a whit better or truer than the infamous myths of
the poets. He excuses Varro's reactionary and—as it seems to
him—fundamentally false attitude towards the whole problem
of State religion by pointing out that Varro was living in a time
of scant political liberty, with the old order crumbling about
him, so that his own conservatism compelled him to defend the
Roman national religion as the very soul of the Roman republic.[6]
But if there be some truth in this observation, yet for the same
reason the old Roman religion, even in its most recent and
strongly Hellenized form, was unable to become the religion of
the empire in which so many different nations were united. To
St. Augustine it is inconceivable that any true religion should be
restricted to a single nation. God is essentially universal and
must be worshipped universally.[7] This, indeed, is a basic
Christian doctrine; but it is in the universalism of Greek philosophy that St. Augustine finds its chief support. Greek philosophy is genuine natural theology because it is based on rational
insight into the nature of reality itself; the theologies of myth
and State, on the contrary, have nothing to do with nature but
are mere artificial conventions, entirely man-made. St. Augustine himself says that this opposition is the very basis of the
concept of natural theology.[8] Obviously he has in mind the
old antithesis of φύσει and θέσει. Even Socrates' pupil Antisthenes, whose influence upon the Stoic philosophy was profound, had distinguished the one φύσει θεός from the many
θέσει θεοί,[9] among whom he included the gods of the poets no
less than those of the official cult. So from the standpoint of
natural theology the gods of the poets and those of the State
were on precisely the same footing. This is a point which St.
Augustine quite properly brings up against Varro.[10] Obviously
Varro's threefold division was intended to blur the sharpness
of this antithesis in order that the State gods might be rescued
from the general repudiation of the θέσει θεοί and thus be permitted to retain their birthright. The division was really
a compromise. We do not know who first introduced it. At
any rate it must have been some Hellenistic (probably Stoic)
philosopher, for Varro still used for his three *genera theologiae* the Greek adjectives *mythicon*, *politicon*, and *physicon*.

St. Augustine was one of the first to replace the Greek word *physicos* by the Latin *naturalis*.[11]

The word 'theology' is much older than the concept of natural theology and the Varronian trichotomy. But theology is also a specific creation of the Greek mind.[12] This fact is not always rightly understood and deserves special emphasis, for it concerns not only the word but even more the thing which it expresses. Theology is a mental attitude which is characteristically Greek, and has something to do with the great importance which the Greek thinkers attribute to the *logos*, for the word *theologia* means the approach to God or the gods (*theoi*) by means of the *logos*. To the Greeks God became a problem. Again, it will be better to trace the development of both the idea and the word in the history of the language, rather than to begin with a systematic discussion of the relations between theology and philosophy, for such general definitions are never valid for more than a limited period.

The words θεολόγος, θεολογία, θεολογεῖν, θεολογικός, were created in the philosophical language of Plato and Aristotle. Plato was the first who used the word 'theology' (θεολογία), and he evidently was the creator of the idea. He introduced it in his *Republic*, where he wanted to set up certain philosophical standards and criteria for poetry. In his ideal state the poets must avoid the errors of Homer, Hesiod, and the poetic tradition in general, and rise in their representation of the gods to the level of philosophic truth. The mythical deities of early Greek poetry were tinged with all kinds of human weakness; but such an idea of the gods was irreconcilable with Plato's and Socrates' rational conception of the divine. Thus, when Plato set forth τύποι περὶ θεολογίας, 'outlines of theology', in the *Republic*,[13] the creation of that new word sprang from the conflict between the mythical tradition and the natural (rational) approach to the problem of God. Both in the *Republic* and the *Laws* Plato's philosophy appears, at its highest level, as theology in this sense. Thereafter every system of Greek philosophy (save only the Sceptic) culminated in theology, and we can distinguish a Platonic, Aristotelian, Epicurean, Stoic, Neopythagorean, and Neoplatonic theology.

The words derived from θεολογία are particularly frequent in the works of Aristotle and his school.[14] In his writings they are used to indicate a special complex of problems and a special intellectual attitude.[15] But his usage apparently involves an inner contradiction. On the one hand, he understands by 'theology' that fundamental branch of philosophical science which he also calls 'first philosophy' or 'science of first principles'—the branch which later acquires the name of 'metaphysics' among his followers. In this sense theology is the ultimate and highest goal of all philosophical study of Being.[16] In historical contexts, however, he uses the term to designate certain non-philosophers such as Hesiod and Pherecydes, whom he contrasts rather sharply with the oldest genuine philosophers or physicists.[17] In this sense one might say of the older period that philosophy begins where theology ends. We can find good evidence of this conception in the first book of Aristotle's lost dialogue *On Philosophy*, which was highly renowned in antiquity. When, for instance, he discusses the historical antecedents of his own scientific philosophy and goes so far as to take the religious systems of the Orient into account, I suspect that the remarkable range of his purview can be most simply explained if we remember that the men who stood for this kind of wisdom (σοφία) impressed him as falling into the category of θεολόγος in the second sense I have described.[18] Aristotle's pupil Eudemus of Rhodes, the first man to write a history of theology, uses the same system of classification. Accordingly he too gives special attention to the Oriental religious systems when he deals with the contributions of the Greek verse- and prose-writers on theogony—the origin of the gods. But Eudemus would never have included his master Aristotle, the creator of metaphysics or theology in the philosophical sense, among the theologians.

I should like to dispel this apparent contradiction by referring to a passage in the twelfth book of the *Metaphysics*, where Aristotle, after developing his own theory of the unmoved mover of the universe and the movers of the spheres, turns back to the ancient religious conception of the gods in heaven. He sees here an intimation of the truth; but religion, he feels, has amplified this true intimation mythologically by inventing the anthropomorphic gods.[19] Thus the theologians represent human thought in its primitive mythological stage. In later years philosophy returns—on a rational plane—to the problem which the theologians have already attacked in their own way. In this hour a conception is born sufficiently comprehensive to take both these stages into account: the conception of theology as we find it in Plato and Aristotle.

Even to-day one might easily begin the history of philosophical theology with this period, as Edward Caird has done in his excellent book *The Evolution of Theology in the Greek Philosophers*, the product of his own Gifford Lectures at the University of Glasgow.[20] Similarly Paul Elmer More, writing with an eye to the origins of Christian theology, began his long series of works on *The Greek Tradition* with a volume on *The Religion of Plato*.[21] It is true that in Plato we find the first systematic approach to this problem. But philosophical assertions about the divine are to be found in pre-Platonic thinkers from the very first. These strike me as extremely significant for the relations between religion and philosophical thought. If one bears in mind certain aspects of the philosophy of the Hellenistic and imperial periods, he will have no desire to maintain that the value and originality of the religious ideas of a philosophical school must always be directly proportionate to the degree of its systematic ambitions. I should like, therefore, to trace in these lectures the very earliest beginnings of theology in Greek philosophic thought, with no attempt to follow its later development.[22] What the Epicurean Velleius tries to do in the first book of Cicero's *De natura deorum* and the Stoic Lucilius Balbus in the second book of that dialogue, and what St. Augustine does in the *De civitate Dei*, where he likewise starts the history of theology with the thinkers of the Milesian school —that we shall undertake once more on the basis of careful philological analysis, without being influenced by any philosophical dogma.[23] We shall find that the problem of the Divine occupies a much larger place in the speculations of the early natural philosophers than we are often ready to acknowledge, and that it receives in actuality a much greater share of their attention than we might be led to expect from Aristotle's picture of the development of philosophy in the first book of the *Metaphysics*.

In later Greek philosophy, which is more systematically worked out, theology is so clearly distinguished from the other branches of thought that it is easy to give it separate treatment.

But in the oldest Greek thought there is no such differentiation. Hence there arises a methodological difficulty; for if we really hope to understand the isolated utterances of Anaximander or Heraclitus on God or 'the Divine', we must always take their philosophy as a whole, as an indivisible organism, never considering the theological components apart from the physical or ontological. On the other hand, there are obvious reasons why it is here impossible to spread out all the traditional material before us and enter into all the special problems in the history of the earliest Greek thought. Since this has been done fairly often, we shall have to presuppose some acquaintance with the traditional field of research.[24] We must now turn our attention to one particular side of philosophical thought, without losing sight of the whole context. In this way we may approach some of the relevant testimonia at rather close range and deal with them by direct interpretation. For herein, I think, lies our only chance of making new headway where the terrain has already been so thoroughly explored.

Ever since the time of Aristotle it has been one of the conventions of the history of philosophy to look at these thinkers from a perspective that emphasizes their achievements as natural scientists.[25] Aristotle called them the φυσικοί (in the ancient sense of the term), which in turn led modern interpreters of the nineteenth century to understand them as the first physicists (in the modern sense). The pioneers of natural science could easily be pardoned, so it seemed, for having mingled their great new scientific intuitions with other half-mythological elements: it was the task of the modern historical mind to separate these features from each other and to select as truly relevant the scientific ideas which can be construed as an anticipation of our own empirical science. The modern historians of Greek philosophy who lived during the period of the metaphysical systems of Hegel and the other German idealists, namely Zeller and his school, dwelt primarily on Plato, Aristotle, and the speculative philosophers. The age of positivism which followed, with such representatives as Burnet and Gomperz, stressed in turn the empirical and scientific character of the early thinkers. In their zeal for proving the modernity of the pre-Socratics they have often minimized or even neglected that aspect of the first philosophers with which this book is concerned in approaching them in the perspective of the origin of natural theology. This is the perspective in which the ancients themselves saw these philosophers. When Cicero in his *De natura deorum* and St. Augustine in the *De civitate Dei* see the physicists from Thales to Anaxagoras as the first theologians, they only repeat what they found in their Greek sources.

If the position of pre-Socratic thought in the history of Greek philosophy needs to be revised and complemented in this sense, our view of its relationship to Greek religion must also be affected. The theology of the early philosophers makes them appear quite as much a part of the history of Greek religion as of the history of philosophy. The usual histories of religion have hardly ever treated their theology seriously in this larger context, presumably because their chief interest has always been more in the cult divinities and the institutions of the religious life than in ideas. Wilamowitz, in his posthumous work *Der Glaube der Hellenen*, has done us the great service of breaking with this prejudice and has given the Greek philosophers a place in the religious development of the Greek people.[26] But, as is natural in a work of such enormous scope, he never really interprets the words of the philosophers in the context of their entire thought or seeks to determine their full meaning. His appreciation of them is seriously handicapped by a Protestant bias that keeps him from seeing any genuine religion in either the intellectual world or cult piety, even when these might teach us something important about what religion meant to the Greeks. So one of our primary aims must be to give the religion of the philosophers—and not only that of the pre-Socratic thinkers—a really positive place in our effort to understand how Greek religion developed. Before we can do this adequately, we must first get a better grasp of the specific form which religious thought takes when it enters the stage of independent philosophical speculation. It is easy to decree *a priori* that the sublime ideas which a certain age of human history formed about the nature of the Divine do not correspond to our average concept of what religion is and therefore should be left to philosophers and physicists, who for their part do not particularly care for them because they are not pure reason. This situation is only another instance of that most unfortunate lack of integration in human life which is characteristic of our modern civilization and which we try to impose on former ages in our historical interpretation of their products. In so doing we often deprive ourselves of the insight into their true nature, and perhaps even of the blessing, which they could afford us. A genuine understanding of the religious intellectualism of the early Greeks is one of the first steps on the road towards a more adequate evaluation of the later historical phases of the Greek mind. Out of these heroic beginnings there gradually developed the philosophical transformation and revival of religion in Plato's theology, in the systems of Aristotle and the Hellenistic schools (Stoics, Epicureans, &c.), and most of all in the system of theology which was the product of the conflict and mutual penetration of Greek tradition with Jewish and other Oriental religions and finally with the Christian faith. The spiritual foundations of this growing humanistic world unity were (1) the *Imperium Romanum*, so far as it was maintained by the idea of a world-wide rule of law and justice; (2) the Greek *paideia*, so far as it was conceived as the start of a universal human culture; and (3) a 'universal' (καθολική) theology as the religious framework of such a civilization. The philosophical theology of the early Greek thinkers, as St. Augustine in his *De civitate Dei* clearly recognized and emphatically enounced, marks the starting-point of this gradually developing universal theology.

I long ago started my work on pre-Socratic philosophy under such men as Hermann Diels and Wilamowitz and am bound to approach it as a part of the history of the Greek genius; but I have also spent a whole life on the study of Christian tradition, especially in its ancient Greek and Roman phase. I therefore am deeply impressed by the continuity of the fundamental forms of thought and expression which triumphantly bridges the chasm between these antithetic periods of the human mind and integrates them into one universal civilization.

Earlier writers than Aristotle have noticed some relationship between certain ideas of the natural philosophers and those of the earliest Greek poets. To be sure, the suggestion that Homer anticipated Thales' theory that water is the basic principle of all things (a suggestion which may have come from the Platonic school) is one which Aristotle himself regards with an air of critical reserve.[27] But as far as the problems of metaphysics are concerned even he seems to look on Hesiod and others like him as forerunners of philosophy. He calls them the πρῶτοι θεολογήσαντες, just as in the same connexion he speaks of the older philosophers as πρῶτοι φιλοσοφήσαντες. This implies that even in the fourth century the word θεολογεῖν could be used in a sense quite properly applicable to the θεολογεῖν of the philosophers.[28] But when Aristotle uses the word πρῶτοι, it involves the further connotation of something undeveloped and primitive—something to be followed by a higher stage of development. In another passage he contrasts the philosophers with the older theologians of the Hesiodic type: the essential thing about the philosophers, he asserts, is that they proceed by strict methods of proof; the theologians, on the other hand, are μυθικῶς σοφιζόμενοι.[29] This is a very pregnant formulation; it brings out both a common factor and an element of difference: the theologians are like the philosophers in that they promulgate certain doctrines (σοφίζονται); unlike them, however, in that they do so 'in mythical form' (μυθικῶς).

In general the former characteristic does not apply to Homer; on the contrary, it indicates precisely the nature of the difference between Hesiod's *Theogony* and the Homeric epic. Only in those isolated passages which furnish the chief excuse for Aristotle's classifying Homer among the theologians does he too appear in this light.[30] When the *Iliad* refers to Oceanus as the origin and source of all the gods, this has a theogonical ring; but when in another verse he is described as the origin and source of all things, this seems like nothing more than a transparent way of expressing in mythical guise the comparatively matter-of-fact conception that everything arose from water.[31] As a rule the heroic legends that form the content of the Homeric poems seldom give occasion for doctrinal application. But this exceptional passage may well belong to one of the later portions of the *Iliad*. If so, we may hazard the inference that the intellectual standpoint which we find here belongs to a later stage of development than that in which the heroic epic of the Homeric type reached its height.[32] Of course, we must not make too sharp a distinction between heroic legend and the myths of the gods, for both were primarily attempts to describe what had already come to pass, and both were originally looked upon as true. On the other hand, the legends

of the gods naturally afforded much more opportunity for
σοφίζεσθαι—that is, for the introduction of original explanations and constructions such as we find in Hesiod's *Theogony*.
It is precisely this coalescence of the traditional representations
of the gods with the element of subjective intellectual activity
that determines the theological character of Hesiod's work.

In the older epic there was no thought of calling the poet by
his name; he was simply an anonymous vehicle for inspiration
from the Muses, carrying far and wide the legends of ancient
times. This fact provides a standard *topos* for *prooimia*; but
Hesiod makes it an occasion for a bit of personal history. He
tells us how the Muses appeared to him, Hesiod, while he was
tending his sheep at the foot of Mount Helicon, and gave him
the rhapsode's staff to betoken his mission as a singer. Here
the new emergence of the subjective is already clearly expressed.
But its appearance also implies a new responsibility. The
Muses say to Hesiod:

We know how to tell many falsehoods that sound like the truth;
But we also know how to utter the truth when we choose.[33]

Obviously Hesiod feels that here he has gone beyond the older
poets; for he claims to tell the truth about the very beings that
it is hardest to know anything about—the gods themselves.[34]
His work shall reveal the origin of all the gods now reigning upon
Olympus; he will also tell us how the world has come to be,
with all its present order.[35] He must, therefore, record all the
relevant myths and show how they fit together; he may perhaps
have to eliminate many versions that strike him as incorrect, or
devise new connexions where tradition has none to supply.

Hesiod's basic postulate is that even the gods have come into
being. This was by no means a new idea at the time. It had
often been presupposed in the legends, even though it might
seem inconsistent with the familiar language about the eternal
gods.[36] Zeus himself and many others of the great cult divinities
had had their own parents and youthful years. Such stories
had even been told of Kronos and Rheia, who were made the
children of Ouranos and Gaia. Farther back than this the series
did not go; the ultimate beginning had been reached, and no
more questions were asked. No one who tried to bring all these
tales of the divine ancestry into a definite sequence, as Hesiod

did, could help coming to view the gods themselves rather differently. The idea of a series of successive procreations, which is Hesiod's solution of the problem, becomes the principle by which all the individuals of the divine world can at last be linked together.[37]

In this way a systematic genealogy of the gods is developed.[38] To Hesiod, who can see divine personalities even in physical forces like heaven and earth, generation is the one real form of becoming. If we bear this fact clearly in mind, we can trace, behind the urge to schematize all the generations of the gods from the very beginning of the world, a type of causal thinking unmistakably rational in the consistency with which it is carried out, even though it takes the form of myth.[39] It makes little difference that the idea of cause and effect had not yet appeared; for this is genuinely σοφίζεσθαι, even if μυθικῶς.

But in Hesiod we find more than passive submission to an urge for mythical narration: when he resorts to telling the old myths he has actual problems in mind which he feels he is now equipped to answer. This is evident everywhere, not merely in his construction of the divine genealogy. In his other surviving poem, the *Works and Days*, where he expounds to the peasantry his doctrine of human labour, its necessity, and its blessings, he raises the problem of toil and hardships and how they have come to mankind. Even in an utterly non-mythological context, which plunges us directly into the poet's immediate environment, he tries to solve the philosophical problem in terms of traditional myths. He tells us how in the beginning men lived in a state of paradise without work or exertion, and how the theft of fire by Prometheus and the creation of Pandora, the first woman, brought grief and responsibility into the world. This is theology in a very real sense, for it gives us a mythical explanation of certain moral and social facts, comparable to the biblical account of the Fall. Hesiod's theology, thus applied to practical life, should give us a keener insight into its true nature.[40] In the doctrine of Eris—the malicious goddess of strife—with which he opens his *Works and Days* as a warning to his greedy and contentious brother Perses, he expressly makes reference to his own *Theogony*,[41] though he does so only to correct his earlier doctrine: for he now gives the spiteful Eris of the *Theogony* a sister goddess, the good Eris, who presides over all the more wholesome competition in this world. The very existence of this later correction is striking evidence of the extent to which Hesiod's attitude towards mythology was affected by the new issues he raised. These questions keep turning up everywhere throughout the *Theogony*; and their scope is broad enough to include all the problems to which the religious consciousness of his period gives rise, whether he seeks to explain the fact of evil and tribulation or to justify the reign of the gods themselves. For even they are not immune from criticism, now that man's own devices for regulation of State and community are beginning to be called into question; and Hesiod's genealogical conception of the divine government makes him see this world as a battlefield for the great new gods of Light, and the dark, wayward, elemental powers of ages long since past. The struggle of these two groups for supremacy has at last raged itself out, and Zeus is victorious; but the earth's murky depths still fume and bubble with the reeking breath of the vanquished. In thus depicting the punishment of the rebels in the world below,[42] no less than in his invectives against man's injustice here on earth as a crime against the authority of Zeus and his divine justice, Hesiod reveals the theological nature of his thought.

While the *Theogony* invades the realm of human life, it never loses touch with the natural world-order. Theogony leads back to cosmogony when the poet proceeds to connect the reigning dynasty of the gods with the primeval Ouranos and Gaia. We have already noted that Hesiod's thought never reaches beyond Heaven and Earth, the two foundations of the visible world; before these was Chaos.[43] In the *Physics* Aristotle speaks of Chaos as empty space (τόπος);[44] and another passage of the *Theogony* shows it to be nothing else than the space that yawns between Earth and Heaven.[45] Apparently the idea of Chaos belongs to the prehistoric heritage of the Indo-European peoples; for the word is connected with χάσκω ('gape'), and from the same stem *gap*- Nordic mythology has formed the word *ginungagap* to express this same notion of the gaping abyss that existed at the beginning of the world. The common idea of Chaos as something in which all things are wildly confused is quite mistaken; and the antithesis between Chaos and Cosmos, which rests on this incorrect view, is purely a modern invention.

Possibly the idea of *tohu wa bohu* has inadvertently been read into the Greek conception from the biblical account of creation in Genesis. To Hesiod, who thinks in terms of genealogies, even Chaos came into being. He does not say, 'In the beginning was Chaos', but, 'First Chaos came to be, and then the Earth', &c.[46] Here the question arises whether there must not have been a beginning (ἀρχή) of becoming—something that has not itself become. Hesiod leaves this question unanswered; indeed he never goes so far as to raise it. To do such a thing would require a degree of consistency that is still quite foreign to his thought. But his *Theogony* is of obvious importance for a future philosophy that sooner or later really will be consistent enough to ask such questions. Nor is it any less obvious that once this question has been raised it cannot help affecting certain conceptions on which religion has laid stress, and that it will by no means be lacking in religious significance in its own right. And the very thing that will have done the most to render the philosophical content of the myths mobile and give it religious significance is Hesiod's *Theogony*, with its theologizing of the old myths of the gods. It seems to me idle to discuss whether the true Greek religion lies in the myth or the cult. In any case Hesiod has genuinely religious motives for treating the myths theologically; and he undoubtedly sees something of religious importance in the cosmic implications he claims to find in certain myths. This fact should be kept in mind in any attempt to judge the theology of the Greek natural philosophers as a religious phenomenon, even though they seek other ways of solving the problems of this twilight realm of mythical theology, and other ways of satisfying the inner need that brought them forth.

After all, there is no reason why we should not look upon Hesiod's *Theogony* as one of the preparatory stages of the philosophy soon to come.[47] History itself has dispelled any doubts about the matter by revealing the decided influence of Hesiod's ideas. In his view of the world there are certain definite points to which the great philosophers are particularly fond of turning their attention. They often refer not only to his conception of Chaos and the beginning of things, but indeed to the whole cosmogonic side of the *Theogony*. While the ideas involved are by no means immediately derived from experience, they can still be subjected to some empirical control, or at worst be found to conflict with experience; so it is quite inevitable that they should become targets of criticism for anyone who, like the natural philosopher, thinks for himself and begins with the evidence of his senses. But negative criticism is not the only response that Hesiod arouses in these men, for there is much in his *Theogony* that is of direct philosophical significance to them. We can see, for instance, the way in which his peculiar conception of Eros as the first of the gods is later developed by Parmenides and Empedocles. Indeed this idea has been of almost unlimited fruitfulness throughout the history of philosophy, even down to the nineteenth-century theories of cosmic love. To Empedocles, Love (or, as he calls it, $\Phi\iota\lambda\acute{\iota}a$) is the efficient cause of every union of cosmic forces. This function has simply been taken over from the Eros of Hesiod. At the very beginning of his account of the world's origin, the poet introduces Eros as one of the oldest and mightiest of gods, coeval with Earth and Heaven, the first couple, who are joined in loving union by his power.[48] The story of Earth and Heaven and their marriage was one of the traditional myths; and Hesiod reasons quite logically when he infers that Eros must have been as old a divinity as they, and so deserving of one of the first places.[49] The union of Heaven and Earth begins the long series of procreations which provides the main content of the *Theogony* and occupies the centre of Hesiod's theological interest. How could he help inquiring into the source of this urge which brought all divine couples together and even joined theogony with cosmogony—the veritable cause by which the world came to be? And how could anyone who thinks of so many natural and moral forces as divine persons fail to see a god in the Eros uniting all things?

Historians of religion have pointed out that Eros had a very old cult in Boeotian Thespiae at the foot of Mount Helicon, though he does not appear elsewhere as a cult divinity in early times. Inasmuch as Hesiod also had a special personal relationship to the Muses of this his own home soil, the fact that he assigns to Eros so great a role might be explained by natural partiality to the god of his own neighbourhood. But this explanation strikes me as rather superficial. It is true enough that the cult may have given him good reason for meditating on this deity; but it is not enough to account for the role that Eros plays in the *Theogony*. The cult god of Thespiae is merely a fructifier of flocks and human marriages; he does not become a cosmic force until he takes his place at the head of the pro-creative series that gives birth to the wide world and the very gods themselves. In thus singling out the power that produces these procreations and setting it at the beginning of the whole series as its divine cause, Hesiod performed a hypostasis such as we find at analogous stages in the theological thought of all times and all peoples. This is precisely what the Hebrew theologians are doing when they take the phrase 'And God said:' (the phrase repeated at every new creative act of Yahweh in the Mosaic account of Creation) and hypostatize it as the creative Word, the *Logos*, treating it as a primordial being in itself and placing it at the head of the series of creative acts that proceed from it. The fact that Eros already received homage from a cult was no more important to Hesiod than the problem of whether Heaven and Earth or Kronos and Rheia were also cult divinities. The point is that the introduction of Eros is altogether typical of Hesiod's theological thinking. Quite apart from the natural philosophers whom we have al-ready mentioned, we shall find that this method of mythical hypostasis becomes a particularly important device for explain-ing the world in the theological cosmology of post-Hesiodic times, where Hesiod's primeval Eros again has a powerful influence.

In other respects, however, if we compare this Greek hypo-stasis of the world-creative Eros with that of the *Logos* in the Hebrew account of creation, we may observe a deep-lying differ-ence in the outlook of the two peoples. The *Logos* is a substan-tialization of an intellectual property or power of God the creator, who is stationed *outside* the world and brings that world into existence by his own personal fiat. The Greek gods are stationed *inside* the world; they are descended from Heaven and Earth, the two greatest and most exalted parts of the uni-verse; and they are generated by the mighty power of Eros, who likewise belongs within the world as an all-engendering primitive force. Thus they are already subject to what we should call natural law, even if the hypostatical mind of Hesiod represents this law as a god among gods rather than as one all-ruling principle. But in the Hesiodic conception we already find the germ of the quest for a single natural principle which we meet in the later philosophers. Its influence will become particularly clear in the new forms which the Hesiodic Eros takes in the works of Parmenides and Empedocles. When Hesiod's thought at last gives way to truly philosophical thinking, the Divine is sought inside the world—not outside it, as in the Jewish-Christian theology that develops out of the book of Genesis. Hesiod will then be reckoned more as cosmogonist than as theogonist, and the divine nature will be sought in those forces by which all things are engendered. In this philosophy Eros will become more important than all the gods whom Hesiod makes him bring into being. The gods are a part of the mythological tradition; and as Hesiod's thinking is utterly rooted in myth, this is all that is needed to make them real for his theology.[50] Accordingly he never has any reason to inquire into the nature of the Divine as such. This fundamental question is one that cannot be raised until a time when all Hesiod's individual divine figures and the very myths themselves have become problematical. And such a stage does not occur until the moment when man comes to recognize that his only source of certainty in dealing with the actual lies in experience and in self-consistent thinking grounded upon experience. While this standpoint is quite different from Hesiod's, I believe I have shown that it is not absolutely alien to him, but is closely connected with his theological explanation of the world, which indeed provides the background for its own peculiar problems. Thus it is quite natural that this new thinking should not be so fundamentally unconcerned with the problem of the Divine as is often supposed; on the contrary, it accepts this problem as one of its essential heritages from the previous period, while at the same time it restates it in a new and generalized philosophical form.

CHAPTER II

THE THEOLOGY OF THE MILESIAN NATURALISTS

AT the gateway of philosophy stand three venerable figures, Thales, Anaximander, and Anaximenes. Ever since the time of Aristotle we have grouped these men together as physicists or philosophers of nature. While it is true that in later years there were other thinkers of similar inclinations, these three are still pre-eminent of their kind, and obviously form a unified group. Even in their place of origin they belong together: they are all sons of Miletus, the metropolis of Greek Asia Minor, which had reached the peak of its political, economic, and intellectual development during the sixth century. It was here, on the colonial soil of Ionia, that the Greek spirit achieved those two general conceptions of the world which have given rise on the one hand to the Homeric epic and on the other to Greek philosophy. We can, of course, show that the Greeks of Asia Minor came into very close contact with the older cultures of the Orient in trade, art, and technics; and there will always be some dispute as to how much this influence contributed to Greek intellectual development. It is not hard to imagine how deeply the sensitive minds of the Greeks must have been impressed by the various Oriental creation-myths and the Babylonian attempt to connect all terrestrial events with the stars. Perhaps we may even trace in the theologizing of Hesiod certain reactions to the theological speculations of the Orientals, particularly in his myths of the first woman and of how sin and evil came to the earth.[1]

In spite of all this, Hesiod's *Theogony* is already thoroughly Greek both in content and in spirit; and the impulse which makes the Ionian philosophers of nature seek to comprehend the world in universal terms takes a form that is utterly and unmistakably their own. The Hesiodic type of rationalism, with its interpretation and synthesis of the traditional myths, has given way to a new and more radical form of rational thinking, which no longer draws its content from the mythic tradition, nor indeed from any other, but takes as its point of departure the given realities of human experience—τὰ ὄντα, 'the things that exist'. Here we have an expression which was used rather commonly, even in later times, to denote a man's household goods and property; in philosophical language its scope is now widened to include everything that human perception finds in the world.[2] In thus broadly defining its subject-matter, philosophy shows that it has reached a new level, even in matters of theology; for among these ὄντα the heavenly forces piously reported in the earlier myths will find no place, and can no longer be taken for granted at the outset, as can the actual presence of things like stars and air, earth and sea, rivers and mountains, plants, animals, and men. Thunder and lightning are given facts; but can this be said of Zeus, the god who sends them? At all events, he does not belong to the realm of things that meet the senses; and beyond that realm we cannot go. Even if we recognize that eyes and ears do not reach very far, and that imagination travels immeasurable distances beyond the bounds of direct perception, the ὄντα that imagination finds will always be of the same sort as the things that present themselves to the senses, or at least very similar.

So reserved an intellectual approach implies a profound alteration in man's state of mind as compared with the mythological stage. His attitude towards myth itself has changed. It is true that the older philosophical thinkers have left us no direct statements about their relationship to the traditional myths; but it is inconceivable that they could have failed to regard their own ideas as most patently antithetical to a way of life grounded on the assumption that any mythical tale in general acceptance must be true. In particular they must have felt that there should be no intrusion of μῦθοι in any genuine knowledge of the world. Now the word μῦθοι had originally been a harmless designation for any speech or narration; but by the time of the Milesians, when men were beginning to turn to a more immediate source of knowledge, it must undoubtedly have started to take on that negative sense which was to become almost universal by the time of Thucydides, and which is expressed with a particularly clear connotation in the adjective μυθώδης: here we have the mythical in the sense of the fabulous and unauthenticated, as contrasted with any verifiable truth or reality. Thucydides uses the word 'mythical' to discredit the traditional verse and prose accounts of the older periods of Greek history; and surely an Ionian philosopher of nature like Anaximander must have felt no less disparaging sentiments when he considered what the myths had told about the gods and the origin of the world. One might well expect anyone with such a point of view to wash his hands of everything which we have been calling theology and banish it to the realm of the imaginary.[3] Indeed, the fact that these new men are referred to as natural philosophers or φυσικοί (the term is comparatively late) might seem to express in the very idea of φύσις a delimitation of interest that automatically rules out any concern with the θεοί. In confining themselves to facts ascertainable by the senses,[4] the Ionians would thus appear to have taken an ontological position which is frankly non-theological.

But the surviving testimonia, scarce as they are, still show clearly that this rather obvious way of interpreting the intellectual attitude of the first philosophers is a false modernization. Quite apart from any testimonia, this falsity must be evident to the philologist, for he need only reflect that to translate the word φύσις by our word 'nature' or φυσικός by 'natural philosopher', fails to do justice to the Greek meaning and is definitely wrong. φύσις is one of those abstract formations with the suffix -σις which become fairly frequent after the period of the later epics. It denotes quite plainly the act of φῦναι—the process of growth and emergence; that is why the Greeks often use it with a genitive, as in φύσις τῶν ὄντων—the origin and growth of the things we find about us. But it also includes their source of origin—that from which they have grown, and from which their growth is constantly renewed—in other words, the reality underlying the things of our experience. We find this same double meaning in the word γένεσις, a synonym of φύσις, which is quite as old and perhaps even older. In the comparatively late Homeric passage where Oceanus is called the origin of all things, the word is already used in this sense. To say that Oceanus is the *genesis* of everything is virtually the same as calling him the *physis* of everything.[5] Now Thales holds that Water is the origin of everything.[6] This does not seem very different, but a difference is unquestionably present: it lies in the fact that the philosopher dispenses with any allegorical or mythical expression for his intuition that all things came from Water. His water is a visible part of the world of experience. But his view of the origin of things brings him very close to the theological creation-myths, or rather leads him to compete with them. For while his theory seems to be purely physical, he evidently thinks of it as also having what we may call a metaphysical character. This fact is revealed by the only one of his utterances that has come down to us in verbal form (if, indeed, it actually goes back to him): πάντα πλήρη θεῶν, 'everything is full of gods'. Two hundred years later, at the end of this first period of philosophical thinking, Plato cites this apophthegm with special emphasis, almost as if it were the primal word and the very quintessence of all philosophy.[7] Plato finds it of profound historical significance that the philosophy of nature, so long regarded as a source of atheism, should, in his own doctrine of the star-gods, have returned to the same basic truth with which it started.[8] And his theologizing disciple, Philip of Opus, cites these words in his *Epinomis*[9] as the ultimate formula of the philosophical study of Being, supposedly substantiated by the most modern astronomical theories of the celestial bodies.

In attaching this new content to Thales' ancient dictum, Plato is naturally interpreting it in his own way; we can only guess what Thales really had in mind. We have several bits of evidence that he was interested in magnets, and Aristotle suggests that he may here have been thinking of magnetic attraction. This would mean that Thales must have used this single phenomenon as a basis for a generalization about the nature of the so-called inorganic world. The assertion that everything is full of gods would then mean something like this: everything is full of mysterious living forces; the distinction between animate and inanimate nature has no foundation in fact; everything has a soul.[10] Thales would thus have made his observation of magnetism a premise for inferring the Oneness of all reality as something alive. This interpretation is still far from certain. But at any rate the words reveal that the man who utters them is aware of a shift in his attitude towards the prevalent ideas about the gods: although he speaks of gods, he is obviously using the word in a sense rather different from that in which the majority of men would use it. In contrast to the usual conception of the gods' nature, he declares that everything is full of gods. This statement cannot refer to those gods with which the imaginative faith of the Greeks peopled mountain and stream, tree and spring, any more than to the inhabitants of Heaven or Olympus of whom we read in Homer. Thales' gods do not dwell apart in some sequestered and inaccessible region, but everything—that is, the whole familiar world about us, which our reason takes so soberly—is full of gods and the effects of their power. This conception is not without its paradox, for it clearly presupposes that these effects can be experienced, and experienced in a new way: they must be something that can be seen with the eyes and grasped with the hands. We no longer need to look for any mythical figures in or behind the given reality in order to discern that it is itself a theatre where higher powers hold sway. So in restricting our cognition to that which we find immediately before us, we are not necessarily compelled to abandon the Divine. Of course our mere understanding is hardly sufficient in itself to give us any adequate evidence for the gods of popular belief; but experience of the reality of φύσις provides it with a new source of knowledge of the Divine: it is there for us to grasp as if with our own hands, everywhere in the world.

We may now introduce for comparison another early utterance of the old Hellenic philosophy, which anecdote has ascribed to Heraclitus. The story goes that as he was standing by the hearth-fire of his house and warming himself, he noticed that visitors stood at the threshold, hesitating to come in. Whereupon he called out to them: 'Enter. Here, too, are gods.'[11] This remark has been taken to refer to the fire, which Heraclitus held to be the original principle of all things. In any case his words presuppose Thales' dictum that everything is full of gods, here wittily applied to the situation of the moment.[12] The story is symbolical of the intellectual advance that characterizes the very beginnings of Greek philosophy, and is particularly significant in its bearing on religion. Over the gates of the philosophy of Being, which begins with Thales, stands the inscription, visible from afar to the eye of the spirit: 'Enter. Here, too, are gods.' These words shall light us on our way as we pass through Greek philosophy.

In dealing with Thales it is of course impossible to know the inner connexion between his bold assertion that everything is full of gods, and his more special views. When we come to

Anaximander we can find our bearings much more precisely. With this philosopher we are for the first time in a position to see clearly how that which we may call his theology is a direct outgrowth from the germ of his new intuition of φύσις. Naturally we cannot here consider all the details of his thought. But in Anaximander we find the first unified and all-embracing world-picture, based on a natural deduction and explanation of all phenomena. This explanation, of course, is a far cry from our present-day science both in method and in results; but as a total achievement it still bears witness to an enormous power of intellect, constructive rather than analytic. Anaximander is striving to find the key to the hidden structure of reality by studying the way in which it has come to be what it is; we can trace this effort in the zeal with which he seeks to discover mathematical proportion and harmony in the relationships of the world-whole and its parts. To-day, of course, there still seems to be something very primitive in the geometrical schematization with which this model of the world is put together, no less than in the uniformity with which Anaximander applies it to cosmology and geography alike; but if we consider it as a work of art, it is an overwhelming expression of the conviction with which he approaches the world as a whole, and of the demand that the universe shall have a rational meaning. This world-view marks the first clear emergence of philosophy in the mind of man. To many of us to-day it seems hardly possible to look back any farther than this primary philosophical experience of significant Being; and yet we can see that man's repose in Being is not to be taken as a matter of course. Philosophy is rather the supreme stage of a new self-assurance on man's part, under whose foundations lie vanquished a wild army of darksome forces. Anaximander's cosmos marks the triumph of the intellect over a whole world of rough and unformed powers which threaten human existence with primeval danger at the very moment when the old order of living, the feudal and mythical order, known to us only in the earliest phase of Greek culture, the Homeric epic, and already past its prime, finally goes to pieces.

Even the old gods are denied admission to the new world-system, though their names and their cults persist. Their passing leaves a gap which the philosopher now must fill, and thus there arises anew the problem of the 'whence'—the origin of all things. While Thales, still thinking in terms of simple sensory intuition, conceived of the world as growing out of the elemental water and taking permanent shape, his successor rejects this conception on purely logical grounds: he cannot understand how a preponderance of any single substance so essentially one-sided as water could ever give rise to qualities of a sort that would make possible the existence of other things differently constituted, such as fire or earth. The same objection applies to any other substance now present in the world, as soon as we try to think of it as the source of everything else. So the thing with which the world begins can only be something that is identical with none of the given substances, and yet is capable of giving rise to the vast immensity of them all. The distinguishing property of this something must therefore be the fact that it is itself unbounded; and so Anaximander calls it by this very name—*apeiron*. The best ancient expositors follow Aristotle in taking this word of many meanings to denote the endless, inexhaustible reservoir or stock from which all Becoming draws its nourishment,[13] not that which is qualitatively undetermined, as certain modern writers have described it. As a matter of fact, the word *apeiron* points unequivocally to boundlessness as the real meaning of this conception. This is the way Burnet has explained it.[14]

According to the testimony of the learned Neoplatonist Simplicius, in his commentary on the *Physics* of Aristotle, Anaximander was the first man to say that the *apeiron* is the *arché* or principle.[15] This would be important evidence if correct; for it would determine how we are to judge a certain passage in Aristotle in which he describes how the older speculation regarding the *apeiron* arose and explains its logical foundations. The question is whether Aristotle is really giving us a kind of historical report or is merely trying to fathom the philosophical motives of the older thinkers from his own point of view. According to Aristotle the relationship between the concept of the Boundless and that of the beginning (in the temporal sense) is one of mutual exclusion: 'Everything either is a beginning or has a beginning. The Boundless, however, has no beginning; for otherwise it would have a boundary.' Here the proposition that the Boundless is itself the principle or

beginning is deduced from the very content of this conception.
Only the Boundless satisfies the requirements which the idea
of an absolute beginning involves; for it is itself without temporal beginning since it has no bounds. Aristotle then proceeds
to deduce the chief properties of the *apeiron* from the concept
of an absolute beginning:

'As a beginning, it must also be something that has not become
and cannot pass away. For that which has become must necessarily
come to an end, and all passing-away likewise has an end. Thus,
as we have said, it is itself without beginning, but is rather—so it is
thought—the beginning of everything else. And it encompasses all
things and governs all things, as those persons declare who posit
no other causes besides the *apeiron*, such as mind [νοῦς] or love
[φιλία].' (Here he is thinking of Anaxagoras and Empedocles.) 'And
this, they say, is the Divine. For it is immortal and indestructible,
as Anaximander and most of the natural philosophers maintain.'[16]

The explicit reference to Anaximander at the end of this
passage makes it quite certain that in this demonstration of the
apeiron we have before us not merely Aristotle's own reflections
but some of the thoughts of Anaximander himself.[17] Aristotle
rules out Anaxagoras and Empedocles on the ground that they
do not represent the theory of the *apeiron* in its purity, but
recognize the efficacy of additional causal factors.[18] Their philosophy is accordingly more complex. Among the genuine representatives of the theory of the *apeiron*, Aristotle rightly singles
out Anaximander rather than anyone else, for he is the pioneer
and leader of this movement. It was he who applied the
epithets 'immortal' and 'indestructible' to the Boundless, from
which he held all becoming to arise. The other predications
which Aristotle mentions obviously are due to him too, for
they all fit together as a whole.[19] We shall have something to
say later about their significance for Anaximander's theology.
But is Anaximander also responsible for the deduction in which
the dialectic of the *peras* and *apeiron* is used to prove that the
Boundless has no beginning?[20] If Simplicius is right in maintaining that Anaximander was the first to use the word *arché*,[21]
his statement would be a valuable signpost in helping us to
answer this question. Simplicius draws this bit of historical
erudition from the foundational work of Aristotle's pupil Theophrastus on the teachings of the natural philosophers, which,

shortly before this passage, as in many other places, he mentions expressly as his source.[22] Another author from later antiquity, Hippolytus, has borrowed the same information from the same source. These two writers are notoriously independent of one another; and as they report the same matters with almost identical words, we can reconstruct Theophrastus' phrasing with fair precision on the basis of their agreement.[23] That the learned Peripatetic, in the passage utilized by both writers, should have made a statement concerning Anaximander's priority in using this concept, is entirely credible. Simplicius reports elsewhere that another pupil of Aristotle, Eudemus, author of a history of geometry and other similar works, has passed on the tradition that Plato was the first to use the concept of element (*stoicheion*).[24] Indeed, the historians of philosophy in the Aristotelian school gave considerable attention to such problems, especially when the first appearance of concepts in their own system was involved, as in the case of *arché* and *stoicheion*.

Burnet, however, has expressed some doubt about the conventional view that Anaximander was the first to use the word *arché*. He sees here a misinterpretation of Simplicius' statement. The point of these words, according to Burnet, is not that Anaximander was the first to designate the *apeiron* as *arché*, but, on the contrary, that he was the first to call the *arché apeiron*.[25] Accordingly Burnet holds that Anaximander really used the word *apeiron*; whether he also used the concept of *arché*, Burnet considers doubtful. He thinks it significant that *arché* in the sense of 'principle' is an Aristotelian term, and he holds that it never assumes this meaning in the actual fragments of the pre-Socratics themselves. Only when their teachings are reported by later authors—all of whom go back to Peripatetic sources—does the concept of *arché* recur, and there he would explain it as part of the standard terminology of the Aristotelian school.[26] Burnet does not profess to see any grammatical impossibility in the interpretation of Simplicius' words which he disputes; he merely considers his own interpretation the more natural. Nevertheless, difficulties arise when we find that Hippolytus, in his parallel to Simplicius' account, has not understood Theophrastus as Burnet has understood him. Burnet holds that Hippolytus' version is a misinterpretation which has become the point of departure for most modern scholars; he thinks that this can be explained by a slight verbal disparity between Hippolytus and Simplicius, which he traces back to a simple mechanical corruption of the text in Hippolytus.[27] But from another passage of Simplicius it is evident that this author has construed Theophrastus in exactly the same way as Hippolytus has done; for he says there quite clearly that Anaximander was the first to designate the substratum (i.e. the *apeiron*) as *arché*.[28] If that which Hippolytus and Simplicius report as a fact were false, then either they must have both independently misunderstood their source, Theophrastus, in the same way (which is not at all likely), or their source, Theophrastus, must himself be looked upon as responsible for the error in the first place. But inasmuch as Theophrastus made direct use of Anaximander's own writings, this is quite improbable, especially since the matter here involved was an important one for him and not difficult to verify. It is far more likely that Hippolytus and Simplicius, following Theophrastus himself, both agreed in holding that Anaximander was the first to use the word *arché*, and it remains most probable that this view is correct.

But how shall we deal with the consideration that the concept of *arché* ('principle') is primarily Aristotelian and not otherwise found in the pre-Socratics? The frequency with which this concept appears in the ancient doxographical tradition about the pre-Socratics is due obviously to the Peripatetic terminology of Theophrastus, who is the principal source for this literature. In the present case, however, the difference lies in the fact that Theophrastus expressly attributes the first appearance of the word *arché* to Anaximander. But this statement no more implies that Anaximander used the word (ὄνομα) *arché* in the sense of Aristotle and Theophrastus, than Eudemus' parallel assertion, that the word 'element' (*stoicheion*) appears in its first philosophical context in Plato,[29] means that Plato used this word in the Aristotelian sense. Theophrastus merely reports that the word *arché* was used by Anaximander. But perhaps it is possible to go back still earlier than either Aristotle or Theophrastus and come closer to Anaximander by tracing the continuity of thought in pre-Socratic philosophy. One avowed follower of Anaximander is Melissus of Samos. He belongs to those who, as Aristotle puts it, 'made the *apeiron* a principle'. Chronologically he falls midway between Anaximander and Aristotle, about a century from each. Like his contemporary, Diogenes of Apollonia, Melissus represents the renascence of the Milesian philosophy of nature, which becomes prominent about the middle of the fifth century. In his speculations on the *apeiron* Melissus uses the concept of *arché* in the same sense which we find in the Aristotelian passage cited above, where the concepts of *apeiron* and *arché* are designated as the point of departure for reasoning about the *apeiron*. Aristotle writes: 'Everything either is itself a beginning or has a beginning. The Boundless, however, has no beginning, for otherwise it would have a boundary.'[30] Melissus says: 'Nothing which has a beginning and end is eternal or boundless.'[31] Here, just as in Aristotle, the relationship between the concept of the *apeiron* and that of the beginning is asserted to be one of mutual exclusiveness, as the beginning would constitute a limit. In a second passage Melissus concludes: 'Since, then, it has not come to be, it is, and ever was, and ever will be; and it has no beginning and no end, but is *apeiron*.'[32] Any such being, without a beginning, is, according to Aristotle, 'a beginning itself'.[33] Melissus does not say this outright in the fragments we possess; but his manner of expression and style of argument show clearly that the idea of beginning, as was indeed natural, played an important and even decisive role among the early speculators about the *apeiron*. Thus Theophrastus' report that the first appearance of the word *arché* in philosophical literature occurs in Anaximander is now fully confirmed; and though we are unable, because of the loss of Anaximander's book, to demonstrate this usage until we reach his follower Melissus, Theophrastus is clearly right in saying that this concept actually derives from the creator of the theory of the *apeiron* himself.

By his introduction of the concept of a Boundless and his consequent denial of the boundary or *peras*, Anaximander has put something without beginning at the beginning of his cosmology. His *apeiron* is, according to the words of his single fragment (which is preserved in the form of an indirect quotation), that from which everything takes rise and to which everything returns.[34] It is thus the beginning (ἀρχή) and end (τελευτή) of everything that exists. Does it really take Aristotelian logic to discover that such a Being, which has neither beginning nor end, is itself the beginning and end of everything? A similar thought is expressed in the well-known Orphic verse, 'Zeus is beginning, middle, and end'. Hesiod could not have made such a statement; it was too much out of keeping with the old genealogy of the gods. The writer of this line is not concerned with the origin of his god, but rather with his eternity and his being. The Orphic writer has already been influenced by philosophical thought; so it is not surprising that the philosophers themselves, from Plato and the author of the treatise *De mundo* on, should find him congenial and refer to his work. For us it is important to see how the concept of a being which is without beginning and end and is therefore itself beginning and end, is connected with the idea of the supreme god. Did it have such an association for Anaximander? We can give this question a final answer only by considering it in connexion with the other predicates which he attributes to his *apeiron*. It is significant that ancient tradition has already ascribed to Thales the statement that the Divine is 'that which has neither beginning nor end'.[35] Naturally there is no real authority for connecting this apophthegm (which appears in an anecdotal context in Diogenes Laertius) with the half-mythical first of philosophers himself. But it is important that the idea of something without beginning or end, which we have restored to Anaximander, is here set back at the very outset of Milesian reflection and associated with speculation concerning the Divine. We shall presently see that the ontological considerations which underlie Anaximander's *apeiron* possess just such a theological significance for him throughout.

Again the statements of Aristotle must serve as our point of departure. He continues:[36]

'And it encompasses all things and governs all things, as those persons declare who posit no other causes besides the *apeiron*, such as mind [Anaxagoras] or love [Empedocles]. And this, they say, is the Divine; for it is immortal [ἀθάνατον] and indestructible [ἀνώλεθρον], as Anaximander and most of the natural philosophers maintain.'

Is Aristotle here freely paraphrasing the thoughts of his predecessor, or do we still hear in this poetical form of speech the bold language of an older race of thinkers? A philologically

trained ear will be convinced of the latter at once; but fortunately we are helped by still another passage in Aristotle, where
he tells us that the *apeiron* of the old philosophers of nature is
the matter (*hylé*) of things; it would therefore be incorrect to
say that it encompasses all things: we must say rather that
it is encompassed by or contained in all things.[37] It is clear
that Aristotle is here criticizing a specific passage which he has
before him, and that it is the same text which he has made use
of in the above-mentioned portion of the *Physics*, where he
quotes it more precisely—that is, the statement that the *apeiron*
'encompasses all things and governs all things'.[38]

If we examine the way in which this fuller version is formulated, we can see at once that when Aristotle contends that the
apeiron must really be that which is encompassed by all things,
he has not kept altogether in line with Anaximander's original
meaning. Anaximander's *apeiron* is not to be understood in
terms of the Aristotelian concept of matter. He has not yet
distinguished between Being as matter and Being as form, and
his *apeiron* is not simply something which, as matter, is en-
veloped by form. It is rather the thing which encompasses
all things and governs all things, something active, indeed
the most active thing in the world. These two predicates,
'governing' and 'encompassing', are used again and again in
pre-Socratic philosophy to describe the activity of the highest
principle.[39] Thereafter they passed into the terminology of the
later philosophers, as Plato himself reports in the *Philebus*.[40]
In recent years it has been well pointed out that when the older
philosophers speak of the highest principle, their style undergoes
a peculiar modification. This fact has been shown to be particularly true of Anaxagoras and Diogenes, whose language in
such passages either approaches that of the hymn in vocabulary,
sentence structure, and rhythm, or introduces some philosophically toned variant of the hymnic style appropriate to the
subject-matter.[41] Anaxagoras and Diogenes are especially good
examples of this tendency, for we still have some fairly long
fragments of their work preserved in its original phrasing. But
I think it is clear from passages such as Aristotle's on Anaximander that these later thinkers were not the first to use this
kind of language in writing about their highest principle. The
way was blazed for them by Anaximander, the first man to

write a philosophical work in prose.[42] The vigour of expression that marks his one surviving fragment still glows through Aristotle's sober account, especially in the series of epithets with which he characterizes his first principle. We can trace these in full detail even now. The Boundless is unborn and imperishable, all-encompassing and all-governing (notice the solemn, hieratic repetition of the word 'all');[43] we are not surprised when Aristotle continues with the words, 'And this is the Divine, for it is immortal and indestructible, as Anaximander and most of the natural philosophers maintain.'

The phrase 'the Divine' does not appear merely as one more predicate applied to the first principle; on the contrary, the substantivization of the adjective with the definite article shows rather that this is introduced as an independent concept, essentially religious in character, and now identified with the rational principle, the Boundless. That this expression is of epoch-making importance in Greek philosophy is clear from the frequency with which we encounter similar statements both in the other pre-Socratics and in later philosophers. Taking the natural world as their starting-point, they develop the idea of some highest principle (for instance, the *ens perfectissimum* of Aristotle and the world-forming fire of the Stoics) and then proceed to assert of it that 'this must be the Divine'.[44] As far as I have been able to discover from the remaining evidence, the concept of the Divine as such does not appear before Anaximander.[45] Later, in the time of Herodotus and the tragic poets, it will become a frequent substitute for the phrase οἱ θεοί ('the gods'), just as in that period we shall often meet the singular ὁ θεός ('the god', or, perhaps better, simply 'God').[46] But any such general locution is still unheard of in the earliest days of Ionian philosophy. Therefore the first appearance of the expression 'the Divine' is all the more noteworthy. We have already observed that while Hesiod's theology admits many kinds of gods, he has not yet inquired into their nature. But whoever first uses the general concept of the Divine must consider this question; and Anaximander does so. When he says that the Boundless 'encompasses all things and governs all things', he is satisfying the loftiest demands which religious thought has required of divinity from time immemorial; for he makes it the bearer of supreme power and dominion. Moreover, since the older poets and the current religious faith looked upon immortality as the outstanding characteristic common to all the gods,[47] Anaximander could see in his argument for the imperishability of the Boundless a proof that there actually is something immortal, and that this is no other than the Boundless itself; so that this and this alone can have any claim to be called the Divine.

But the *apeiron*, as we have seen, is also something that has never become. This is a property peculiarly appropriate to the original principle of all things. In mythical thought, while the chief distinguishing feature of the gods is found in the fact that they are not mortal as men are, they are otherwise represented in human guise. Rational thought, on the contrary, has arrived at the idea of something immortal and divine by seeking an origin for all things which shall itself be without an origin. This aspect is either entirely absent or only potentially present in the old conception of the gods as the αἰὲν ἐόντες, which is often employed in Homer and Hesiod, and shows merely that the gods are thought of as immortal, living for ever. The possibility that the gods should have had no beginning is expressly ruled out by such a theology as Hesiod's, who constructed a genealogy of all the gods, and held that everything, even Chaos, came into being. Anyone who traces the gods' ancestry back to Ouranos and Gaia and thinks of them quite concretely as the actual heaven and the actual earth, which in their turn, too, came into being, has no conception of the eternity of the gods in the strict sense of the word. That the Greeks saw here one of the weaknesses of the older theogonies will often be clear in the later theogonies themselves;[48] but this difficulty, which comes to the fore in the final, theologizing phase of the mythical religion, does not exist for Anaximander. His first principle is immortal and without beginning. It is not only infinite but also truly eternal. It would be a mistake to blind ourselves to the religious significance implicit in this exalted conception of the Divine because of any preconceived notions of what genuine religion ought to be and what kind of knowledge it should seek. We have no right, for instance, to complain that Anaximander's god is not a god one can pray to, or that physical speculation is not true religion. Surely no one will deny that we simply cannot conceive of any advanced form of religion as lacking the idea of endlessness and eternity which Anaximander links with his new concept of the Divine.

In other respects his teachings are not so sharply opposed to the Greek polytheism as might appear from what we have said. Sources from the later years of the ancient period have left us a number of remarkable testimonia which certainly go back to Theophrastus and must accordingly have been based on direct acquaintance with Anaximander's writings.[49] These testimonia all agree in stating that he believed in innumerable worlds—an indication that he took the Boundless quite seriously. Apparently this belief involved not only an infinite succession of worlds in time, but also the simultaneous existence of innumerable worlds or heavens, for the equidistance of the *kosmoi* from one another is expressly mentioned. I see no reason not to take this tradition literally.[50] Anaximander is said to have called these worlds 'gods', thus teaching that there are innumerable gods; and as these worlds arise and pass away periodically, Cicero can speak of the *nativi dei* of Anaximander, who are not eternal but merely long-lived.[51] The conception of the δολιχαίωνες is a familiar one in Greek religion; we find it again in Empedocles[52]—another reason for attributing it to Anaximander. But if this is so, then the gods of the innumerable worlds, which have come into existence, must differ somehow from the *apeiron*, which is the sole complete realization of the Divine as such, without beginning and without end. And just as our philosopher has followed traditional Greek conceptions in identifying the primal substance of the world with that which is divine and eternal, he likewise betrays the influence of Hesiodic thought-patterns when he maintains that these innumerable god-worlds issue genealogically from this same divine substance and after unimaginable intervals of time sink back again into its bosom. We may, in fact, see in this view a kind of philosophical theogony.

We find the θεῖον and the individual gods side by side again in Herodotus. But as they here mean something quite different from what Anaximander the philosopher has in mind, we must not attach too much weight to their juxtaposition; it merely serves to show that for Greek sensibility, if not for ours, they are by no means incompatible. We shall discuss later the relationship between the One God of Xenophanes and the other gods of whom he speaks. In Plato and Aristotle, too, the realm of the Divine displays a similar hierarchy; and Buddhistic theology distinguishes between the eternal divine One and the long-lived but mortal gods who, like man and the rest of creation, are caught in the wheel of birth and becoming.

Anaximander is the first Greek thinker whom we know not only from the reports of later authors but also from a fragment of his own work. This fragment consists merely of a single sentence, which, moreover, has come down to us in the form of indirect discourse. Nevertheless it is a jewel precious beyond estimate. As opinions differ about its proper interpretation, I must quote the whole sentence. Out of the *apeiron*, says Simplicius in his account of Anaximander, the worlds arise. 'But from whatever things is the genesis of the things that are, into these they must pass away according to necessity; for they must pay the penalty and make atonement to one another for their injustice according to Time's decree.'[53] These are unquestionably Anaximander's own words. Simplicius describes the diction as 'somewhat poetic' and suggests that it veils a quite dispassionate observation of the intertransformations of the four elements. This interpretation is unhistorical not only in that it reads into Anaximander a much later philosophical theory, but also in that it misses the force of his language by explaining its picturesqueness as mere metaphor. In these very images there lies a philosophical interpretation of the *rationale* of the world. Nietzsche and Rohde have explained Anaximander's reference to the penalty which things must undergo for the injustice of their existence, by supposing that he sees in the very individuation of things an offence for which they must atone. This offence would therefore consist in the emergence of individuals themselves, which would be 'an apostasy from the primordial unity'.[54] While there once seemed to be some hope of tracing this idea back to the Orphic religion, it cannot have come from this source.[55] The only theory in the Greek mystery religion that is at all similar is the view mentioned by Aristotle that human life is a punishment for some great guilt. But even if it is not clear what manner of guilt this is, life cannot very well be both crime and punishment at once.[56]

Burnet has already pointed out that since the time when the

Orphic interpretation was first proposed, the wording of the sentence itself has undergone some revision. From the best manuscripts Diels has brought the word ἀλλήλοις back to light— a word that is missing in the older printed versions of Simplicius. This makes the sentence read: 'Things must pay the penalty and make atonement to one another for their injustice.'[57] This is something quite different, and not at all hard to visualize. It involves the image of a scene in a courtroom. When there are two parties to a dispute, the one who has taken more than his share, whether by force or by trickery, must pay damages for his pleonexy to the party he has wronged. To the Greeks, for whom the just is the equal, this pleonexy, or taking-too-much, is the essence of injustice. We must not think of civil and constitutional rights, but simply of property rights— the daily quarrel over mine and thine. When Anaximander proposes this image as an explanation of the coming-to-be and passing-away of things in the natural world, he is obviously thinking of their very existence as dependent on a state of having-too-much, for which they must make amends by ceding to others the things they now enjoy. A very similar idea appears in Heraclitus when he says that 'these live the death of those, while those die the life of these'.[58] And this atonement occurs 'according to the ordering of Time', or rather, as I prefer to explain it, 'according to Time's decree'.

For this is what τάττω and τάξις mean in the law-courts.[59] The conception of Time as a judge can be found among other writers of this period—in Solon, for instance, who defends himself 'before the bench of Time'. The underlying idea is that Time will always discover and avenge any act of injustice, even without human co-operation. This was an age when the idea of justice was being made the basis upon which state and society were to be built; it was not looked upon as a mere convention, but as an immanently effective norm inherent in reality itself.[60] If we see this political analogue clearly, we can no longer be in doubt as to the meaning of Anaximander's image. Not only in the world of politics but in the whole realm of Being there is just such an immanent justice; whatever happens, this justice will still prevail, and coming-to-be and passing-away take place in accordance with it. In the life of politics the Greek language refers to the reign of justice by the term *kosmos*; but the life of nature is a *kosmos* too, and indeed this cosmic view of the universe really begins with Anaximander's dictum. To him everything that happens in the natural world is rational through and through and subject to a rigid norm. Some writers have tried to read our idea of the laws of nature into Anaximander's words, but what we have found is something else altogether. Here is no sober rehearsal of the regular sequence of cause and effect in the outer world, but a world-norm that demands complete allegiance, for it is nothing less than divine justice itself. Coming-to-be and passing-away, which have furnished the lyric poets of the time with a theme for sighing and plaintive melancholy, are here objectively vindicated.[61] Anaximander's explanation of nature is something more than mere explanation of nature: it is the first philosophical theodicy.

In this so-called philosophy of nature we have thus found theology, theogony, and theodicy functioning side by side. And when we consider the comprehensiveness of Greek thought, what else could we expect than that as soon as it becomes philosophically conscious, it should endeavour to seize in a single grasp the totality of Being and of Spirit? The development of the idea of *kosmos* means both a new way of looking upon the organization of the State as derived from eternal laws of Being, and a re-creation of religion in terms of the idea of God and the divine government of the world as revealed in nature. That this is not peculiar to Anaximander but remains intrinsically bound up with the new philosophical approach, is clear from the way it recurs in Anaximenes. In his attempt to identify Anaximander's infinite first principle with air and to derive everything from the metamorphoses which air undergoes, Anaximenes has undoubtedly been guided also by a feeling that the first principle ought to explain the presence of life in the world; for he maintains that air controls the cosmos and holds it together in the same way as the psyche controls our bodies.[62] In thus animizing the *apeiron* of Anaximander, Anaximenes is obviously thinking of mental and not merely physiological phenomena. He clearly feels that the divine nature of the *apeiron* should include the power of thought, as indispensable for governing the All.[63] That he also retains Anaximander's 'innumerable gods', which he thinks of as emerging from the

Air as their primordial element, shows how firmly this feature is connected with the whole Anaximandrian philosophy as he sees it.[64] His successors, too, have retained it; and this in itself is a sufficient basis for the claims of the pre-Socratic philosophy to be regarded as natural theology.

CHAPTER III

XENOPHANES' DOCTRINE OF GOD

THE ancients distinguished two schools of Greek philosophy,[1] one in Ionia, the other in Italy, and thought of the Italian school as including Xenophanes, Pythagoras, and Parmenides. This geographical classification is not altogether unjustified, but it is rather superficial. It is true that these men lived in southern Italy and Sicily and evidently devoted considerable energy to coming to terms socially and intellectually with their environment, as we shall have occasion to point out later in connexion with Pythagoras and Parmenides. But the mere fact that Italy was the region of their chief activity tells us nothing about their real intellectual antecedence, which was determined far more by their ancestral background. Xenophanes came from Colophon on the coast of Asia Minor, Pythagoras from Samos: both were emigrants. The former left his native city after its conquest by the Medes; the latter left Samos to escape the tyranny of Polycrates. Elea, the southern Italian home of Parmenides, was a colony newly founded by refugees from Asia Minor who had abandoned their homes for the same reasons as Xenophanes, and whose exodus to Italy was the subject of an epic by Xenophanes himself. Whether Parmenides was one of these emigrants or a son of emigrant stock, is of little importance. In any case, he is intellectually a child of Ionia like the rest. All three men are obviously in close contact with the Ionian philosophy of nature, and carry its ideas forward in various directions.

Xenophanes is the first Greek thinker whom we can know as a personality. The human contours of the older natural philosophers have either vanished behind the monuments of their intellectual achievements or survived only in anecdotes. The comparative intimacy of our acquaintance with Xenophanes is directly connected with the fact that he was no such original thinker as they, though his influence was of inestimable value in the dissemination of their philosophy. His struggle on behalf of philosophy brought him fame; and in those of his poems which have come down to us, he is always an impassioned warrior in this cause. By his time Greek poetry had long since become an instrument by which the poet could publicize any of his convictions about the common welfare, whether critical or didactic; and it is characteristic of Xenophanes that he did not, as Anaximander did, set forth a complete theory of the world in the new, untrammeled form of prose, but asserted in poetry his views on various problems of philosophy. At this time it was customary for all poetry to be recited in public, and tradition states explicitly that Xenophanes recited his own poems in person.[2] What is new is that his verses are not concerned with practical or personal matters, but with problems of *Weltanschauung*—the nature of the gods, natural phenomena, the origin of all things, truth, doubt, and false authority. In these fervid pronouncements, the poet's ego emerges quite unabashed at the slightest excuse. Thus we learn that even as an old man of ninety-two he is still wandering through the Greek lands, and that he has been leading this irregular life for the past sixty-seven years[3]—presumably ever since his migration from Colophon to the Greek West, where he seems to have spent most of his time. He recalls the elegance of the Ionian culture in his old home,[4] describes the Medic invasion, and tells of sitting by the fire in winter-time, engaged in pleasant conversation, and being asked how old he was when the Medes appeared.[5]

The poems in which all these personal references appear can hardly have been devoted to presenting a philosophical system. Xenophanes was not the man to write a connected didactic poem in the manner of Hesiod or Parmenides.[6] In the main his works were quite unphilosophical. This is obviously true of his great historical epic on the founding of his native city Colophon, for which he may have found a stimulus in the tales of the city's history by another fellow-townsman and equally famous contemporary poet, Mimnermus. We have already noted that Xenophanes also wrote an epic on the colonization of Elea in southern Italy—an event that occurred in his own lifetime, although he did not take part in it himself.[7] Even these two long narrative poems were therefore decidedly personal in origin.

But the personal character of Xenophanes' work is most clearly revealed in his invention of a new type of poetry—the *silloi*.[8] These poems were satirical in character. Although they were generally written in elegiac distichs, I am convinced that they sometimes took the form of pure hexameters such as we find in Xenophanes' later imitator Timon, author of a collection of caustic satires on all the important philosophers.[9] To be sure, it has long been customary to assign the hexametrical fragments with philosophical content to a lost didactic work by Xenophanes *On Nature*; this has been done by Diels, for instance, in his collection of the fragments of the pre-Socratics, as well as by Reinhardt, whose book on Parmenides has put Xenophanes, too, in an entirely new light.[10] But I agree with Burnet that no such didactic poem ever existed. The mere fact that two late grammarians speak of Ξενοφάνης ἐν τῷ περὶ φύσεως no more proves the existence of a didactic epic of this sort than Plutarch's reference to Σόλων ἐν τοῖς φυσικοῖς proves that Solon had a system of physics or wrote a philosophical poem on nature. Plutarch's statement means nothing more than that somewhere in his poems Solon spoke of lightning and thunder or of a storm at sea—that is, of φυσικά.[11] If we find, therefore, that Xenophanes is the very same satirist and critic in his purely hexametrical fragments as he is in the distichs, we can only conclude that both verse-forms were used in the satires or *silloi*, and that a philosopher Xenophanes with a system of his own never really existed. We possess no fragments by Xenophanes of purely philosophical content which compel us to assume the existence of a coherent didactic epos by him on the nature of the universe. What we do have points rather to a discussion of certain natural phenomena and problems in his *silloi*, in which, as we are told, he criticized the views of other philosophers and poets. Even Aristotle and Theophrastus did not count him as a natural philosopher; Aristotle called his thought 'rather primitive', and Theophrastus excluded his views from his great historical work on the theories of the natural philosophers, because he seemed to belong to a different category of thinkers.[12]

Then what sort of man was he? Gomperz has called attention to a testimonium which reads: 'But he also recited his own poems like a rhapsode.'[13] At that time the rhapsode's profession was well esteemed. The rhapsodes gave public recitations of the Homeric epics; and as I interpret this statement about Xenophanes, it means nothing more than that he recited his own verses, just as the itinerant rhapsodes recited those of Homer. But Gomperz lays special stress on the word 'also': 'he recited his own verses *also*'. Gomperz concludes from this that Xenophanes was primarily a reciter of Homer, and read his own poems only as an added attraction. But the *silloi* are well known to be full of mordant satire and scorn directed against Homer and Hesiod—a fact quite out of accord with the assumption that Xenophanes was a rhapsode. The easiest way out of this difficulty for Gomperz was to suggest that while the poet spent his days in the market-place reciting Homer and eulogizing him, he spent his evenings at the banquets of the rich and mighty (of which he has given us a detailed picture),[14] where he voiced his own enlightened views and castigated the very gods to whom he was forced to render public allegiance in order to earn his daily bread.[15]

Examples of such double-entry book-keeping are by no means lacking in the history of later periods of enlightenment, but the age of Pindar and Aeschylus did not call it forth; and if there ever was a man with whose character such a game of hide-and-seek was incompatible, that man was Xenophanes. We must abandon any attempt to think of him as a rhapsode. He was not at all as Gomperz depicts him—a counterpart of Plato's rhapsode Ion, wandering through the cities of Greece solemnly attired in purple, with the plaudits of the crowd continually ringing in his ears; still less was he a man to sweep his listeners off their feet with counterfeit enthusiasm for Homer, only to unmask himself with cynical abandon in a small circle after his public performance. This bold champion, brusque to the point of intolerance, was himself and utterly himself. His sole enthusiasm was his championship of a truth which he saw emerging from the ruins of all previous ways of viewing the world; and this enthusiasm was genuine and natural. The only mistaken idea in this conception of him is the one which modern interpreters have erroneously read into it—the supposed rhapsode's professional relationship to Homer. For the chief business of the rhapsode was to maintain Homer's official classical prestige, and this is what Xenophanes attacks most vehemently. Only by his polemic against the *laudatores Homeri* can he really be understood.[16]

Xenophanes was an intellectual revolutionary. The earlier philosophers had presented their new conceptions of reality to their contemporaries as a plain, well-rounded whole. But Xenophanes was a man of an altogether different sort, who

perceived the devastating novelty of their approach and loudly
proclaimed that it was irreconcilable with the traditional views.
The dominant intellectual and moral tradition of the time had
no more distinguished representative than Homer, by whom,
as Plato remarks, all Hellas had been educated. Xenophanes
thought the same: to him Homer was the man

From whom all men have learned since the beginning.[17]

These words reveal a clear awareness of Homer's overpowering
authority throughout the realm of Greek culture. And it was
precisely because of this awareness that Xenophanes felt compelled to attack Homer as the mainstay of the prevailing errors.
At this moment the latent antagonism between the new philosophical thinking and the old world of myth, which had dominated the earlier achievements of the Greek spirit, broke into
open conflict. The clash was inevitable. While the pioneer
thinkers of the new philosophy had not marshalled their discoveries polemically, Xenophanes made the world of myth a
focal point for his opposition. It was not unreasonable that he,
the poet, should be the one to see in this situation implications
which spelled disaster for all previous poetry. It seemed to
him self-evident that the poet is the one real educator of the
people, and his work the only genuinely responsible authority
of *paideia*. And so it was with Xenophanes that the work of
deliberately transfusing the new philosophical ideas into the
intellectual blood-stream of Greece began.

It is characteristic of the effect of Ionian philosophy upon the
most enlightened contemporary minds that the problem of God
is central for Xenophanes. This is the best evidence of the
extent to which the new doctrines of the origin of the world had
encroached upon the domain of religion. Naturally, Anaximander must have sensed his own opposition to the traditional
anthropomorphic deities when he boldly asserted the Boundless
to be the Divine, and thus refused to let divine nature take the
form of distinct individual gods; but it is Xenophanes who first
declares war on the old gods with the impressive words:

. . . One god is the highest among gods and men;
In neither his form nor his thought is he like unto mortals.[18]

By this negation the poet gives his newly discovered knowledge
a fixed direction and propulsive force which it hitherto lacked.

These are words which catch men's fancy far more easily than those of Anaximander, despite the genius with which he first expressed this knowledge. For not only did Xenophanes choose to put his message in poetical form; he also consciously applied his philosophical insight to the whole world of the anthropomorphic gods of Homer and Hesiod—a world which had previously counted as plain historical fact, but which now was collapsing. In these two lines the bearing of the new knowledge upon the old divinities is made explicit for the first time, not only in its positive aspects, but also negatively and critically. The philosophical intuition of a single world-ground, of course, involves new riddles more difficult than those for which it provides an answer. Xenophanes himself points out in another context that even when one sees the truth, this knowledge can never give its possessor complete assurance of its validity; about the highest questions there must always be widespread doubt.[19] This insight, which, though tinged with resignation, is still far removed from the thorough-going scepticism of later centuries,[20] inevitably appears whenever man first starts to reason about these problems. But one thing at least is certain for Xenophanes: the human mind is an inadequate form through which to comprehend that infinite, all-governing unity which the philosophers have recognized as the principle of all things. It never occurs to Xenophanes to suggest that God may be without form altogether. It is significant that in all the time that the Greeks gave their philosophical attention to these matters, the problem of the form ($\mu o \rho \phi \acute{\eta}$) of the Divine was one that never lost its importance. It always remained an essential part of the problem *de natura deorum*,[21] and in the Stoic philosophy it acquired new impetus in the doctrine of God's immanence in the world, which was represented as a sphere.[22] But Xenophanes does not express his views of the divine form in positive terms. He does not say that the world is God, so that God's form is merely the world's form; for Xenophanes is not to be dismissed with the word pantheist. He merely makes way for a philosophic conception by denying that God's form is human.[23]

In other respects he retains the conventional Greek pluralism. For understandable reasons Christian writers have always tended to read their own monotheism into Xenophanes' proclamation of the One God; but while he extols this God as more than human, he also describes him explicitly as 'the greatest among gods and men'.[24] This manner of speaking, with its polar juxtaposition of gods and men, follows the old epic formulas; nevertheless, it still makes it perfectly clear that besides the One God there must be others, just as there are men. On the other hand, it would be wrong to conclude that these must be the anthropomorphic gods of the epic, which would rank side by side with the one highest God and would enable Xenophanes to compromise with the popular religion. It is more plausible to think of the dictum of Thales that all things are full of gods, or of Anaximander's doctrine of the one divine primal ground and the innumerable gods (that is, the innumerable worlds) that have come into being,[25] even if we have no right to ascribe to Xenophanes any specific dogma of this sort. In any case the one all-embracing God is so far. superior to all the other lesser divine forces that he alone could really seem important to Xenophanes.

But Xenophanes goes even farther in draining off the residue of anthropomorphism from his conception of the One God. He writes that God 'sees as a whole, thinks as a whole, hears as a whole'.[26] Thus God's consciousness is not dependent upon sense organs or anything comparable. On the other hand, Xenophanes' God is unquestionably represented as a conscious, personal being, a fact which distinguishes him from what Anaximander calls the Divine. The philosophical attempt to divest the gods of their forms, which Stenzel sees in Anaximander's conception, is quite foreign to Xenophanes. The fact that he speaks very definitely of the One God who is more than all others is hardly to be explained as a mere reversion to traditional poetic language. One would not be likely to say of Anaximander's 'Boundless' that it sees as a whole, thinks as a whole, hears as a whole. Moreover, Anaximander, unlike Xenophanes, does not attack the gods in order to supplant them with his own divine Being. But no one can doubt that Xenophanes actually prays to his God; we could be sure of this even if we did not have his banquet elegy to show us how seriously and directly he puts his religious ideas into practice.[27]

These ideas, however, continue to unfold in sharp opposition to the prevailing faith, just as if they were intended to become a prevailing faith themselves. God, says Xenophanes:

> . . . ever abides
> In the selfsame place without moving; nor is it fitting
> For him to move hither and thither, changing his place.[28]

Here Xenophanes is again criticizing the Homeric representation. In Homer the gods' quickness of movement is construed as a veritable token of the divine power.[29] Xenophanes, however, demands that his God be immobile, for he sees in this a mark of the highest dignity, as is clear from the words: 'Nor is it fitting for him to move.' (We meet the same religious intuition again in the contemporary statues and paintings which represent the gods as sitting in full majesty upon thrones, though naturally the artists had to express this insight in anthropomorphic terms.) Furthermore, the idea of God's absolute calm and immobility leads inevitably to an altered conception of his manner of acting upon things:

> But effortlessly he sets all things astir
> By the power of his mind alone.[30]

This conjunction of omnipotence and repose is of tremendous importance in paving the way for the idea of God that we meet in later years. We think at once of the Aristotelian unmoved mover, an idea which really originates here in Xenophanes. Aristotle's doctrine attempts, by adopting the Platonic formula κινεῖ ὡς ἐρώμενον,[31] to give greater plausibility to this noble conception of divine action upon the world. In Aeschylus we find much earlier evidence of the power and vigour of the idea, particularly in the great prayer to Zeus in *The Suppliants*. The poet depicts the divine dominion in a way that reveals not only the critical significance of Xenophanes' pioneering for a purer conception of God, but also its positive religious significance for his own time. The notion that God can sway the world merely by the power of his mind is shifted from the cosmic to the ethical sphere.

> Down from their high-towered hopes
> He flings poor, wretched mortals,
> Donning no armour of might.
> For gods act without effort:
> High from their hallowed seats
> They somehow make their own thinking
> Come all at once to pass.[32]

Aeschylus' expressive but almost prosaic 'somehow' (πως) shows that he is moved by a great and difficult idea which is readily perceptible to his religious feeling, though his reason cannot grasp the 'how' of this activity. This is not the only place in which the poet reveals that he has been directly influenced by contemporary philosophical thought and scientific discoveries. When he imagines the divine powers dwelling on high, he still clings to the old conception of the gods as throned in heaven; but we must bear in mind that even Xenophanes, as Aristotle rightly declares, conceived his idea of the One God by 'looking up at the sky', thus bringing the divine unity before his very eyes.[33]

According to Auguste Comte, the metaphysical stage, which follows the mythical stage of intellectual development and is itself superseded by positive science, is the critical crucible through which the mythical consciousness must pass. We need not discuss the value of Comte's whole system as a contribution to intellectual history; but it does at least help us to formulate the relation between mythical religion and Xenophanes' metaphysical thought in a manner quite consistent with his own genius. In Xenophanes the critical side of the new philosophical theology becomes fully conscious. The idea of an omnipotent Being, transcending all the other powers in the world, even the gods themselves, was one which the later epic-writers had already associated with their highest god. In the eighth book of the *Iliad*, for example, the poet makes Zeus say to the other gods:

> ... And if
> You should try to dangle a cable of gold from the sky,
> And hang on it, all you goddesses and all you gods,
> You could not drag great Counsellor Zeus from his heaven
> Down to the plain, no matter how mighty your straining.
> But I—were I once of a mind to lift, I'd pull
> The whole pack of you up, with all the land and the ocean,
> And fasten the cable to one of the peaks of Olympus,
> And leave you swinging.[34]

Aristotle cites this passage as the first intimation of the power of the unmoved mover in the early history of Greek thought.[35] But the all-too-human form of this conception would have struck Xenophanes as childish. In his century thinking men had not yet learned to hunt for their primitive forbears. Xeno-

phanes' God has no need to nod his head like the Homeric
Zeus to make Olympus quake with terror.[36] Only the phrase
νόου φρενὶ πάντα κραδαίνει betrays the unconscious persistence
of the old Homeric tendency to humanize the sublime.[37]

The fragments reveal further characteristic evidence of Xenophanes' critique of anthropomorphism. He finds his task
easiest in the realm of ethics, where the way has already been
prepared, largely by the progressive moralization of the gods
during the sixth century.

> . . . Homer and Hesiod say that the gods
> Do all manner of things which men would consider disgraceful:
> Adultery, stealing, deceiving each other.[38]

Godhead must certainly be free from any moral weakness which
even men consider blameworthy: this is a point on which
Xenophanes and all his more thoughtful contemporaries would
agree. But he is not content with so easy a victory. He
launches another attack at the very root of the epic theogonies:

> . . . But mortals suppose that the gods undergo generation;
> They dress them with clothes like their own, as well as with voices
> And figures.[39]

The idea of the un-becoming and the unending, with which
Anaximander characterized his divinity, the *apeiron*, put an
end to such notions. Xenophanes merely works out some of the
consequences of this philosophy in detail,[40] a process which
must have brought him up against the problem of the origin of
anthropomorphism:

> . . . But if cattle and horses had hands, and were able
> To paint with their hands, and to fashion such pictures as men do,
> Then horses would pattern the forms of the gods after horses,
> And cows after cattle, giving them just such a shape
> As those which they find in themselves.[41]

Then there would be theriomorphic gods as well as anthropomorphic ones. Apparently Xenophanes was not aware that
there were already just such animal-gods in Egypt, and man-
made at that; but he would have found this only a little disturbing to his theory, which he proceeds to develop with further
ethnological details:

> . . . The gods of the Ethiopians are black with snub noses,
> While those of the Thracians are blond, with blue eyes and red hair.[42]

Thus each race apotheosizes its own type. The gods of the

Greeks, to be sure, are more beautiful; but this does not give them any better claim to be regarded as the only true gods. They, too, are merely copied after one particular human race, and so they confirm the words of the poet:

> Dass jeglicher das Beste, was er kennt,
> Er Gott, ja seinen Gott benennt.[43]

Xenophanes was the first to formulate that religious universalism which, both in later antiquity and more especially in the Christian era, was deemed to be an essential feature in the idea of God, indispensable to any true religion. This does not mean, of course, that its opposite, religious particularism, was ever a conscious article of faith even in the earlier mythical stage of Greek religion; Homer himself thought of his Greeks and Trojans as praying to the same gods, despite the division of their sympathies between the two warring parties. Since Homer's time, however, the Greeks had come to recognize how various the ideals of the gods were among individual nations; and this realization could only lead them to deduce, from the very fact of this particularism, the vanity of all such distinctions between gods, however naturally they may have come about. In the western world, universalism began neither with the Christians nor with the prophets of Israel, but with the Greek philosophers. When St. Augustine in his *De civitate Dei* speaks of Greek philosophy in this connexion as the precursor of the Christian religion, he is giving a thoroughly correct account of the historical relationship between the two.[44]

In this development Xenophanes was not an isolated phenomenon. He merely brought to the full light of consciousness the inevitable consequences of the philosophical revolution in religious faith to which the Ionian theories of nature led; from his time on, universalism had a place in the theology of all the Greek thinkers as one of their basic assumptions, whether or not they took the trouble to express it.[45] True, the time was not yet ripe for the new conception to play any decisive role in the history of Greece as a nation. The public status of the *polis*-gods in the Greek city-states was as yet unimpaired, although a personage like Xenophanes had already broadcast his criticism of them far and wide. Even Xenophanes still thought of his own refined conception of God in connexion with the *polis* and the problem of its legal order. This fact is clear from an elegy that has come down to us in its entirety, where he praises the cultivation of the intellect (σοφίη). Xenophanes considered himself uniquely equipped to propagate σοφίη in his new home in the west of the Greek world; and it is only because he saw in it the highest political virtue that he considered his own efforts justified.[46] Not until the fourth century, when the gods of the *polis* had died and the *polis* itself was losing its identity in the world-empire of Alexander, did the universalistic theology come into its own and emerge from the background of philosophy to cushion the impending collapse of all established authority.[47]

We have already pointed out that while Xenophanes' utterances presuppose the new and profoundly disturbing experience of the Anaximandrian cosmology, they also contain something peculiarly his own. Anaximander's conception of the Divine was deduced by pure speculation about the idea of an absolute beginning, from which it acquired its attributes—its boundlessness and its property of never having become. But in Xenophanes we find a new motif, which is the actual source of his theology. It is nothing that rests on logical proof, nor is it really philosophical at all, but springs from an immediate sense of awe at the sublimity of the Divine. It is a feeling of reverence that leads Xenophanes to deny all the finite shortcomings and limitations laid upon the gods by traditional religion, and makes him a unique theological figure, despite his dependence on the views of the natural philosophers. Only as a theologian, indeed, can he really be understood. His religious motif—the demand for utter sublimity in the Godhead—is expressed with particular clarity in the assertion that it is not seemly for God to move hither and thither.[48] Unrest is not appropriate to the divine majesty. The word ἐπιπρέπει, which Xenophanes uses here, is not, as a matter of fact, repeated in any of the other fragments; but it reveals the criterion on which his entire criticism of anthropomorphism is based: all these human frailties are out of keeping with God's essential nature. The misdeeds of the Homeric and Hesiodic gods are incompatible with the moral elevation of the Divine; nor are clothing, speech, human form, and birth any more appropriate. In the concept of the appropriate, which here appears for the first time in the Greek tradition,

we strike one of the distinctive aspects of Greek genius,
the significance of which for later ages is incalculable.[49] It
originates in that feeling for harmony and proportion which is
peculiarly characteristic of the Greek artistic temper.[50] But it
is no less important in the realm of ethics and politics and in
the theoretical approach to reality. In the history of this basic
category of the Greek spirit a special chapter (and a particularly
important one in the light of its enormous influence) should be
devoted to its application to the problem of God—the problem
of what things befit the divine nature and what things do not.

Such a chapter must begin with Xenophanes. His own for-
mulations are so striking that nothing is left for posterity but
to quote his celebrated words and ring the changes upon them.
We need only mention a few main stages in the history of his
influence. Euripides' treatment of the gods in his tragedies is
largely determined by Xenophanes' criticism of the inappro-
priateness of the way in which they were represented in the
traditional myths;[51] so are Plato's recommendations for the
use of myth as an educational device in the *Republic*.[52] Xenophanes' doctrine provides the basis for the discourse of the
Stoic in Cicero's dialogue, *De natura deorum*.[53] The Stoic distinction between mythical and philosophical theology, which
reached St. Augustine by way of Varro,[54] eventually goes back
to Xenophanes; and in St. Augustine's critique of the gods of
the heathen poets (where he follows Varro rather closely)—*ut
furati sint, ut adulterarint*[55]—we still hear the echo of Xenophanes' κλέπτειν μοιχεύειν τε nearly a thousand years afterwards.
Late Greek invents a special term to designate the theological
category of 'that which befits the divine nature'—the θεοπρεπές.
Probably this word was coined by the Stoics; at any rate,
through them it came down to the Church Fathers, who made
it one of the corner-stones of Christian theology.[56] The postulate
of the θεοπρεπές is fundamental to the allegorical interpretation
of Homer's tales of the gods in Stoicism.[57] In the first century
of our era, when the Greeks, artists and philosophers alike,
sensed a greater need for sublimity in conceiving of the divine
nature, the author of the treatise *On the Sublime* (whose taste
was much too refined for allegorizing) rejected the Homeric
gods as falling short of his standards of true sublimity, and
pointed to the Mosaic account of Creation with its 'Let there

be light' as a far more satisfactory model.[58] Of course the conception of the Creation has little to do with Xenophanes; but clearly his philosophical theology has done more than anything else to smooth the way for accepting Judaeo-Christian monotheism.

Xenophanes' conception of the One God has always roused the interest of monistic philosophers (ἐνίζοντες) because he was the first, as Aristotle tells us, to teach the unity of the highest principle.[59] His conception seems to have a close connexion with Parmenides' theory of the One Being and consequently with the philosophy of the Eleatics. Inasmuch as he wrote an epic of the founding of Elea, the ancient historians of philosophy, who were on the watch for school successions, saw in him the father of Eleaticism. The One God of Xenophanes was thought to be an earlier version of the One Being of Parmenides, as if the religious intuition of the All-one had preceded the logical conception of the ὄν.[60] This view long dominated our own histories until it was vigorously upset by Karl Reinhardt's pioneer work on Parmenides.[61] Reinhardt triumphantly demonstrated Parmenides' complete originality, and succeeded in showing that it was he and not Xenophanes who created the Eleatic theory of unity. His argument broke the traditional link between Xenophanes and the Eleatics, and allowed the problem of Xenophanes' position in history and his chronological relations with Parmenides to come up for fresh discussion. But Reinhardt also tried to give this problem a new solution by supplementing the direct fragments with the anonymous later work *On Xenophanes, Melissus, and Gorgias* as source material. Modern historians of philosophy, such as Zeller, Burnet, and Diels, had questioned the authenticity of this work so far as it dealt with Xenophanes' teachings, and accordingly refused to make any use of it. The little treatise was generally regarded as a product of the school philosophy of the later ancient period, and no one was ready to believe that its material came directly from Xenophanes' poems. It seemed much more likely that its author had taken Xenophanes' well-known assertions about the One God and his attributes, combined them with certain constituents of Parmenides' logic of Being, and thus tried to bring them into a strictly systematic dialectical form. But Reinhardt saw it all quite differently. Nothing seemed to him

to exclude the possibility that Xenophanes, supposedly a
rhapsode and inveterate popularizer, quite devoid of philosophical originality but clever enough to learn from everybody,
had also borrowed a large number of Parmenides' ideas, and
that therefore the strange hodge-podge in the tract *On Xenophanes*, the derivative quality of which had been rightly recognized by the critics, actually went back to Xenophanes himself.
If this view should prove correct, then we already possess not
only the few fragments of Xenophanes on which we have re-
lied heretofore, but also a whole theological system after the
Eleatic pattern. In that case, Xenophanes' idea of God would be
nothing but the ὄν of Parmenides in a theological mask; for the
theological arguments of the tract *On Xenophanes* actually do
not demonstrate the One God at all, but merely the One Being.
Far from having been the father of Eleaticism, Xenophanes
would thus simply have been a follower of the school, and not
a particularly original one.

This view fails to explain Xenophanes' enormous influence
on later religious development. But the only ideas that have
exerted such an influence are those with which the remaining
fragments of his poems have given us some familiarity; we do
not find the influence of the elaborate theology ascribed to
him by the author of the tract *On Xenophanes*, the dialectical
arguments and systematic structure of which stand in such
striking contrast with the intuitive reasoning of the fragments.
The only kind of work upon which this elaborate, connected
treatise could have been based must have been a good-sized
didactic poem; but, as we have seen already, it is quite impossible to prove that such a poem ever existed. Even if Xenophanes had written a work *On Nature*, it is hard to imagine
how this theological dialectic would fit into it. Certainly its
logical form never gives us the impression of being immediately
derived from Parmenides. From him, of course, comes the list
of attributes which the alleged Xenophanes tries to deduce as
the properties of his God; but the inferences we find in his arguments could hardly have been possible before the century of
Plato and Aristotle. We must therefore attribute them to some
later writer, presumably the author of the treatise himself.
Also, we must discount the unknown writer's authority in the
light of the plain statements of Aristotle. To be sure, while

Aristotle is still our most valuable source of information about the pre-Socratics, the weight of his testimony has been decidedly impaired during the last fifty years as we have become more and more clearly aware of his inability to grasp the ideas of his predecessors except in the fixed categories of his own system. But here we are dealing with facts that are almost unmistakable. Let us examine them briefly.

Aristotle reports that Parmenides thought of the One in terms of its λόγος or essence, while the Eleatic Melissus thought of it in terms of its matter, so that for Parmenides the One was limited, for Melissus unlimited. But Xenophanes, Aristotle continues, knew nothing of such a problem and did not aim at either the logical or the material One, but merely looked up at the whole heaven and said that the One was God.[62] Now if we are to believe the author of the tract *On Xenophanes*, we must regard this account as false, for he says that according to Xenophanes the world is neither limited nor unlimited. If that is true, then Aristotle simply cannot have read Xenophanes; otherwise he could not have maintained that Xenophanes fails to distinguish between the logical and the material One, and therefore says nothing about whether it is limited or unlimited.[63] But it is really much more probable that the author of the late tract had not read Xenophanes at all. Instead he took his data from Aristotle and misunderstood it. After reading this good witness's statement that Xenophanes neither called the One limited nor called it unlimited, he drew the absurd conclusion that, according to Xenophanes, the One was neither limited nor unlimited. Out of Aristotle's merely negative statement he thus fashioned an utterly preposterous positive dogma, which he then proceeded to put in Xenophanes' mouth.[64] This is quite enough to prove the untrustworthiness of the author. It is undoubtedly true that all the arguments for the One which he attributes to Xenophanes actually point to the Being of Parmenides and not to the One God; but this fact merely proves that he has inserted Xenophanes' God into the Parmenidean ontology.

On the other hand, we can well understand how the author of the tract *On Xenophanes*, writing at a later period, can have come to devise this Eleatic *rationale* for the philosopher's idea of God. Evidently he felt that Eleaticism was precisely the sort of thing that Xenophanes stood for. Like all of us, he had learned in school that Xenophanes was the father of Eleaticism,[65] and accordingly he attempted to understand the theory of the One God in terms of the Eleatic logic of Being. He therefore had some reason to suppose that the Parmenidean ontology must have been potentially present in Xenophanes' theology from the first. But as a matter of fact, the God of his Xenophanes is only the Being of Parmenides in disguise, and has nothing to do with the historical Xenophanes, nor is it the germ-cell of Parmenides' philosophy. The whole theological Eleatic Xenophanes is a chimaera. He is purely synthetic, the product of a doxographical attempt to build up a set of teacher–pupil relationships which, as Reinhardt himself has admirably shown, never existed in the form we have always imagined. But if Xenophanes is far from being the father of Eleatic philosophy, he is just as far from being its unoriginal devotee; we cannot even think of him as a person who has translated this philosophy into theological terms. Here Reinhardt himself has not sufficiently escaped the Eleaticizing view of Xenophanes which he himself has refuted. He has accordingly made him a popularizing eclectic—an hypothesis rendered possible only by Gomperz's view of Xenophanes as a rhapsode. Each of these theories is as impossible as the other. The fragments of Xenophanes' poems tell us something entirely different. It is these that we must follow; and the reports of the best authorities, Aristotle and Theophrastus, agree with them throughout. Xenophanes was never a philosopher of the type of Parmenides, least of all an eclectic pseudo-philosopher.[66] He had many interests, as his poems reveal. To the extent that he participated in the philosophical thought of his time—and this did not yet include the Eleatic doctrines but merely the Ionian philosophy of nature—he was an enlightened man with an alert sense for the natural causes of all phenomena. But above all he was profoundly impressed by the way in which philosophy was disturbing the old religion, and it was this that made him insist upon a new and purer conception of the divine nature. His peculiar piety alone is enough to assure him a place in the history of ideas. Accordingly we cannot really understand him as an historical figure except by tracing the development of rational theology as it emerges from Greek philosophical thinking.

CHAPTER IV

THE SO-CALLED ORPHIC THEOGONIES

THE fewer the petrified remains of doctrine from which we can still hammer out the sparks of genius as we study the earliest thinkers, so much the more precious is a man like Xenophanes, who shows us how widely that genius radiated—from the edge of Asia, the birthplace of Greek philosophical thought, to the westernmost borders of Greek civilization. Xenophanes is by no means the only Greek poet of his time to be touched by the rising philosophy. The Sicilian Epicharmus, for example, the first writer of literary comedies, resident at the court of the tyrant Hieron of Syracuse, has left us some clever verbal fencing over the origin of things, in which one of his characters shrewdly criticizes the venerable Hesiodic *Theogony* because it speaks of Chaos, the ultimate beginning itself, as having come into being.[1] Clearly the playwright had had some acquaintance with the natural philosophers' conception of a first principle which itself has had no beginning. Epicharmus also bears witness to the whirlpool of doubt into which this conception had drawn the religious thought of the time. When we see the whole problem aired before thousands of listeners as a field for comedians' glibness, it is evident that the intellectual dispute which philosophy had stirred up had already begun to have an unsettling effect upon wider and wider strata of society.

Nevertheless, the old style of theogonic thinking is by no means dead, as this very discussion in Epicharmus shows. Even in its oldest Hesiodic form, theogony is a typical transition-product, not unconnected with the new philosophical spirit, an offshoot of a religious attitude which has already become more thoughtful; so it is hardly surprising to find it flourishing steadily with the quickening growth of philosophy throughout the whole sixth century in an imposing array of theogonic works, most of which still retain the poetical form of their model, Hesiod. The very closeness of this association shows us that these two types of intellectual attitude are sister branches of a single root reaching deep into the parent soil of religion. In the theogonies religious interest is focused directly upon the problem from which all philosophical thinking in this early period arises—the problem of cosmogony—while philosophy reveals its close relationship with its theogonic sister by assigning direct theological significance to its own cosmogonical discoveries. Thus it is inevitable that the philosophical conception of God should also prove positively fruitful for the old mythical theology in its vitalizing counter-effects upon theogonic speculation. Indeed, religious speculation, far from having its principles overthrown, acquires from this stimulus certain new incentives of extreme importance; for though it becomes indirectly dependent upon philosophy, it is now able to guard itself from the strongest attacks of a philosophical naturalism by taking full advantage of its own position. This advantage lies in the fact that while the philosopher must work with rational concepts of his own devising, theology always operates with the images and symbols of a living world of religious ideas firmly rooted in the popular consciousness. Even philosophy must fall back on such symbolism when it faces the ultimate enigmas. Xenophanes has already remarked that the very wisest of men never knows whether he really has found the truth about God and the universe.[2] Alcmaeon, the physician and student of nature, expresses the same conviction in an important passage at the beginning of his work;[3] and his later successor, the author of the treatise *On Ancient Medicine*, which has come down to us in the Hippocratic collection, agrees whole-heartedly.[4] How could any defender of the mythical theology fail to perceive here a vindication of his faith and keep from turning it to account? The more loudly the philosopher insists upon the sublimity of his own conception of God, all the more must anyone who accepts the old idea of a plurality of divine beings see a basic weakness in the indefiniteness and incomprehensibility of this philosophical God, and all the more readily will he exercise his inherited Greek impulse to endow his gods with definite forms and names.[5]

From this introduction to our special treatment of the sixth-century theogonic literature, we can see how inevitably misleading are those older accounts of the history of Greek philosophy which, following Aristotle, put the so-called Orphic systems at the very beginning, along with Hesiod, as a primitive stage of the philosophical spirit.[6] Diels evaded the problem by

placing the remains of these writings as an appendix at the end
of his collection of the fragments of the pre-Socratics. The
latest editor of this classical work has now shifted them back
to the beginning, so that they are again at the starting-point
of their wanderings.[7] The truth is that the theogonic writers
cannot be understood except in the light of their close reciprocal
relationships with the philosophers of their own period who are
connected with them by the common bond of theological
speculation, no matter how much they may differ in intellectual
type. We must make this fact especially clear. To neglect it
would be to obscure the organic interconnexions of the development of religious thought, in which philosophy has played a
role from the very beginning.

For the most part recent research in the history of religion
sees in the sixth-century theogonies, as we have remarked, a
branch of the great religious development we call Orphism.
Generally speaking, the sixth century meant for Greece a re-
newal of the religious life which the wave of naturalism in the
previous period had threatened to drown out. The devotions
of the official cult of the *polis*-gods were always in danger of
becoming merely external. They were largely under the control
of an enlightened stratum of high-born patricians. This was a
period when the individual was beginning to enjoy much greater
freedom of movement; both in art and poetry old forms lost
their rigidity, and naturalness became the supreme standard
for the depiction of reality no less than for the conduct of life.[8]
But in the course of the social upheaval caused by the widespread class struggles which were then beginning throughout
Greece and which were to reach their peak during the sixth
century, the social and political rise of the lower classes was
accompanied also by the penetration of their religious conceptions into the higher intellectual life, thus smoothing the way
for decisive changes. This revolution was heralded by the
mounting esteem in which the cult of Dionysus now came to
be held. Even as late as the Homeric epics this cult had hardly
been deemed worth considering; now, however, it began to
spread from the plains to the cities, where it soon found a place
in the public festivals and divine ceremonies. Originally the
orgiastic character of the Dionysiac religion had been looked
upon as something quite alien, an insult to all municipal

order, as is clear from the myths of Pentheus and Lycurgus. But in the sixth century—often for political reasons—it came into favour with the tyrants, who were the representatives of the social stratum newly coming into power. We can see this change, for example, in the displacement of the old civic hero Adrastus of Sicyon by the Dionysiac cult under the rule of the tyrant Cleisthenes, and in the mighty rise of the Dionysiac festivals in Corinth under Periander and in Athens under the Peisistratidae, to which ceremonies the dithyramb and Attic tragedy and comedy owe their origin.[9]

Hand in hand with the rise of the cult of Dionysus went a revival of the ancient local mysteries, which were favoured by much the same political forces. We know that Peisistratus built the new Telesterion at Eleusis; and the mysteries were flourishing everywhere else as well, a sure sign of the new inward religious fervour which the movement had inspired. In the Orphic orgies, which were restricted to no one place, we find a kind of religious rites (τελεταί) of which there is no evidence before this time, though they were supposed to have been founded by the mythical singer Orpheus. Rules for the purification of man from sins which he had committed were, as Plato ironically remarks, promulgated by itinerant beggar-prophets and other devotees both by word of mouth and by whole piles of tracts.[10] They also called Orphic certain ascetic rules of abstinence. Along with demands for abstention from meat and a purely vegetarian diet went a commandment enjoining justice in the conduct of life.[11] Thus the Orphic piety took the form of a definite βίος or way of living; but it also involved the observation of certain rites of sacrifice, exorcism, and expiation, which demanded some degree of training and accordingly necessitated a class of men professionally equipped for their performance.[12]

Modern students of the history of religion have gone a long way both in working out the details of this Orphic piety and in showing its influence on philosophy. According to Macchioro, who, to be sure, is an extreme partisan of the theory of Orphic influence, the teachings of Heraclitus and Plato are largely Orphic in origin.[13] Many have seen in Orphism a religion of an oriental type, working its way into the organic development of the Greek spirit from outside like a bit of foreign matter in the body. The problem is complicated by the fact that in later antiquity the name of Orpheus was so comprehensive a symbol that it tended more and more to include everything in the realm of mystical literature and mystical orgies. Almost all the initiatory rites to be found anywhere in Greece came to be looked upon as having Orpheus for their founder, even when they were not at all similar to those we have described. We must steer completely clear of these latter if we hope to determine what could properly be called Orphic religion during the sixth century. On the whole our most reliable evidence comes from writers of the fifth and fourth centuries, but the information they give us is very scanty.[14] Even the so-called Orphic hymns (which positively revel in the unions of the gods—a subject particularly dear to the Greeks of the later period) are of comparatively recent date.[15] In late antiquity there was also a so-called Orphic theogony by Hieronymus or Hellanicus, the chief features of which we can still reconstruct from Neoplatonic sources. But the principal work of this type was the set of *Sacred Discourses* or *Rhapsodies*—a long poem in twenty-four cantos like the *Iliad* and the *Odyssey*, on which it was obviously patterned.[16] The poem must have been of post-Alexandrian origin at the earliest, for the division of the Homeric poems into twenty-four books by the grammarians goes back no farther than this. Even Lobeck, the shrewd and inexorable older critic of the whole tangled problem of Orphism, thought it possible to put the *Rhapsodies* in the sixth century B.C.; and in this he was long followed by more recent scholars, such as Kern and others. Kern, however, in his useful collection of the fragments of the Orphic writings, in which both earlier and later fragments lie peacefully side by side, has himself abandoned the early dating for this long work.[17]

A sobering critical blow was struck by Wilamowitz in the posthumous second volume of his *Der Glaube der Hellenen*.[18] Whenever we used to find verses or phrases of Parmenides or Empedocles occurring in the *Rhapsodies*, it seemed obvious that these thinkers had made use of the Orphic theogony;[19] now, however, we recognize the error fostered by an exaggerated notion of the influence of the Orphics on philosophy. So when we find anyone looking for Orphic theories in all the philosophers and seeking to trace the Orphic conception of sin in

Anaximander's clear and simple words about the passing-away of things as a punishment (see p. 34 ff., above), we may regard him with the utmost scepticism.[20]

The question arises whether we can prove that there ever were any theogonies in the early period which can properly be designated as Orphic. Aristotle certainly speaks of some Orphic poems with theogonic subject-matter; these, however, were not the work of Orpheus, as he is careful to explain, but of the poet Onomacritus.[21] Onomacritus lived at the tyrant court of the Peisistratids in Athens during the sixth century, and eventually had to be banished by his princely patrons because his colleague Lasus of Hermione caught him in the act of forging some verses under the name of another celebrated prophet, Epimenides the Cretan, and a great scandal seemed imminent. Later, when the tyrants themselves went into exile, they again joined company with Onomacritus.[22] This affair is typical of the whole pseud-onymous theogonic literature. Diels, for instance, has shown that while the collection of oracles that goes under the pseud-onym of Epimenides probably antedates the Persian wars (it would fit into Onomacritus' period rather nicely), it must have had a number of *vaticinia ex eventu* interpolated into it during the war period.[23] This may remind us of the way in which some of the early Christian writings were falsely ascribed to the apostles. But the difference lies in the fact that the apostles really belonged exclusively to the Christian community, so that if any works were placed under their names it merely indicated that those works were intended for Christian readers. When, however, we find a forgery attributed to Orpheus, it does not necessarily mean that it was written for the faithful of a definite sect that called itself Orphic; for Orpheus was not the monopoly of any particular sect. He belonged to the Greek saga in general; he was not a specifically religious figure but rather a mythical singer of primeval times.[24] If poems were composed under his name, that meant no more than did use of the names of singers like Thamyris, Linus, or Musaeus, which were often borrowed as authors' pseudonyms in poems of the period. Even when the poems are theogonic in content, it is more difficult to prove that they are based on the tenets of any particular religious community. The fact is simply that the name of some authority from the earliest times, preferably of divine descent, would lend more prestige to the cosmic doctrines of the theogony than would that of some more commonplace individual; and when the name of Orpheus was utilized by adherents of the so-called Orphic rites, it did not mean that they had any connexion with the epics of the Pseudo-Orpheus. So we are not yet dealing with anything like a revelation in the Christian sense.

In modern works on the history of religion, however, these matters are handled quite differently. We read of an organized Orphic religious community whose tenets presumably came from the Orient. This community is supposed to have taught the first revealed religion; it is, indeed, a genuine Church with everything a Christian would consider appropriate. The initiates are its parishioners, the Orphic rites its sacraments, the mendicant priests its apostles; the later Orphic hymns constitute its parish hymnal and must therefore be of extreme antiquity. The dogma alone is lacking, and this is promptly found in the theogonies attributed to Orpheus. Onomacritus would be considered a dogmatic theologian, so to speak, the Origen of the Orphic church. But this attractive picture is drawn too closely after a fixed *a priori* pattern. This early precursor of Christianity is in fact merely a replica of the Christian religion projected back into the sixth century. The germ of the idea is already present in Erwin Rohde's famous book *Psyche*, and has more recently been worked out in greater detail, particularly in Kern's history of Greek religion.[25] Kern's attempt to solve the Orphic problem by approaching it with the yardstick of a specific religious type familiar to us in history, and correcting the Greek tradition to tally with it, leads me to remark on a few matters of principle that may not be irrelevant in the light of certain preconceived opinions which at present are rather widespread.

This reconstruction of the Orphic religion is based on the expressed assumption that theology and dogma are symptoms of a definitely oriental type of mentality.[26] If there is any probability that such a mentality is present in the Orphic faith of the Greeks, it depends on the hypothesis that that faith is of oriental origin. Kern thinks that all dogma, and therefore all theology in our sense of the word, is alien to the Greeks; but to make so sharp an antithesis between the Greeks and the

Christian Church by representing them in the naïve modern fashion as a race of liberal free-thinkers is to narrow the horizon of comparison far too much. Naturally the Greek religion was without either theological dogma or creed. Nevertheless it was the Greeks who brought the Christian faith into the form of dogma, and the very history of Christian dogma was enacted on the soil of Greek culture. The only way the Greeks could make the oriental religion conform with their own nature was to approach it through the problems and the methods of Greek philosophy.[27] But on no account is the dogmatic and theological element in Christianity, which was developed in the first four centuries of our era, an oriental product. The Church Father, Gregory of Nyssa, who, as a man of Asia Minor, stands virtually at the watershed dividing the Greek mind from the Oriental, was fully aware of this fact and formulated it with masterly clarity: nothing, he says, is so characteristic of the Greeks as the erroneous notion that 'all Christianity rests entirely on dogmas'.[28] Sects, dogma, and theology, indeed, are definitely products of the Greek mind, and their intellectual structure is such that nothing else could have given them their characteristic stamp. It is not, however, from the Greek religion that they arise, but from philosophy, which, at the time of its impact on Christianity, was split up among a number of sects, each distinguished by its own rigid dogmatical system. Even if we cannot characterize the intellectual attitude of the early Greek thinkers as dogma in the rigid sense of the Stoics or Epicureans of the Hellenistic age,[29] theirs is the root from which both concept and word have grown; and if there was anything at all comparable to a dogma among the Greeks of the sixth century B.C., it must be sought among the philosophers and not in the Orphic rites. A figure like Xenophanes shows well enough how philosophy, with the peculiar firmness of intellectual conviction that characterizes it, can give rise to a dogmatic pathos—an entirely new phenomenon, not quite untouched by that impatience with which we usually view the religious opinions of our fellow-men whenever they strike us as erroneous. But a truly religious dogma is something of which this period has as yet no inkling. The theogonic theories arising as a Hesiodic aftermath have no such significance in contemporary religious life. They merely represent a constantly renewed endeavour to solve the problems of the origin of the world and the nature of the divine powers (which philosophy attacks with its own methods) without abandoning the forms in which the old faith conceived them, though more and more reliance is placed on the help of constructive intelligence. No speculation so unexacting can lead to any rigid theory. I grant that this is already theology, but it is theology without dogma. It is quite as unattached to any particular credal sect as the *Theogony* of old Hesiod himself. In spite of the fact that it makes use of a rich religious tradition, it is essentially a free, individual creation.

In no other way can we explain the peculiar variability of the views appearing in the remains of these older theogonies. That their authors should have taken over many features from Hesiod or from one another is only natural among the Greeks, where a poet's relation to his predecessors is often very close even in fields less bound by tradition. For that reason any departure from the earlier works usually indicates a conscious attempt at correction.[30] If we are not careful, many of these variants will look rather inconsequential at first glance, as when, for instance, Aristotle reports that 'certain old poets' made the world begin with Night rather than with Chaos.[31] Eudemus corroborates this in his history of theology and expressly vouches for the fact that this doctrine belongs to a theogony ascribed to Orpheus.[32] The very idea of Chaos obviously implies that the yawning empty space at the beginning of things lay in nocturnal darkness. In the parabasis of Aristophanes' *Birds*, the chorus of birds, who are to become the gods of the new kingdom, rehearse an amusing bird-theogony cleverly parodying an actual poem of this type— indeed an Orphic theogony of the very sort described by Eudemus and Aristotle.[33] Chaos and Night are actually named together as the origin of all coming-to-be; so, too, are Primeval Darkness and Tartarus. Night has already appeared in Hesiod, but only in a subordinate role and not at the beginning.[34] Perhaps one of the reasons why Night is introduced in Aristophanes' verse is that the word Chaos is a neuter, and he needs as the first mother for his genealogy a female who has existed even before Heaven and Earth and is obviously of cosmogonic importance. But the poet is also going back to certain venerable ideas from the pre-Hellenic Chthonic religion, which knew a primeval goddess of this name. This is the same ancient Mother Night whom Aeschylus invokes with such genuine awe as the mother of the Erinyes.[35] The old struggle between these darksome powers and the bright Olympians, which lives again in Aeschylean tragedy, is no less present in the sixth century. In the primeval antithesis of Light and Night, from which the Pythagorean cosmology derives the origin of the world,[36] this struggle is presupposed as a truth directly evident to the religious sensibility. Aristotle is correct when he sees the significance of the conception of Night as opposed to Light in the Orphic theogony, and infers that in this genealogy the imperfect is consciously regarded as an earlier stage of the perfect and good, so that the Olympic pantheon becomes the culminating point in the world's development.[37] According to Plato the theogony of the so-called Orpheus brought the gods into the world in six generations, the last of which must have been the Olympians.[38]

If we compare this religious cosmology with the oldest natural philosophy, we are struck by the thoroughness with which the values have been transposed. The fact becomes even clearer when we observe that Aristophanes' parody-theogony is directly reminiscent of the philosophical conception of the infinite; for this is quite apparent in the words:

But first in the endless gulfs of Darkness, Night, black of pinion,
Gives birth to a wind-egg, from which, in the cycle of seasons,
Springs Eros, who wakens desire.[39]

That yawning, darksome infinity which existed in the beginning is not, as it was for Anaximander, the thing that is really divine, while all things that issue from it are ordained by time to return to its bosom as if by way of punishment;[40] rather, the true divinities are the gods whom Eros creates out of infinity— the powers of Light and Goodness. Time again plays a part; but its present function is that of bringing these later and higher stages of becoming out of the endless primeval night into individual existence.[41] The later writer has clearly perceived the significance of the Eros in Hesiod's *Theogony*;[42] he has emphasized Eros's position as an independent positive principle in the origin of the world by lifting him out of the procreative series and making him the first to be born from the world-egg that Night has hatched.[43] While the conception of the world-egg is not Hesiodic, we have evidence of its presence elsewhere on Greek soil. It is so closely in accord with the early zoomorphic feeling for nature that there is very little likelihood of its being derived from the Orient. For a moment it might seem that Aristophanes introduces the world-egg only in order that his Eros, who is a winged creature like the bird-gods descended from him, may be properly hatched. But since Eros had long been regarded as winged, it was very simple for the poets of the theogonies to hatch him out of the world-egg. That this is really an old conception is shown by the theogony written under the pseudonym of Epimenides and cited by Eudemus, which likewise involves a world-egg.[44] There is nothing specifically Orphic in this idea, but it was taken over by the later so-called Orphic theogony. In this recent poem the god Phanes originated from the egg. In the documents of later Hellenistic syncretism Phanes was identified with Erikepaios.[45] It used to be thought that both these names could be deciphered in old Orphic documents (though these documents, the gold plates of Thurii, have not been preserved in a form earlier than the second or third century B.C.); but Diels has seen the erroneousness of such an assumption.[46] There is therefore no evidence for the presence of Phanes in the sixth-century theogonies. Still less may we conclude from the discovery of a mystical papyrus of the third century B.C., containing the appeal 'Erikepaios, save me!',[47] that the sixth-century Orphic theogonies provided the dogmas for a redemption religion.

The theogony of the so-called Epimenides, to which we have already referred, unfortunately remains no more than a name to us; but it is important that the testimony of Eudemus proves it to be old.[48] The little that we can gather from his account of it allows us to put it side by side with the theogony of the so-called Orpheus. In the beginning, according to Epimenides, were Air and Night.[49] As in the older philosophy, Air ($\dot{a}\eta\rho$) is thought of as the void.[50] Air thus takes the place of Chaos; and as the word $\dot{a}\eta\rho$ is masculine, the neuter Chaos and feminine Night have now given way to a genuine male and female— Air and Night. We have here a correction of Hesiod similar to

4384   F

that in the Pseudo-Orpheus.[51] The author must next come
to some compromise with the Homeric doctrine according to
which Oceanus and Tethys are the progenitors of all things.[52]
So he simply combines it with the corrected Hesiodic theory of
Air and Night as the first couple, by making the 'two Titans',
who seem to be identical with Oceanus and Tethys, their children.[53] We get an impression of a similar contamination when
he makes the new couple Oceanus and Tethys produce the
world-egg.[54] If this generation has any meaning at all, it can
only be explained allegorically as a way of expressing the theory
that the world has arisen out of the primal water. Possibly the
philosophy of Thales has been influential here; if so, we could
then explain why the author has gone back to the isolated
Homeric passage on Oceanus as the origin of all things and given
it a place in the theogonic tradition. At all events, the sequence
of empty air or space, primeval water, and *terra firma*, has
something in common with a physical explanation, especially
if we may rely on another tradition passed on by Philodemus,
according to which the (second) couple in the theogony of
Epimenides were not Oceanus and Tethys, but Oceanus and
Gē.[55] Tethys is merely the female counterpart of Oceanus in
the language of mythical genealogy, just as Phos and Erebos,
Light and Darkness, are the male counterparts of Hemera and
Nyx in Hesiod. Oceanus and Gē, however, are simply water
and earth, the familiar elements (though we must not take this
word too abstractly); and the suggestion that the world-egg
is derived from these two would be only an allegorical way of
expressing the theory held also by Xenophanes that the world
arose from water and earth.[56] It may be said for the correctness
of this reconstruction of Epimenides' ideas that this feature
reappears in the Hellenistic theogony of Hieronymus,[57] a system put together from a number of heterogeneous components.
Obviously we have no right to date any of the details of this
later system in the sixth century as long as we have no other
way of proving that they belong there; on the other hand, we
have valuable confirmation of their presence at this time as
well as of their subsequent influence, when we find demonstrably
older features recurring in the later work.

We learn more about the so-called Orphic theogony of the
sixth century in Pherecydes of Syros. Ancient chronology

places this author in the time of the Seven Wise Men; but as he must have known the philosophy of the Milesians, he can hardly have lived much before the end of the sixth century. Our records about him and our small collection of fragments have in recent years been supplemented with a comparatively long papyrus fragment that gives us a much clearer idea of his work. He wrote in prose, which at that time was still something new. Of course there was nothing epoch-making about this, as there was in the work of Anaximander, who was the first to put his philosophical doctrines in writing. Since Anaximander's time the process of converting the contents of the learned genealogical and theogonic poems into prose discourses had already begun; Hecataeus of Miletus, Pherecydes of Syros, and Acusilaus of Argos were the chief writers of this type. Pherecydes must have sought his originality largely in his stylistic form—a simple narrative art almost charming in its *naïveté*, though far less influential in the long run than the solemn pomp and already antiquated epic diction of the contemporary verse theogonies. But of course Pherecydes must have introduced a good deal that was new in content as well. In his writing there is nothing dry or impersonal like a pronouncement of dogma; the tone is quite conversational. He prattles away like this: 'Zas and Chronos and Chthonié always existed; but Chthonié came to be called Gē [Earth] because Zas gave her Gē as a *geras* [gift].'[58] Here not only the style but also the teachings of Hesiod have been abandoned, as we may perhaps infer to have been the case in a smaller degree with the less individual Acusilaus of Argos, who, as later authors report,[59] turned Hesiod partly into prose and partly improved upon him. Pherecydes' *diorthosis* goes deeper; it reminds us of the rationalistic way Hecataeus of Miletus goes about his criticism of the ancient myths.

But obviously Pherecydes does not base his criticism solely on what his common sense tells him is possible or impossible. When he says that Zas, Chronos, and Chthonié always existed, this is a correction of Hesiod, who had said that even Chaos had come into being This correction was in the air at the time, as is clear from the criticisms of Xenophanes, who takes Hesiod to task for believing that the gods could have come into existence, as well as from the jibes of Epicharmus, who particularly

attacks the notion that even Chaos should at some time have
come into being just like everything else.[60] All these criticisms
of the older theogony indicate some acquaintance with the
philosophic notion of an ἀρχή of the world—an originative
source that never has come into being and never will pass away.
This implies a definite change in the prevailing views, which
Pherecydes takes into account when he puts something eternal
at the beginning of things. His triad of primal forces presupposes the philosophical conception of the ἀρχή, which he has
merely fused with the genealogical principle. Instead of the
single ἀρχή, we now have a pair of gods. But Pherecydes has
again deviated boldly from the theogonic tradition in deciding
whom this pair is to include. He does not follow Hesiod in
choosing Ouranos and Gaia, the visible heaven and the visible
earth; his Zas and Chthonié stand for two universal principles
philosophically opposed, which by their union bring all the rest
of the world into existence. This is immediately made manifest
in the change of names. The words Zas, 'he who liveth'
(derived from the verb ζῆν) and Chthonié, 'she who is under the
earth'—despite their connexion with the gods of the cult and
the theogonies, show by their very expressiveness of form that
they denote something newer and deeper. Symbol and allegory
here appear as a legitimate form of religious thought. It is
quite right in principle when one of the later ancient expositors
interprets Zas as Ether and Chthonié as Earth, that is, as the
Light and the Dark, the active and the passive.[61] In the name
Chronos, the third of this series, which the same late authority
spells with a kappa instead of a chi,[62] there is certainly an
allusion to Kronos, an indispensable personage in the old theogonies, who is now changed into Chronos or Time by a transparent bit of etymologizing. But this notion is also borrowed
from philosophical speculation: it is according to Time's decree
that coming-to-be and passing-away are brought to pass in the
cosmogony of Anaximander.[63] Therefore we need not worry
about any oriental influences, for the influence of the theologizing philosophy upon this theogony grown speculative is far
more evident. Etymologizing is an old method that we have
already found used rather extensively in the Theogony of Hesiod,
and indeed it is one that has always played an important role
in Greek theology. It rests on the assumption that the names of

mysterious divine powers, when rightly interpreted, give the key to their nature.[64] But in Pherecydes the situation is reversed: the new names merely express the recent utterances of speculative thought. Even Aristotle includes Pherecydes among the mixed rather than among the pure theologians,[65] because he does not always put what he has to say in mythical form (τῷ μὴ μυθικῶς ἅπαντα λέγειν), and thus departs from what Aristotle describes in another passage as Hesiod's characteristic way of thinking (μυθικῶς σοφίζεσθαι).[66] Aristotle reads still more into our fragment: he holds that, unlike the older theogonies, Pherecydes preferred to have something perfect and good at the beginning of all things, rather than something essentially incomplete, such as Chaos or Night;[67] for the idea of the perfect and good has always been connected with the name Zas. This is also presumably true of the Milesian philosophers, who understand by their first principle something that 'governs all things and embraces all things'. The distinguishing feature of Pherecydes' theory is his assumption of an original dualism, for which the theogonic idea of a union between a male and a female divinity provides an appropriate symbolic expression.

Pherecydes depicts the sacred marriage in almost novelistic terms, and far more anthropomorphically than Hesiod;[68] but we may venture to suspect that this anthropomorphism is no longer naïve. It has, so to speak, assimilated the philosophical criticisms of anthropomorphism; and the representation of the Divine in human terms is already consciously allegorical. A great palace is built for Zas and Chthonié, and as soon as it has been fitted out with everything necessary—furniture and household servants—the wedding is celebrated. On the third day of the festivities Zas weaves a large and splendid tapestry, with Earth and Ogénos and the palace of Ogénos woven in. The tapestry is obviously to be his wedding-gift for Chthonié. Earth and Oceanus (of whose name the obscure form Ogénos is probably a variant) appear as figures embroidered on her gown. She herself, therefore, is more than these—the very essence of the depths by which they are all sustained. Earth and Sea are merely the adornment with which Zas the All-living has decked her out in token of his love. He now presents her with the garment and speaks to her as follows: 'As I wish that this marriage be sacred to you, so with this gift I honour you. Be welcome, and become my wife.' This was the first ceremony of the *Anacalypteria*. The presentation of gifts from bridegroom to bride was a regular part of the Greek wedding; Pherecydes' story, however, is not so naïvely aetiological as it appears, but is a development of the idea of the sacred marriage of the first couple, in the light of a marriage custom that opened up unusually good opportunities for speculative understanding.

The hidden philosophical significance of Pherecydes' teaching is constantly emerging at other points. His work later received the title of 'Pentemychos' because it dealt with five caves or recesses (μυχοί, ἄντρα), also called ditches (βόθροι) or gates (πύλαι).[69] To these respectively were assigned Fire, Vapour, Water, and so forth. Unfortunately there are lacunae in Damascius' account of the way these were distributed, but at any rate the whole was parcelled out among what later came to be known as the four elements.[70] Pherecydes thinks in terms of cosmic powers and regions. He tells of a subterranean precinct to which Zeus banishes culprit deities, putting them under the guard of the Harpies and Thyella, daughters of Boreas—figures evidently conceived quite concretely as meteorological forces.[71] Accordingly we must also see natural forces in the hostile Titanic powers whom they hold in their bonds. In this way the Titanomachy, which is one of the traditional elements in the theogonies, is given a systematic cosmogonical interpretation. These dark forces contending against the world-order of Zas under the leadership of Ophioneus, the Snaky One (a detail that permits us to infer a chthonic origin), are vanquished and hurled into Oceanus.[72] It seems obvious to me that the volcanic phenomena of the Mediterranean world are responsible for this elaboration of the old Titanomachy, especially since this is the way Aeschylus and Pindar interpret the tale of the wild Typhos over whose head Zeus rolled Mount Aetna.[73] The winged oak of which Pherecydes speaks presupposes Anaximander's theory of the cylindrical earth freely suspended in space, as Diels has remarked. The idea of the roots of the earth was extremely old; so it was not hard to think of the earth as a gnarled tree. and express its floating movement by giving it wings.[74]

All this is evidently not the ancient sacred doctrine of a

sect, but the mythopoeic fancy of a theologian—a new. and interesting 'mixed' type of person, stimulated by the revolutionary ideas of philosophy. The philosophers' way of looking at the world has impelled the more intelligent of their contemporaries to come to terms with their approach, particularly where religion is concerned. This extension makes for an extraordinary increase in the philosophical capacity of the religious consciousness and gives it an entirely new direction. The ability to construct theogonies is one that never dies out of Greek religion. Even in Hesiod many new creations appear (there are just as many, whether they are the work of Hesiod himself or merely a product of his times)—particularly the personifications of those ethical powers which imperiously crave admittance to Olympus in every period, such as Diké, Eunomia, Eirené, and others.[75] In Pherecydes the problem is not so much one of inventing new gods as it is one of reinterpretation on a large scale. He is led to create allegorical divinities representing certain cosmical forces, and to set up equivalences between the old names of the gods and the natural forces of the new cosmology. Such a naturalistic interpretation is later applied systematically to all the Greek gods and legendary figures; but the process begins in the sixth century. Both Anaximander and Anaximenes speak of their first principle as divine. From the spiritualization of nature, theogony draws new strength. At bottom, of course, this spiritualization is all mere fantasy of the same sort as that which has made the Greeks people tree, mountain, and spring with Dryads, Oreads, and Nymphs, and do homage to Helios and Selené as gods. Such a view of the world inevitably takes on the form of pantheism as soon as the idea of the All and its unity is pushed to the fore by philosophy. That this view does not begin in Hellenistic times with the Stoics, but as early as the sixth century, is made clear in the well-known lines of Aeschylus:[76]

> Zeus is the Ether, Zeus the Earth, and Zeus the Sky;
> Zeus is the All, and what is higher yet than this.

By an unimpaired capacity for animizing the world pantheistically, the old gods are reborn in a new sense. The course of development leads from the divine personages of the old Greek folk-religion to the divine powers and divine Nature of the

philosophers and theologians. The deified forces of nature constitute an intermediate stratum between the old realistic faith
in particular divine personages and the stage when the Divine
is completely dissolved in the All. Though they are thought of
as natural forces and even as parts of nature, they still bear
personal names. In this regard they still represent the deeply
rooted pluralism of Greek religion. But despite this point of
contact, they are a far cry from the old cult divinities. Their
names are merely a transparent archaistic veil which by no
means obscures their purely speculative character. Though
philosophy means death to the old gods, it is itself religion; and
the seeds it has sown now thrive in the new theogony.

CHAPTER V

ORIGIN OF THE DOCTRINE OF THE SOUL'S DIVINITY

T HE Greeks (as one modern student has remarked) share with the Jews the honour of creating an intellectualized faith in God; but it was the Greeks alone who were to determine for several millennia the way in which civilized man would conceive the nature and destiny of the soul. Their ideas contribᵘted much that was essential in forming the Christian world-view; and by becoming part of the Christian religion these ideas acquired in their turn the widest possible diffusion. We may think of this Greek conception of the soul as beginning to develop in the sixth century. Its roots may well reach deep into the prehistoric strata of human existence; but during the sixth century the belief that the soul was divine and had a meta-physical destination took on the intellectual form that enabled it to conquer the world, and this will always remain a decisive historical event. The Greek soul-myths were not a fruit of the philosophical spirit, but sprang rather from the religious move-ment which we have described briefly in our previous chapter. That movement, however, lay directly in line with philosophy. Its influence took the form not of the absorption of a complete religious dogma by philosophy, but rather of a free intellectual catharsis of the religious beliefs about the soul; in any case it implied that these beliefs provided a new point of orientation from which philosophical thought could set forth. It accordingly falls within the frame of our study.

But we must first consider the general forms that the Greek idea of the soul took, so far as we can know from our extant tradition. Since the appearance of Erwin Rohde's classic volume *Psyche*, which was for the philology of his time a supreme achievement of scholarly synthesis and artistic skill,[1] research has not been idle, and the Homeric conception of the soul has been particularly favoured as the subject of penetrating studies which undermine the basic assumptions of Rohde's treatment. Rohde had been much impressed by the theory of an animistic stage in the history of religion such as E. B. Tylor and Herbert Spencer had worked out; he accordingly attempted to bring the general ideas of this theory into harmony with the text of Homer. Taking the Christian belief in immortality as his point of departure, he first proceeded to show that there is nothing at all comparable in Homer,[2] and then turned his attention to that side of the Homeric conception of the psyche which has to do with the world beyond. But in beginning here he made his first mistake. For however important Homer may have found the role of the psyche as the shade of the dead person in the lower world, this meaning of the word ψυχή nevertheless remains derivative and secondary, as we shall presently show. Rohde himself says correctly enough that as soon as a Homeric man dies, his existence as an individual ceases; there is no soul in him which could live on after death.[3] The shades of the dead which have entered Hades enjoy no conscious existence there; and several times when Homer uses the expression 'the man himself' as contrasted with the shade, he is thinking of the corporeal remains as such, even if life is now gone from them. Thus in the very first lines of the *Iliad* we read that the souls (ψυχαί) of the heroes, i.e. their shades, were hurled into Hades, while 'they themselves' (αὐτοί) became feasts for dogs and birds of prey.[4]

But before we turn to what is really the chief meaning of the word in Homer, the psyche of the living person, let us spend a while longer with that unsubstantial, shadowy image from the world below, which he also calls simply an idol because of its close outward resemblance to the dead person; and let us ask with Rohde where it came from and how it was related to the man during his life.[5] There are a number of passages in Homer where we read that the psyche has severed itself from the dying person, flown away from his mouth or his body (more exactly, from his limbs), and hurried off to the underworld. It must have dwelt for a while in the living person, but what was its activity there? That which we call 'soul' or 'consciousness', which is also what the later Greeks understand by the word ψυχή, is never given this name in Homer, but is called θυμός, or referred to by words denoting the heart, the diaphragm, or some other bodily organ involved in the affective or volitional reactions. Now Homer often uses the word ψυχή in connexion with living persons, in the sense of life.[6] But Rohde felt that this usage was not enough to explain how the same word could come to designate the man-like idol of the dead in Hades. It seemed to him that this disembodied double must have lived in the man during his lifetime, though without any assignable function to perform, for certainly none was evident in the state of waking consciousness. Rohde, however, was of the opinion that such an activity was really to be found in the dream-activity of the consciousness in sleep, which he interpreted as analogous to the final release of the psyche from the body at the moment of death, and different only in degree. He found support for this interpretation in a parallel passage from Pindar, which is actually very significant. The passage reads:

> And all men's bodies follow the call
>   Of overpowering death.
> And yet there still will linger behind
>   A living image of life,
> For this alone has come from the gods.
>   It sleeps while the members are active;
>   But to those who sleep themselves
>   It reveals in myriad visions
>   The fateful approach
>   Of adversities or delights.

Though the psyche is not directly mentioned, Pindar represents it as an idol or image of life, almost exactly as in Homer.[7] He asserts the psyche to be the only thing remaining after the body's death. Accordingly Rohde saw all the more significance in Pindar's explicit statement that the idol of the living person is present in him even during his lifetime but asleep when he is awake. This explanation seemed the only way of accounting for the curious fact that Homer never speaks of the presence or activity of any such double housed in man's body as an invisible second ego. That this double should become active only in dreams—that is, in temporary emancipation from the body—was for Rohde the decisive point, for this seemed to give him the final proof that the whole conception rested on a logical inference of primitive man from the actual experience of dreaming and other similar phenomena, such as ecstatic conditions and fainting spells. This explanation coincided with the theory of animism.

At this point W. F. Otto made some effective criticisms in his little book *Die Manen*.[8] For several decades Rohde's apparently conclusive argument had been granted tranquil acceptance; but from a purely philological standpoint it was vitiated by his complacent assumption that Pindar's conceptions could legitimately be read back into the Homeric epic, several centuries earlier. Otto rightly pointed out that a single statement in Pindar's lines was enough to prove the methodological inadequacy of this promiscuous approach. The poet asserts that when the body undergoes death the idol of the living person remains alive, for this alone is derived from the gods. There is nothing so un-Homeric as the idea that the human soul is of divine origin; and no less strange to Homer is the dualistic division of man into body and soul which this theory presupposes and which Pindar expresses very clearly. To ignore this basic mystical conception and claim the rest to be Homeric, as Rohde proposes, simply will not do.[9] For in Pindar the idea of the soul as a stranger from a higher world dwelling in the body as a guest is intimately connected with one of the details that Rohde reads into Homer, namely that the soul sleeps while the man is awake, becoming active only when he is asleep and dreaming. There is no trace of this conception in Homer, as Otto's excellent analysis of his treatment of dreams has shown.[10] In Homer the dream is always a genuine apparition that comes to the sleeper. It is true that he occasionally calls this dream-apparition an *eidolon*, but he never applies this term to the soul as an organ for dreaming, as Pindar does.[11] It would be quite unthinkable for Homer to conceive of the truthful dream as a vision in which the soul is set free from the body and again exalted to the divine power that was originally hers. We have here two altogether different conceptions of the soul's nature, and they should be kept as distinct as possible. Rohde's animistic theory of the Homeric psyche as a sort of double, a second ego which slumbers in man while he lives, and abandons his body at death to depart for Hades and there lead an impotent, vaporous shadow-existence, has nothing left to stand upon.

Otto himself was led to this problem, not so much in studying the development of Greek theories of the soul, as in tracing the forms of the oldest beliefs about death, as the title of his book, *Die Manen, oder Von den Urformen des Totenglaubens*, indicates. Consequently he does not start by asking what words Homer

uses to designate the various aspects of all that we summarily
refer to as 'soul'; he does not even ask what the particular
meaning of the Homeric conception of the psyche may be; but
he approaches the problem of the psyche with special attention
to that sense of the word in which it betokens the spirit of the
dead, just as Rohde began with the fact that in Homer the
psyche as a being from Hades is an image of the living man.
But while Rohde tried to use this creature from Hades, this
idol and double, as a basis for inferences about the nature of
the psyche in general and even about its function as the psyche
of the living man, Otto distinguishes sharply between these two
significations. In the Homeric creature from Hades he sees
merely a Greek manifestation of the primitive belief in the
ghost of the dead, quite untouched by reflection, a product of
the fear of the dead which is part of the common experience
of all peoples. But since Otto insists upon this origin for the
shadowy image from the world below, it becomes problematical
why such an image should ever be called a ψυχή; for, as we have
already remarked, when Homer uses the word ψυχή in connexion
with a living person, he uses it to designate his life,[12] which is
at quite the opposite pole from using it to refer to the dead.
Here we must notice a further distinction: the psyche that
hovers about as an idol in Hades has a strictly individual
character by reason of its manifest resemblance to the form of
the living person,[13] but the psyche of the living person is simply
the animal life that is in him; it is in no way personal. How are
these two conflicting meanings of the single word ψυχή in Homer
to be reconciled? The conception of psyche as life will not
explain the employment of the same term to denote the ghost
of the dead. Otto accordingly assumes that there has been
some transference of meaning. He suggests that conceivably
the apparition of the ghost has been connected with the impression which the moment of death makes upon the beholder:[14]
the thing that separates itself from the body and escapes is
the life, the *psyche*, which must then have been identical with
the ghost in Hades. Now if this identification had occurred as
a conscious inference, it would be hard to imagine how those
who made it could have failed to notice the distinction we have
just mentioned. Moreover, it would have been ill in accord
with Otto's own ideas of the primitive intellectual processes

underlying these Homeric conceptions, to think of them as involving a sort of primitive logic—a conscious procedure of inference.[15] Hence when Otto found the Homeric creature from Hades designated by the term ψυχή, his only recourse was to consider this a purely superficial substitution, with nothing to justify our supposing that life and the ghost of the dead were actually equated, as the associative identification seemed to imply.

If one sees clearly the difficulties of this position, he will understand why Otto's efforts to get at the facts behind the Homeric beliefs about the soul and the dead could not help bringing another attempt in their wake before long. This attempt was made by Ernst Bickel in his book *Homerischer Seelenglaube*, which appeared in 1925.[16] Bickel started with the postulate that the designation of the ghost of the dead as a ψυχή could not be a mere later contamination of two concepts so basically different as those of life and ghost, and that the Homeric ψυχή must rather have included from the outset something to bridge the gap between them; he assumed further that the key to this must lie in the basic etymological meaning of ψυχή as 'breath' or 'exhalation'.[17] The pysche of the living person, he maintained, was originally the exhalation-soul or breath-soul, the existence of which was a matter of immediate certainty in man's animal experience, particularly at moments of fainting or dying, when life departs with the breath. Otto had set himself in opposition to many earlier Homeric expositors by vigorously denying that in Homer the word ψυχή as applied to the living ever meant anything else than life. He claimed that it had already become a completely abstract conception, and that there was no passage in Homer where the meaning 'breath' could be proved beyond refutation. Bickel, however, demonstrated that in Homer the verb ἀποψύχω means to 'exhale' or to 'breathe out', and that we also find the phrase ψυχὴν καπύσσαι, which can be translated only as *animam efflare* —'to breathe out his soul'.[18] In the Latin word *anima* the ideas of life, soul, and breath are still clearly combined. Though it must be conceded that Homer's ψυχή has not retained the sensory connotation of breath to the same degree as the Latin *anima*, which is cognate with ἄνεμος or 'wind', the instances where it is associated with the verb for breathing out, or where such a verb is formed from the stem ψυχ- itself, show plainly that even in Greek the concept of psyche goes back to this sensory representation.[19] As late as the time of Homer, when this origin is already becoming obscure, it is still often consciously felt. This is evident from expressions like 'his psyche flew out of his mouth' or 'out of his body'.[20] The idea of the flight to Hades, which is often connected with that of the psyche, combines rather badly with the abstract concept 'life' but quite well with the idea of breath, according to the old Greek ways of thinking. In the sixth-century Orphic epics we find the conception of the psyche entering man at birth, borne on the breath of the wind.[21] This idea, to be sure, is not to be found in Homer; but it is the exact complement of the Homeric belief that the psyche escapes from the dying person by flying away. The Homeric conception must be extremely old. Even outside the sphere of literature we encounter it in the figure of the psyche fluttering about as a soul-bird or butterfly after quitting its human host.[22] Whether the image of flying was originally meant in this literal sense or in the purely metaphorical sense of hovering in the air, which would be especially appropriate for the soul as breath, Homer still conceived it in perceptual terms.

The post-Homeric literature is known to us in such a fragmentary state that we cannot find out very much about its nomenclature for the soul. It is only natural that the poets imitating Homer should have retained his terms with their old significations.[23] The tradition has left us nothing to show how the language of daily life expressed itself. With the introduction of prose in the sixth century, the philosopher Anaximenes, in the one remaining fragment of his treatise, uses the word ψυχή in the sense of soul, not in that of life. 'Just as our psyche, which is air, holds us together and rules us,' he writes, 'so do *pneuma* and air encompass the whole cosmos.'[24] When Anaximenes says that the boundless substance that underlies all Becoming is air, he does so chiefly because he looks upon air as the bearer of life. For him the primal principle itself is already animate and related to the visible corporeal world as the soul to the human body. In identifying the air with the soul, the philosopher apparently has no need to do more than take advantage of the word ψυχή, for evidently anyone hearing it would understand the connotation of breath. Bickel has rightly declared it improbable that Anaximenes revived this original sense of ψυχή simply by his own lucubrations. Presumably this is how he had understood Homer; at any rate it is how he understood his mother tongue. Xenophanes is said to have argued against the theory that the world breathes.[25] This conception too, like many others, was one that he had found in the Ionian philosophy of nature and repudiated as altogether too outlandish. It would fit Anaximenes nicely; and it is chronologically possible that it originated with him. Aristotle expressly states that the idea of the world's breathing was to be found among the older Pythagoreans, who connected it with their theory that the world contained empty space.[26] But in itself the idea may well be older and go back to Anaximenes. Moreover, the Orphic theogony, when it represents the soul as entering the new-born child on the wings of the wind, already presupposes the philosophical theory that air is the principle of life.[27] It would be interesting to know whether Anaximenes already thinks of the word ψυχή as including the idea of consciousness; at any rate this will soon be the case with Heraclitus, for whom, as for Aeschylus and Pindar, this connotation is well established. This need not necessarily be true for Anaximenes, inasmuch as his chief concern is with the physiological aspects of the psyche. But at least his expression 'the soul rules us' (συγκρατεῖ ἡμᾶς) tempts us to interpret this with an eye to the intellectual powers as well;[28] and since the endless air is just as divine for Anaximenes as the *apeiron* is for Anaximander, and at the same time governs the world, it is hard to follow this analogy with the soul of man if consciousness and reason are left out. In any case the step from Anaximenes' airpsyche to the psyche as conscious soul would be only a short one. The meaning must be at least potentially present, and for us that is the deciding factor. Whether this whole development occurred in Ionia we cannot tell, for unfortunately we do not know what was going on in the mother country. Certainly it did not begin with Homer, though we must begin with him in the absence of other sources. Even Homer's conception of the psyche shows some departure from the original form; and the real starting-point for this development lies far more in the living language and imagery of the folk. From this alone and not from the two disparate Homeric ideas of life and ghost can we explain how the one word ψυχή could come to express them both. Only the word 'spirit' with its breath-connotation, like the analogous concepts in English and German, suggests both of the two widely different aspects here involved: on the one hand, life; on the other, the supernatural apparition of the ghost. This, then, is the original notion. There is no way of jumping from the psyche as life-in-the-abstract to the idol in Hades.

However, we have not yet really solved the problem of how the word ψυχή in Homer can mean both the impersonal concept 'life' and 'ghost of the dead' appearing in individual form. The double significance with which this word is conceived in Homer cannot have grown from a single conceptual root. Otto's hypothesis that the idea of the life that soars away from the body at death has been combined with the experience of 'seeing ghosts' does not, of course, suffice to explain how the word ψυχή can have been transferred to the idol in Hades; but the hypothesis that some such transference occurred strikes me as inescapable. It becomes much easier to understand if the original meaning of ψυχή was not merely 'life', as Otto assumes, and if this transference was not consummated in Homer, for whom the prevailing meaning of ψυχή was already 'life', but rather at an earlier stage, when the word still meant quite literally the 'breath-soul'. It was then fairly easy to think of the breath-soul that escaped at death as identical with what primitive belief held to be the one thing remaining from the dead person which could under certain circumstances become an object of human sense-perception—namely, the ghost. From this identification the concept of psyche acquired its contrast of meanings; and this contrast is not to be explained away, for the breath of life is essentially nothing individual, while the apparition from the realm of phantasms naturally resembles the dead person himself. It is worth our while to notice that it was obviously much easier for the word ψυχή to have its range of meaning widened to include this creature of the dead than to take in those conscious processes which it would pre-eminently denote later on. Consciousness and animal life are never originally conceived as a unity. Accordingly they are indicated by different words.[29] While this may seem curious in the light of the later psychological meaning of ψυχή, it is quite understandable if we bear in mind the basic linguistic meanings of the Homeric words θυμός and ψυχή. In Homer the predominant meanings of θυμός are 'passion', 'will', 'soul', 'mind', while that of ψυχή is 'life'; these, however, are obviously all secondary meanings which only gradually developed. Etymologically it is clear that θυμός is connected with the Latin *fumus* or 'smoke' and the Greek θύω ('to sacrifice'), so that it really suggests a hot welling-up of blood; ψυχή likewise means originally something quite concrete and perceptible, the 'breath', and belongs to the same family as ψύχω ('to breathe') and ψυχρός ('cold'). The two words indicate quite different and separate psychophysical phenomena and make no pretence of being reducible to any common denominator. But by the time of Homer there was already an inner tendency to merge the phenomena of consciousness (θυμός) and of animal life (ψυχή) in a single soul-concept, though the language contained no one word embracing both meanings; this is evident in double expressions such as ψυχὴ καὶ θυμός ('soul and mind').[30] Since the poetic language of the epic was extremely old and the significance of the words had long since become fixed, the meaning of a word like ψυχή could not be extended towards the mental side so easily here as it probably could in the imperceptible transitions of popular speech, where this process was already completed by the sixth century.[31] We find parallels to this development elsewhere, for instance in the realm of ethical thought. While in the language of the epic the word ἀρετή has the specific, narrowly restricted sense of 'strength' and 'manly bravery', which goes back to the earliest heroic lays and continues under Homeric influence to reappear now and then in the language of poets centuries later, we also see in post-Homeric times an extension of the meaning of this word, coming partly from the language of daily life, partly from the poetical language itself. By this time ἀρετή has come to stand for every kind of human excellence and perfection, even outside the realm of warfare; it can denote justice, prudence, wisdom, or piety. Obviously the chief factor that made this extension of meaning possible was the extent of its basic etymological significance, which could include any sort of excellence whatsoever. So the development of this idea must simply have depended upon what each succeeding period felt man's highest excellence to be.[32] But the shift in the meaning of ψυχή followed a different course. The idea of breath was not general enough to take on any new mental connotations at random. It could not be broadened to acquire the meaning of soul in anything like our present sense until that which had hitherto been called θυμός was understood to be dependent on the psyche, and sheer animal living accordingly recognized as fundamental for the higher life of consciousness. So we do not need to explain why the word ψυχή was bound to defeat the word θυμός in their rivalry to determine which would better suggest both the mere fact of living and the life of the soul in the fullest sense. In the end ψυχή entirely absorbed the meaning of θυμός as soul or mind. As a matter of fact, θυμός frequently shows a tendency in Homer to rise to this more general meaning and include animal life as well;[33] but in the living language ψυχή carries the day, and θυμός becomes more and more confined to the special meaning of 'courage'.[34]

Now this complete coalescence of life-soul and consciousness in the conception of the psyche appears in the religious beliefs of the sixth-century Orphics and Pythagoreans as a presupposition of their doctrine of the so-called transmigration of souls. It is impossible not to see in this doctrine one of the most important causes of the diffusion of the un-Homeric meaning of the word ψυχή and its ultimate triumph. But it is certainly wrong to suppose that this comprehensive conception of psyche was confined exclusively to these late mystical groups, and to regard it as a foreign substance in the intellectual life of the Greeks. Of course if we should contrast Homer and the Orphics as representing two distinct types of belief about the soul, the gap between them might seem so unbridgeable that we might as well be dealing with the typical opposition of popular belief and mysticism or with the philosophical views of two opposing races,[35] Homer representing the Greeks, and the Orphic dualism the Orientals.[36] But we have already observed that the non-Homeric and pre-Homeric Greek conception of the psyche as the breath-soul possessed a native tendency to widen its meaning to include something like our present idea of the soul, and that out of all the Homeric words for indicating either the physical life or the life of the conscious soul, this was by far the one best suited to express the new intuition of the inner connexion and indeed the very unity of these two aspects of life.[37] So it is not surprising that the new doctrine of transmigration should have adopted this most comprehensive way of referring to the soul, for obviously the doctrine itself was based on the unity of life-soul and consciousness.

The idea of a soul independent of the body, wandering incessantly through various existences, was quite impossible so long as the Homeric distinction between a life-soul ($\psi\upsilon\chi\acute{\eta}$) that leaves the body at death but neither thinks nor feels, and a consciousness-soul ($\theta\upsilon\mu\acute{o}\varsigma$) entirely bound up with bodily organs and processes, was still taken for granted. A transmigration of the soul as a person's moral and intellectual ego was possible only if the animal basis, without which such a thing was inconceivable even to the Orphics, could be separated from the body at the same time and could itself be as incorporeal as possible. This, however, was precisely the case with the breath-soul as it was conceived in the philosophy of Anaximenes and his contemporaries. Leaving aside the problem of how and where the doctrine of metempsychosis arose (insoluble because nearly all the relevant traditional material has been lost), it is plain that what was really fruitful in this doctrine and pregnant with future influence was not the mythical conception of transmigration, but the impetus the theory was to give to the development of the idea of the soul as the unity of life and spirit, and the vigour with which it conceived this psyche as a spiritual being in its own right, quite independent of the corporeal.[38] If we recall that at this very time the Pythagoreans were identifying air with the empty space between bodies, thus conceiving of air itself as incorporeal,[39] it at last becomes thoroughly clear that in archaic thought the breath-soul must have served as the vehicle for the spirit in its full incorporeality and independence.

In this period there were a number of factors paving the way for this increased independence and enrichment of the idea of psyche. Even when Anaximenes equated psyche with air, he did not identify it with any corporeal substance of the world of experience. Air to him is the originative source of all coming-to-be and passing-away, active both within and behind these processes as their divine ground. It is quite fitting, even from the beginning, that this divine ground should include both life and consciousness; at least this is how we have felt that the philosopher's words must be interpreted.[40] From such a standpoint death can be nothing other than the return of the individual to the primal ground and his entry into new forms. The distinguishing feature of the transmigration theory is the preservation of the identity of the ego both before and after this life. In contrast to the pantheism of the Milesian philosophy, a genuinely religious motif now appears in the permanence of the person as an intellectually and morally responsible agent, actively co-operating in his own fate, though immersed in the general natural processes of coming-to-be and passing-away, to which even man seems irresistibly subjected. By this contrast with the pantheistic and naturalistic conception of man, the religious anthropology of the transmigration theory acquires a dignity that lifts it well above the level of mere primitive mythology. Moreover, the idea of the permanence of the person is not one that emerges suddenly and unpreparedly. In the Greek mysteries, the pre-Greek origin of which is attested by many facts in the history of religion and even of architecture, a man was deemed blessed if he had witnessed the sacred pageantry of the epopts and come to share in the higher wisdom. Our authorities tell us that he had also some hope of a better lot after death, though they fail to indicate whether this promise involved the idea of a continuing personal life.[41] Still less can we say whether it involved any continued existence of the soul as a conscious being separate from the body. Such a separation of soul from body was perhaps more likely to be intimated in the practices of the Dionysiac cult, which were designed to lead to ecstasy; for the devotee would then behold the god and become one with him. Yet even here we have no tradition of any special soul-theory, no matter how often the Orphic and Dionysiac cults were merged. So the Dionysiac religion can at most be regarded merely as a forerunner of the Orphic belief in the possibility of the soul's independent existence outside the body.

In expounding the Orphic soul-theory itself, recent scholars have, as in other cases, produced such a heedless mixture of views reported by the older writers and material from comparatively late sources that we are inevitably faced with the sceptical question of whether even the theory of metempsychosis can be traced at all confidently to any Orphic sect which ever actually existed. Let us therefore leave all later material out of account. Our oldest and surest evidence is to be found in Pindar's lines in the second Olympian ode, addressed to Theron of Akragas, where he speaks of Theron's religious convictions about the life after death; and here we must again consider that same Pindaric fragment which Erwin Rohde used in interpreting the Homeric beliefs about the soul.[42] However little this latter passage can contribute to our knowledge of those beliefs, it is all the more precious as a document of a particular form of religious conception of the world beyond which was current in Pindar's time. Of course Pindar does not tell us that this is an Orphic doctrine; but even if someone should accordingly doubt its Orphic origin, we should willingly dispense with the name if our critic will only acknowledge that this fragment marks the first appearance of a new and extremely influential religious conception of the soul's nature, the chief features of which emerge very clearly as Pindar presents them.

In the second Olympian the poet praises the manly virtue and god-sent benison of wealth and power with which Theron is graced; we meet both *Areta* and *Ploutos*, inseparable companions in the human ideal of the old Greek aristocracy. But along with these, as a third and novel element, Pindar includes the assurance of reward and punishment in the hereafter, thus paying his respects to the devout faith of the religious community to which Theron presumably belongs. Perhaps it was through him that Pindar became familiar with this doctrine.[43] We have little business to ask whether the poet himself belonged to the band of initiates; in any case their theory of the world beyond gave his fancy wings for one of its boldest flights. According to their beliefs there is an after-world, the gates of which are unbolted only at the moment of death. For those whose lives have been remiss, stern judgement waits. But those who are truly noble shall enjoy a less troubled existence, free from tears. For them the sun never sets; they know neither toil nor need. The wicked must suffer such torments as the eye cannot bear to look upon. But he who has three times persevered in both lives, here and there alike, without polluting his soul, shall enter Kronos' lofty hall on the Islands of the Blest.

> There the ocean breezes blow;
> And golden flowers are blazing,
> Some on the land in glistening trees,
> While others are fed by the sea.
> And the blessed ones weave them in crowns for themselves.

We find another no less exuberant and visually concrete description of the sorrows and joys of the beyond in a fragment from a lost Pindaric threnody.[44] In still another fragmentary series of lines we read of souls who must do penance there until the ninth year, when Persephone sends them back to the upper sun: from these come illustrious princes, men of swift strength and utmost wisdom, henceforth to be honoured as heroes.[45]

With this eschatology the mystics associated a call for purity of life in accordance with certain specified rules. In particular this βίος required abstention from any form of bloodshed, including even blood-sacrifice and the eating of animal flesh[46]—a prescription that led to a precise ritualistic regulation of diet. Man sees himself as responsible for the future fate of his soul in the beyond, and no longer feels fully at home in this world, whether he expects to obtain his salvation by mere adherence to outward ritual or rather by some ethical sanctification in the course of his wanderings. His soul, which has come from a higher and diviner sphere, is a transient guest in the house of the body. Only in dreams and in the hour of death, when released by the body, is it ever completely itself.[47] We must notice that Aristotle uses almost the same words with regard to the nature of the soul in a famous fragment of one of his early and still Platonistic dialogues.[48] He, too, speaks of the dream-vision and the intimations of the future at death as the only moments when the soul exists entirely by itself and reveals its true nature. The Orphic soul-theory is a direct precursor of Plato's and Aristotle's view of the divine nature of soul or mind, though they have stripped away all the material features still clinging to this conception. The passage from Aristotle that agrees so closely with the Pindaric fragment stands in a lengthy exposition of how the idea of God originated. This fact alone is enough to prove the significance of the Orphic soul-theory for Greek theology. In the teachings of Plato and

Aristotle the deepest source of our experience of the Divine
lies partly in the intuition of the ordered movements of the
heavenly bodies (that is, in the experience of the cosmos) and
partly (perhaps even more) in the soul's inner experience of
its connexion with a higher world.[49]

We know so little about the Orphic rites that it is no longer
possible to discern clearly how the chief Orphic ideas about the
nature of the soul are connected with the experience of the
Divine; but undoubtedly the theory of the divinity of the soul
marks a turning-point in the early history of the philosophical
idea of God. Of course this religion was no philosophy in the
strict sense, but it was closely akin to the kind of thought that
takes the transcendent world for its province. Since the time
of Plato and Aristotle philosophical theology has always supplemented its rational arguments for God's existence by stressing
the reality of the soul's inner experience of the Divine; but the
development of this idea goes back to the doctrines and ceremonies of the mysteries. It is here that we first meet the kind
of religious experience described in another important Aristotelian fragment,[50] where we read that those who participate
in the initiation ceremonies are not supposed to learn ($\mu a\theta\epsilon\hat{\iota}\nu$)
something, but rather to experience or suffer it ($\pi a\theta\epsilon\hat{\iota}\nu$), and
to acquire a certain inward disposition, provided that they
are properly qualified.[51] The experience of the Divine in the
initiations is characterized as a true passion of the soul as
contrasted with mere intellectual knowledge, which needs no
special qualifying relationship with its object. A statement
like this leads us to conclude that for the initiates the divine
nature of the soul itself, guarded from all distress by its own
unsullied purity, served as a guarantee of its susceptibility to
divine influences. But the philosophy of the Platonic school
was not the first to devote attention to the mystery religion.
It is well known that the Orphic doctrine of transmigration is
also to be found in Pythagoras, who associates it with his
mathematical researches in a remarkable manner. The Pythagorean rule of life reminds us of the βios of the Orphic community, though it does not resemble it in every detail, and the
Pythagoreans have a good deal besides that is peculiar to themselves. Parmenides, Heraclitus, and Empedocles show themselves familiar with the Orphic soul-theory.[52] And when

Socrates holds that the preservation of man's soul from harm is the thing most important in life, and that in comparison with this everything else must recede, his emphasis on the value of the soul,[53] so incomprehensible to the Greece of an earlier age, would have been inexplicable if the Orphic religion had not turned its attention inward with that faith which the watchword of this βίος expresses: 'I, too, am of godly race.'[54]

CHAPTER VI

PARMENIDES' MYSTERY OF BEING

XENOPHANES' criticism of the popular religion and the revival of theogonic speculation have shown us how profoundly the broad religious currents of the sixth century were influenced by the Ionian philosophy of nature. With Parmenides of Elea we now return to philosophy in a stricter sense. Hitherto all philosophical thinking had been of the physical type, taking as its point of departure the problem of the permanent ground of coming-to-be and passing-away, the originative source or ἀρχή. But in Parmenides' theory of the Existent (ὄν) we find a new and original point of departure. Karl Reinhardt, whose book on Parmenides has the great merit of making us understand him anew, has, in his final pages, dealt briefly with the problem of the relation between philosophical reasoning and religious feeling in Parmenides' thought. He calls him 'a thinker who knows no other desire than knowledge, feels no other manacle than logic, and is left indifferent by God and by feeling'.[1] The creator of the metaphysic of Being, which subsequently becomes in Plato and Aristotle an 'instrument for satisfying the longing for immortality and the presence of the Divine in man',[2] would, if Reinhardt's characterization is correct, fall completely outside the range of the perspective from which we are here examining the Greek thinkers. His philosophy would frankly become a kind of symbol for that basic human impulse of pure intellectualism which, 'free from any religious or moral scruple . . . follows the path marked out for it, in a spirit of the most ruthless analysis'. Reinhardt finds this spirit present not only in Parmenides but also in Anaxagoras, Empedocles, and Democritus, while he feels that in Pythagoras and Heraclitus the pursuit of scientific knowledge has become strangely pervaded with an interpretation of the world basically mystical and religious.

Certainly we are following one of the less admirable fashions of our period when we permit our interest in the history of religion to lead us to find in religion the single root of every form that the human spirit assumes, including even the deeply-lying desire for knowledge, towards which, according to Aristotle, all human beings strive. Nothing could be more false to the inner motivation of the heroic thinkers who meet us at the outset of Greek philosophy than to look on them as a company of pious doctrinaires or scholastics ambitious to demonstrate with the tools of the intellect what their feeling accepts on faith. An established confession of faith never played any part in the veneration accorded to the deities of the Greek cults. Their significance and their nature fluctuated with the universal change; and as life and human experience advanced from one stage to another, there were always new ways of discovering the divine presence in reality. For that very reason, however, we must take pains not to go to the other extreme and think of pure thought as something hermetically sealed and isolated, essentially opposed to religion and shut off from it with as sharp a cleavage as that with which modern science sometimes cuts itself off from the Christian faith. The Greeks were as yet unaware of any such autonomous realms of the spirit. Among the sources of those human experiences which helped in transforming the traditional mythical concept of the Divine, the rational investigation of reality was one of the most important; and just as religious inquiry itself had whetted the appetite for knowledge, so the philosophical speculation with which the Greeks were constantly aiming to grasp the totality of existence performed a truly religious function and gave rise to a peculiar religion of the intellect, reflecting in its structure the shift in the relationship between reason and feeling which confronts us in that new intellectual type—the philosopher. We have, I think, shown that it is impossible to follow Reinhardt (and here Reinhardt himself seems to vacillate) when he counts Anaximander and Anaximenes among the men of pure science but sets Xenophanes apart from all other thinkers as a radical theologian. For while Xenophanes clearly differs from them in the way he expresses his religious feelings, their rational style of thinking gives them a new conception of the world which is deeply satisfying to their own religious sense. And the very fact that Xenophanes was not originally a student of physics is all the more indicative of the latent religious force in the world-view of the natural philosophers.

Our problem is similar when we come to Parmenides. We need not ask whether his study of pure Being has a religious

purpose, such as proving the existence of God in the traditional
Christian manner; our question is rather whether his speculations about true Being strike him as having some significance
that is in any sense religious, even though he does not call this
Being God. As long as the relationship between Parmenides
and Xenophanes was still generally conceived according to the
old view, which saw in Xenophanes the father of the Eleatic
school and made his single God an earlier theological stage of
Parmenides' purely logical Being, the question of whether Parmenides' teachings had any religious content could hardly have
been answered affirmatively; for it was then almost impossible
to see anything in his theory of Being but a deliberate effort
to strip off the shell of theology and devote himself to working
out the ontological content of his master's speculations about
the One.[3] If, however, Parmenides' theory is a wholly original
achievement, utterly different from Xenophanes' mystical intuition of the divine One in the world of nature, as Reinhardt
himself has shown, the problem of its religious content must be
raised afresh. This problem is not to be solved by comparing
Parmenides with Xenophanes, but only by studying his own
words.

Parmenides expounded his doctrine in the form of an epic.
If we are correct in maintaining that Xenophanes never wrote
a systematic poem on nature but put his criticisms of the old
gods and the traditional cosmology in his satires or *silloi*,[4]
Parmenides' choice of the didactic epic as the form best suited
to his own philosophy was a bold and extremely significant
innovation. It is clear that he quite consciously disdained the
new form of prose, which Anaximander had introduced. One may
even conjecture that this Ionian, living as he did in southern
Italy, where there was a large Doric population and where
Doric was spoken, could not have written in modern Ionic,
but had to fall back on the Panhellenic language of Homer
and consequently on verse if he hoped to make himself widely
understood. But obviously Parmenides was not concerned
merely with the problem of making his language as easily
understandable as possible and choosing the best-known dialect.
His epic is by no means so closely akin to Homer as it is to
Hesiod's *Theogony*, the first work to use the form of epic poetry
for a rational and didactic exposition of the world of the gods.

The Hesiodic gods, to be sure, had since been supplanted in the Ionian natural philosophy by a single divine substance like Anaximander's primordial ground; but how could the Greeks, with their fondness for any sort of contest, have helped seeing in Parmenides' adoption of the verse-form of his venerable theological predecessor an avowed intention to compete with him on his own territory, however sharply the rigorous conceptual deductions of the Eleatic must have contrasted with Hesiod's fanciful *mythopoiia*? That we need consider only the *Theogony* as Parmenides' model, and need not concern ourselves with the *Works and Days*, is evident upon closer comparison. The parallelism between Parmenides and Hesiod's *Theogony* becomes particularly evident in the second part of Parmenides' poem. There not only the cosmogonic Eros of Hesiod appears, but with it, if we may trust Cicero's philosophical source in the first book of his *De natura deorum*, a large number of allegorical deities such as War, Strife, Desire, &c., whose origin from Hesiod's *Theogony* cannot be questioned.[5] But what prompted Parmenides to relegate these deities of Hesiod to the second part of his work, which is concerned with the world of mere appearance, and to contrast with it what he calls the Truth: his conception of eternal Being?

The *Theogony* had been introduced in the proem as a revelation from divine beings. By this time it had already become conventional for any epic to begin with a short invocation of the Muses; but Hesiod, the shepherd of Ascra, had quite deliberately developed this feature into a striking and detailed narration of his own personal experience: he told how the goddesses had appeared to him as he tended his flocks near his home at the foot of Helicon, their sacred mountain, and how they had inspired him[6] with a mission such as no poet before him had ever received—the truly prophetic inspiration of proclaiming the eternally existing gods and expounding their origin. It must have been this emphasis on the gods' eternal existence[7] that moved Parmenides to present himself as one who had followed in Hesiod's footsteps and beaten him at his own game. For it is again as a direct and unique divine revelation that he introduces his poem on that which exists eternally with a grandiose proem describing his heavenward journey.[8] This proem used to be lightly laid aside as a pure matter of artistic formalism

quite without significance for the abstract thinker, a mere concession to the style of the didactic epic, just as Plato's dialogue
form was neglected for centuries as something quite superficial.
But in more recent years the form of the proem has received
well-deserved attention from the philological side, and its importance for the understanding of the philosophical content
has rightly been pointed out. In criticizing Parmenides, one
really has no right to speak of conventionalities of style, for
everything is characteristically the author's own, personally
felt in the highest degree, as his conscious deviation from the
Hesiodic pattern indicates. How different, for instance, is the
proem of Empedocles' poem on the philosophy of nature, which
we can much better accuse of conventionality! Parmenides,
however, carries his parallelism with Hesiod even farther: he
seeks to proclaim the 'truth' (*aletheia*) which he has learned
from the mouth of the goddess herself, and the whole body of
his poem professes to be her direct address to him.[9] The goddess
is thus an exact counterpart of the Muses who revealed the
truth to Hesiod.[10] Of all the Greek writers who have come
down to us, Hesiod was the first to give the word 'truth' such
a pregnant and almost philosophical sense;[11] and it is in this
sense that Parmenides now uses it, carrying it on to a new stage
of meaning. He proclaims the 'truth' about Being, which is
eternal and without beginning, opposed to appearance and all
the deceptive 'opinions of mortals'.[12] This very opposition, so
sharply stressed, will show his truth to be of divine origin,
which Parmenides reinforces quite explicitly by his poetical
device of the goddess who reveals this message to him, the only
mortal so to be favoured.

Let us hear his own words:[13]

The team of mares that conveys me has carried me on
As far as my heart desired, after leading me down
The sagacious road of the goddess, which leads him who knows
Unscathed wherever he goes. It was there that I sped, for there
I was borne by the sapient horses drawing my car,
And maidens were driving. The axles shed sparks in the hubs
And creaked with the clamour of piping (for, one on each side,
A couple of whirling wheels hastened them on)
When the daughters of Helios quickened the speed of my ride,
Forsaking the dwelling of Night as they drove towards the light,

And tossing their veils away from their heads with their hands.
There stand the gates of the pathways of Night and of Day,
And round about them a lintel and threshold of stone.
The aethereal gateway is closed with immense folding doors,
And the keys with their versatile changes are kept in the hands
Of Diké, the manifold punisher. She, then, it was
Whom the maidens persuaded with carefully coaxing words
To be swift in pushing the bolt with its peg from the gate.
And as it flew open, the gap of its doors gaped wide,
While the bronze-fitted posts with their pivots and bolts
Swung forward and back in their sockets. And there, driving straight
Through the portal, the maidens conducted both horses and car
In the travelled track of the wagons. And graciously
Did the goddess receive me. Taking my right hand in hers,
She addressed me these words and bespoke me: 'O youth, you who come
To our house with your escort of deathless charioteers
And these fine mares that have brought you, welcome and hail!
It is no evil Moira that leads you to come by this road
(For indeed it lies far from the pathways frequented by men),
But Themis and Diké. And now you must study all things:
Not only the unshaken heart of well-rounded Truth
But also mortals' opinions, in which there is no true reliance.'

The concreteness with which the various details are depicted
—the goddesses, the team, the chariot-ride, and the entrance
gate to the upper world—must be attributed to the poetic
medium. The language, indeed, with its sturdy compactness
(which no translation can reproduce) is very far removed from
the pallid allegory which the academic aesthetician traditionally expects of a philosopher's experiments in verse. But the
thing which really justifies the presence of all this imagery at
the beginning of a philosophical poem is its transparent double
significance. Naturally it will not do to follow the source used
by Sextus Empiricus, to whom we owe thanks for preserving
this precious section of the lost work, and interpret the horse-
drawn car Platonically as the chariot of the human soul.[14] But
it is quite plain that the chariot conveying the poet to his goal
is driven by higher powers. The road that he takes is com-
mended as 'far from the pathways of men'. No mortal can find

the way to it. Only the daughters of Helios himself can show
him the way; and they must first lift the veils from their heads,
which they always keep covered in this our world of night.
Only by their intercession, not by his own powers, may he enter
the gates of the realm of light, where they are at home. The
mistress of this realm, the goddess who greets him, tells him
explicitly that in being admitted to this world he is receiving
a special favour that is more than human; and his entire
account of it includes nothing that he has observed there himself, but is rather an exact word-for-word rehearsal of the
revelation he has received with full credence from her lips.
This revelation exalts him above all his fellow-men, but it
also lays upon him the obligation of zealously proclaiming the
divine truth and fighting the 'delusions of men' with the utmost
trenchancy.

No one who studies this supernatural overture could ever
suppose that the philosopher's aim in this passage is merely to
provide an effective stage-setting. His mysterious vision in the
realm of light is a genuine religious experience: when the weak
human eye turns towards the hidden truth, life itself becomes
transfigured. This is a kind of experience that has no place in
the religion of the official cults. Its prototype is rather to be
sought in the devotions we find in the mysteries and initiation
ceremonies; and as these were flourishing with some vigour in
southern Italy in Parmenides' time, he presumably had become
acquainted with them there.[15] It would probably be fashion-
able to speak of these rites as 'Orphic' in view of the widespread
inclination to believe that this key will unlock all doors.[16] But
the name is of little consequence for our present purpose. The
less we worry about it, the clearer will be the fixed features of
the particular type of religion which underlies Parmenides'
description, where we encounter a highly individual inner experience of the Divine, combined with the fervour of a devotee
who feels himself charged with proclaiming the truths of his
own personal revelation and who seeks to establish a community
of the faithful among his converts. Indeed, the 'philosophical
school' was originally nothing but the secularized form of just
such a religious conventicle. When Parmenides laments that
mortals 'roam about' on the path of error, or speaks of their
'wandering minds',[17] this suggests the language of the religious

revival. Similarly Aeschylus, in the great speech where Prometheus boasts of being the εὑρετής of human τέχναι, borrows
a number of intonations from this sphere of prophetic discourse,
the influence of which can still occasionally be traced, though
it is otherwise lost to us:

> Seeing, they saw in vain;
> Listening, they failed to hear.[18]

To Parmenides, of course, eyes and ears were precisely the
organs by which men were led astray;[19] so he could speak only
in more general terms of 'wandering off the track' and 'roving
about'.

Naturally we have no reason to suppose that Parmenides was
trying to build up a case for any particular religious sect, or
was even following some such prototype point by point in
describing his remarkable experiences. If such a model may
have helped him find suitable ways of expressing his own
position, it was at any rate a highly original device for giving
it intellectual form. It amounts to far more than mere metaphor.
What Parmenides has done is to take over the religious form
of expression and transpose it to the sphere of philosophy, so
that in truth a whole new intellectual world takes shape. Indeed, the one thing that distinguishes the achievement of the
major Greek philosophers from the so-called special sciences
(which were already beginning to emerge at this time, sometimes alongside philosophy and sometimes directly out of philosophy itself) is this very ability not merely to assemble their
facts or make out a case for their theories, but to build up a
full-sized intellectual world. Throughout the history of Greek
thought we shall notice again and again how the philosophical
spirit constructs its own *kosmos* and *bios* out of concepts and
forms taken over from the religious and political life of the
community, and remoulded until they have become genuinely
philosophical in character. These matters have often been
regarded as irrelevant to the philosophical content; but from
our standpoint, which is really no longer that of a simple history
of dogma, their value is peculiarly enhanced. In the wider
intellectual life of Greece the philosopher who devises new
symbols is no less important than the man who arrives at new
doctrines. They are (mostly) one and the same person. Often

it is only in the language of its symbols that the spirit underlying these doctrines acquires its peculiar tonal colour.

So if we are fully to understand the inner meaning of Parmenides' approach, we must remember that, unlike the Ionian
philosophers, he does not retreat behind his subject-matter with
truly Homeric self-effacement, but, like Hesiod, announces in his
own name a special revelation. His proem is a testament to the
religious depth of his message and to the compelling experience
which had enabled him to penetrate to the nature of true
Being. The road along which he was driven by the sun-maidens
did not go 'through all the cities', as the wording of our best
manuscript would seem to require.[20] This reading, which has
properly always been criticized, would make Parmenides a
second Odysseus, wandering through the lands and towns of
men,[21] with an endless craving for knowledge purely for the
sake of increasing his information. Parmenides' 'roadway'
(ὁδός) is nowhere to be found on this earth; it is rather the
way of salvation, of which he had learned in the mystery
religions. Obviously it was here that the concept of the 'way'—
innocent enough in itself—first acquired that pregnant significance which it constantly has in Parmenides' writing: the one
right way that brings salvation and leads to the goal of knowledge.[22] The philosophical language of a later era was to coin
the similar word μέθοδος, which also stands for the way to a
goal; but how empty, how merely methodical this metaphor
seems in comparison with the 'way' of Parmenides, which (if
this attempt at restoring the text is correct) 'leads him who
knows unscathed wherever he goes'?[23] Only the way of salvation brings a man through unscathed, and no road but the road
of truth does this for 'the man who knows'.[24] For the first time
in Greek philosophical language we meet the philosophical personality considered as a bearer of knowledge. There is no intention of boasting of this knowledge; the philosopher chooses
rather to look upon it as a gift from some divine power and to
depict himself with modest pride as a mere instrument of that
power. This is the real meaning behind the conception of 'the
man who knows': he is one who has come to share in a knowledge of a higher origin—an analogue of the 'knower' or 'mystes'
of the religious initiation rites, who is thus distinguished from
the uninitiated.

The verses with which the main portion of Parmenides' poem begins are contained in fragments 2 and 3 (4 and 5 in editions previous to the fifth) of Diels's collection:

Come then, I shall tell you (and please listen well to my words)
Which ways of inquiry alone can be thought. The first
Maintains that *it is* and *cannot not be*; and this
Is the path of conviction, which follows the truth. But the next
Asserts: *it is not* and *this not-being must be.*
This latter path, I must tell you, cannot be explored.
For that which is not, you neither can know (for this
Is beyond our achieving) nor can you express it in words,
For thinking and being are one and the same.

The truth already proclaimed in the proem, from which the veil is now lifted for the first time, is so overwhelming in its simplicity that it comes as a shock to the listener, whom the solemn pronouncements of the goddess have prepared for some more pyrotechnic display. But this very simplicity reminds us of the actual experiences of the 'mystai' whose minds first had to be freed entirely from all confusing earthly entanglements so that they might be ready for the holy things that the initiation rites would reveal. The founders of the mysteries knew well that the deepest secrets are found only in things that are seemingly obvious.[25]

The two ways—the right way and the way of error—appear again in the religious symbolism of later Pythagoreanism. There they serve as an emblem for the choice between a morally good life and a bad one—the choice confronting every man as a moral agent.[26] We meet a similar conception in the sacred two-branched Y on the gravestones of a later era, which seems to symbolize the dead person's membership in the sect as a decision rightly made, and holds forth a promise of eternal peace in the hereafter.[27] Unfortunately we do not know how far the idea of the two ways goes back. That it was already familiar in early times is clear from Hesiod's *Works and Days*, with its doctrine of the narrow path of *areté* and the broad highway of misery.[28] It is tempting to suppose that the image of the way was also employed in those pious doctrines of the other world which we have encountered in Pindar, for the

religion in which they appeared was definitely based on the
idea of the soul's incessant wanderings. Perhaps it is no accident
that in the passage already cited in the previous chapter Pindar
speaks of a 'way of Zeus' which the soul must travel after death·
if man has led his life aright and entered into blessedness.[29]
At any rate, it would seem quite likely that this symbolism of
the way and the conscious choice thereof was also applied to
our life in this world; for religion has always assumed that man's
conduct in this life can exert considerable influence upon his
fate in the life to come.[30] So Parmenides' image of the two
ways, like the other material of his proem, is presumably based
on a carry-over of religious symbolism into the intellectual
processes of philosophy.

Although he speaks definitely of two ways, that of Being
and that of Not-being, the image is expanded in another
passage. He seems to recognize a third way on which the
ignorant wander perplexed: this way takes for granted that
both Being and Not-being possess real existence.[31] It is obvious
that the two ways so clearly differentiated at the outset are
not to be reconciled. But there are men who still wander in
error—men of two heads, dumb and unseeing—who hope to
perform a reconciliation by regarding the same thing first as
existent and then as non-existent, and who suppose that in
dealing with anything that exists they can first go the one way
and then return and go the other. Thus the third way is no
proper highway distinct from the two others (the explorable
way and the way that cannot be explored), but is merely an
inadmissible combination of the two, disregarding their mutual
exclusiveness. This impossible unification, however, is the chief
thing that Parmenides is fighting against; for men's delusions
invariably lend it plausibility and lead them to pursue it, while
no man would so lightly venture to start on the way of Not-
being alone. This is the sole reason why Parmenides speaks
of a third way at all. Here we need only remember that ever
since Homer the Greek word for 'way' (ὁδός) has meant not
only the beaten track or road but also any course that a man
pursues in going towards a goal. Only in this latter sense can
one speak of a third 'way' when a person takes first one way
and then the other.

Why does Parmenides pose the sharp alternatives of Being

and Not-being at the outset as basic for his whole doctrine?
And who are the 'men of two heads', the 'know-nothings'
(εἰδότες οὐδέν),[32] who serve as butt for the polemic of 'the man
who knows'[33] because their failure to grasp the exclusiveness of
this alternative has led them to think that they can go both
ways at once? Let us begin by answering the second question—
the question of the historical background of Parmenides' philosophy. It used to be rather widely supposed that Parmenides
has a certain definite thinker in mind when he speaks of the
men of two heads; for the view that the same thing both is and
is not, and that one can always go both the way from and the
way towards when dealing with anything that exists, seems
quite exactly to fit Heraclitus and his doctrine of the unity of
opposites.[34] I must add my own misgivings to the doubts that
have recently been raised against this interpretation.[35] Parmenides' prophet-like invective against the men of two heads
who wander in error, eternally dumb and blind, cannot be
directed at any one ingenious person who has gathered a few
aspiring disciples about him; it must rather be aimed at the
whole race of mortals. To them Parmenides himself has given
ear, even up to the moment when the goddess pronounces her
revelation; for it is she, not he, who speaks these words. Naturally mankind has never expressed its naïve conception of reality
in any form so epigrammatic as that of asserting that Being
and Not-being are one and the same. It is only Parmenides
himself who sums up in this paradoxical formulation the
absurd consequences of a cosmology by which all men alike—
the unscientific multitude no less than the philosophers of
nature—are held in the bonds of a single error. That this naïve
cosmology is the target of his attack is shown with particular
clearness in the great fragment on the Existent (the eighth in
Diels's collection), where Parmenides tries to deduce a number
of the essential attributes of that which truly is. Starting with
the concept of Being itself, he finds implied in it the constituent
properties of never having come into being and never passing
away; motion and multiplicity he rules out of it altogether.
But these rejected properties are quite fundamental for that
which is counted as genuine reality by the naïve man in the
street no less than by the Ionian philosophers of nature. The
nature with which they are concerned takes the form of an

incessant coming-to-be and passing-away: the thing that is now present will soon exist no more. But Parmenides' basic idea is that the eternal One, which the philosophy of nature discerns in the process of coming-to-be and passing-away and seeks to identify with the ever-moving primal substance of all things, falls far short of the requirements which a strict conception of Being involves.

This also enables us to understand the remarkable term 'the Existent' or 'that which is' (ὄν), which is the real subject of Parmenides' disquisition from the very first line. Evidently this is an expression of his own coining. It is not, however, one that has been simply brought down from heaven with nothing to prepare the way for it, but is clearly connected with the language and thought of the Ionian natural philosophers. Undoubtedly they had already spoken of the world of things that arise out of the primal ground and then return to it as τὰ ὄντα—the things that are present or given. The innovation of the Ionians lay in the fact that they did not begin with uncontrolled traditions and fictions, as did the mythical thinking of earlier times, but took as their point of departure the things they found given in experience, which they tried to explain in terms of itself alone. Parmenides now takes seriously the claims of these ὄντα to be true Being, and finds that the things which men have hitherto called by this name do not really fulfil the requirements.[36] True Being can have nothing in common with Not-being. Neither can it be many. It must rather be one alone; for anything manifold is subject to change and motion, and this would be contrary to the persistence that is essential to the very nature of Being. Thus there are no ὄντα in the plural, but only a single ὄν.[37] Of course, this conclusion does not agree with the evidence of the senses; but that means merely that the senses must be deceptive and need to be subjected to the strict scrutiny of the understanding (λόγος).[38] If the understanding finds room for only a single Existent, that does not mean that this Existent is something purely mental, such as modern idealism might postulate. This cannot possibly be what Parmenides has in mind in his famous assertion that 'thinking and being are one and the same'.[39] In announcing this identity he is simply attacking the conceivability and knowableness of the Non-existent—a matter which he considers

of decisive importance. The verb νοεῖν does not mean at all the
same to Parmenides as it will to Plato, who contrasts νοῦς
sharply with sense-perception. Ever since Homer νοεῖν has
always meant 'to become aware' of an object and identify it
as the thing that it is.[40] Moreover, the object of νοεῖν that
Parmenides is talking about—'the Existent', or 'that which is'
—is something taken directly from human experience. Parmenides can have no doubts about the existence of this object,
inasmuch as νοεῖν itself is never really νοεῖν except when it
knows the actual. What the understanding or λόγος contributes
is the all-important consideration that the Existent cannot be
as our senses reveal it to us—namely, something manifold and
in motion.

Parmenides' understanding compels him to be consistent, and
this consistency leads him inevitably to a critique of human
knowledge. The very fact that he uses the image of the two
ways in expounding his theory[41] shows how much he is dominated by this motif. This is also confirmed by the way he distinguishes the two sections of his work as dealing with 'truth'
and 'appearance' respectively,[42] thus putting both the metaphysics of the first part and the physics of the second in an
avowedly critical epistemological perspective.[43] Parmenides'
thought, with its amazing self-assurance, has an underlying
necessity that makes it peculiarly compelling—the logical necessity inherent in the very concept of Being.[44] But Parmenides
is quite innocent of our formal logic and does not yet think of
the concept as a mere vehicle; he is convinced that his own
logical reasoning will actually enable him to get a firm grasp
of the Existent itself. To be sure, the Being that he approaches
along this path is quite different from the things of whose
existence the physicists have been talking. But it is significant
that when he claims this Being to be the one true Being, he is
definitely contrasting it with that of the physicists. So even
when he seeks to vanquish the philosophy of nature, he has
the same soil under his feet—the world of objective reality.
And even when he faces the inevitable question of how the
appearance by which all men have been victimized can have
arisen at all, and how it can have obtained such universal
respect, he cannot help putting his answer in the form of a
physical system.

It is well known that this system is presented in the second part of his work. Parmenides does not yet distinguish the subject and object of knowledge as sharply as we do. The only way he has of representing the origin of appearance is by describing the origin of the world of appearance.[45] He expounds a whole cosmogony, always with the intention of showing that the world whose origin he depicts is not a real world but merely an apparent one, and why this is so.[46] Now that he has proved that Being is one alone, the chief problem of the cosmogony of this world of appearance is to explain how the apparent multiplicity of things has arisen. This multiplicity, thinks Parmenides, is implied whenever one posits a duality of first principles such as human thought has heedlessly assumed from the first. So Parmenides accordingly makes the whole world of appearance issue from the primal opposition of light and night as two co-ordinate forces holding the balance between them.[47] Mixture is the underlying principle of this seeming world-order, and the philosopher takes over the god Eros from Hesiod's *Theogony* as the symbolic author of this mixture.[48] Above him stands the goddess who rules all things, with her throne situated in the middle between the two concentric rings surrounding the world—the ring of fire and the ring of night.[49] But the second part of the poem does not always confine itself to explaining the origin and structure of appearance; it seems rather to have been a complete cosmogony, describing among other things the origin of the sky, the Milky Way, the sun, moon, and stars, as Parmenides announces at the beginning.[50] Corresponding to the mixture of light and dark in the world outside is a similar mixture in those portions of the human body from which thought proceeds.[51] Since our knowledge is based on the principle that like is known by like, and since thought is itself a product of mixture, thought can know only that mixed world of appearance in which night and light, Not-being and Being, are accounted of equal worth. Thus the bifurcation of the one Being extends not only through the outer world but also through man and his thinking. The symbolism of light which we find in the proem with its depiction of the journey from the world of night to the world of truth and of Being[52] is resumed in the second part, where the origin of the world of appearance is described in terms of a dualism of light and night.[53]

It has been maintained that the second part is a polemic against certain doctrines of the natural philosophers, possibly those of the Pythagoreans; and indeed there is much that reminds us of Pythagorean views. But it is impossible to show a complete correspondence between the Parmenidean δόξα and Pythagoreanism; and to assume, as some have done, that the thinker's polemical zeal has driven him to burden his work with such a mass of extraneous matter is to miss the point of the whole structure.[54] Parmenides' attempt to explain the origin of the world of appearance is thoroughly original, however unsatisfactory we may find it. Without it we could hardly appreciate all the boldness of the first part, where the philosopher tears himself loose from the world of illusion and mounts upward towards the truth.

In recent years the problem of the relation between the two sections on truth and on appearance has been raised many times and has called forth various answers. One of the reasons for this lay in the feeling (which may perhaps betray too modern an approach) that Parmenides' Being was essentially empty. It appeared possible to overcome this difficulty by assuming a closer connexion between the worlds of Being and Becoming and seeking evidence for it in Parmenides' work. It was then decided that Parmenides must have intended his conception of the Existent to solve the riddle of the universe by performing the same function as the natural philosophers' doctrine of the one original principle. In this way Parmenides' Existent came to be looked upon as something closely akin to that principle: it became the ἀρχή or principle of the world of Becoming as such. The next step was to contrast it with Plato's abstract conception of the Existent, which is simply what remains when one ignores all the particular characteristics by which various kinds of things are differentiated. Comparison with Plato's abstraction made the Existent of Parmenides seem sturdier and more dense, with a solidity quite appropriate to the structure of forces holding the world of appearance together.[55] But this would mean that the Existent must have included the world of coming-to-be and passing-away all the while, which is quite out of accord with Parmenides' explicit statement that Diké, the force of law unchangeable, holds the Existent firmly in her bonds and never sets it free to become or to perish.[56] It

also conflicts with another passage, where we read of the
Existent that

. . . thus

Becoming is quenched, and destruction is utterly lost.[57]

Such an interpretation, moreover, makes the Existent too much
like the simple fact of being as such: it makes the whole doctrine of the Existent too much a mere consideration of one
aspect of the world in the special light of its being. Parmenides
is not like Aristotle: he does not think of the world as having
two distinct aspects on an equal footing with each other—its
aspect as something existent and its aspect as something
moved.[58] To Parmenides our world of Becoming is mere appearance; the world of Being is truth itself. He has no intention
that his doctrine of the Existent should explain the natural
world of multiplicity and motion; but in his remarkable doctrine of the world of appearance he endeavours to explain the
errors of those men who have put duality in place of the One
as the primal substance, and motion in place of that which
persists unchanged.[59]

In the great eighth fragment, which has come down to us as
a connected whole, Parmenides attempts to expound a number
of properties of the Existent which determine its nature more
closely.[60] It is significant that all these properties are obtained
by negating certain properties of the sense-world. The Existent
is un-become and imperishable, whole, single, unshakable,
temporally without limits, and complete. These predicates
show clearly the direction in which Parmenides' thought tends:
he is headed away from the world of Becoming and towards
an absolute Being that is something else altogether; and he
considers it his own special achievement to have lifted Being
out of the realm of immediate sense-experience. He thinks of
his absolute neither as something that supports the facts of
experience from beneath nor as their unmoved mover. Stenzel
has characterized the thought of Ionian natural philosophy as
a process of stripping the world of its form;[61] one might say
of Parmenides that his thought does not stop at this level, but
proceeds to strip reality of its character as a world by removing
every feature that goes to make it a world at all. When Parmenides asserts that the Existent is equidistant on all sides

like a sphere[62] (an obviously Pythagoreanizing comparison), this is, so to speak, its one last vestige of world-form which he has not succeeded in removing; and even in this passage he makes it plain that he is dealing merely with a comparison. His Existent is not to be approached by later conceptions such as that of matter.[63]

It seems, indeed, far more like the pure form of that idea in which all the earlier philosophical research was rooted: the idea of eternal existence as the basis of all knowledge. The Milesians had found this eternal existence in their primal principle and claimed it to be divine. Similarly, Parmenides contrasts his Existent with the world of 'mortals' delusions' and proclaims its gospel as a revelation from the goddess of light— a purely theological figure introduced to emphasize the importance of true Being. Now if we are not mistaken, we have here a new stage in the approach to the same problem which the older thinkers had answered by equating their first principle with the Divine. Like them, Parmenides connects the knowledge of existence with the sphere of religion; indeed, he does so with peculiar effectiveness. On the other hand, he definitely fails to identify Being with God, even though in later times his theory of absolute Being and its predicates has been construed again and again as a philosophical theology. Therefore it may well be more in keeping with the character of his thought if we speak of his Mystery of Being. This will at least do justice to the form he has given his doctrine. A theologian will, of course, deplore the absence of a God in this mystery; but no one with a live religious sense will refuse to count his pure ontology as a genuine mystery and revelation; nor will he fail to be deeply stirred when he sees how much it meant to Parmenides to experience the nature of Being. To put it otherwise, the religious element lies more in the way the man has been affected by his discovery, and in his firm and decided handling of the alternatives of truth and appearance, than in any classification of the object of his research as divine.

In the long run, however, a Greek would feel that the real basis of this religious attitude of 'the man who knows'[64] must lie in the value and significance of that which is known. In this connexion we cannot keep Parmenides' Existent too sharply distinguished from our own idea of reality, tempered as it has been by the abstract approach of modern natural science. What differentiates it from our view is its perfect completeness, which is affirmed explicitly,[65] and which is the very thing that would impress the Greek mind as something of at least divine rank, even if not as a personal God.[66] The comparison of the Existent with the sphere is also relevant here; and we must remember that in the Pythagorean table of opposites both light and the 'limit' (πέρας) are placed in the same column as the good. When Parmenides, who generally combats any such dualism, puts so much weight on the limitedness of the Existent and its affinity to light, it is clear that he is striking out his own peculiar course between the monism of the Milesian *apeiron* theory and the Pythagorean dualism of *peras* and *apeiron*: on the one hand, he refuses to agree with the Milesians that true Being is un-limited, and describes it rather as limited; on the other, he declares that the world in which limit and limitless combine is mere appearance. At this time the strongest religious motive for viewing the world philosophically still lies in the concept of unity. But Parmenides gives it new strength by endowing this unity with the properties of completeness, immobility, and limitation.

CHAPTER VII

HERACLITUS

THE end of the sixth century and the first decades of the fifth mark a general renascence of the religious spirit among the Greeks. In individual works of poetry and art this spirit manifests itself even more impressively than in the religion of the cult-divinities and the newly arisen sects that are usually cited as evidence for it. Along with poetry and art, philosophy now provides a peculiarly fertile soil for the emergence of the great religious personalities these new times bring forth. What is called religion in the narrower sense offers nothing comparable. The line begins with Pythagoras, who founds a sort of religious order. In Xenophanes we meet a person of a very different stamp. He is the bold herald of enlightenment, who attacks the Pythagorean transmigration-theory as mystification with the same ruthlessness that he applies to the gods of the popular religion and the poets; yet he wages his warfare inwardly confident that he has achieved a higher philosophical knowledge of God. Similarly it is in the form of a religious mystical revelation that Parmenides chooses to express his vision of true Being in which he shows the sense-world to be mere appearance; for he sees his new-found knowledge as the answer to the religious questions agitating the whole world about him. Pythagoras, Xenophanes, and Parmenides all belong to the new southern Italian culture resulting from the fusion of imported Ionian intellectualism with the social and religious background of the native stock. In Heraclitus, who appears at the end of the line, we see these same religious questions disturbing Ionia, the birthplace of philosophy. All these thinkers, despite their constitutional differences, possess a kind of prophetic fervour and eagerness to testify to their own personal experience that is especially characteristic of their period and puts them in company with the great contemporary poets Aeschylus and Pindar. This passionate emergence of the personality had not always accompanied philosophical thinking. In the Ionian naturalism of the old Milesians the spirit of observation and pure research had prevailed. We can hardly go wrong by assuming that in the writings of an Anaximander or Anaximenes the

author's personality never obtruded itself, except in the critical
first person singular of the scholar who candidly voices his own
opinions against those more generally held, as in the geographical work of their follower, Hecataeus of Miletus. None
of these earlier men was proclaiming a gospel—not even when
their theory of nature led them to describe their basic principle
as 'the Divine'.[1] Their impulse for rational explanation left no
room for anything so impassioned. Only the restless religious
search that followed the initial period of dispassionate boldness
and self-assurance in the use of reason could produce the philosophical revolutionary or the type of man who founds a religion,
striding over the ruins of the traditional world towards a new
interpretation of existence.

This way of approaching Heraclitus is very different from
that which long seemed unavoidable in the light of the ancient
accounts of his work, particularly those of Plato and Aristotle.
The ancient writers, to be sure, were not trying to grasp his
doctrine as a whole complete in itself, but were considering it
from the standpoint of the Platonic and Aristotelian philosophy.
They inevitably placed Heraclitus among the philosophers of
nature, along with Thales, Anaximander, and Anaximenes, and
found that he differed from them chiefly in choosing fire as his
basic principle.[2] They also contrasted him with Parmenides—
as the philosopher of Becoming versus the philosopher of
Being.[3] According to Plato and Aristotle, Heraclitus' thought
had culminated in the theory of the eternal flux of all things—
the πάντα ρεῖ—only to have the range of this principle restricted
to the sense-world when Plato found in his realm of Ideas that
eternal Being which is the sole and incontestable object of true
knowledge.[4] Thus Heraclitus' theory came to be regarded as
one of the foundation-stones of the absolute truth and an important stage in the history of philosophy that had to be
traversed before the summit was reached in Plato's own achievement. In itself the Heraclitean theory of flux seemed a bril-
liantly one-sided *tour de force*, the chief significance of which lay
in the fact that it summed up the metaphysical contribution
of the older Ionian philosophy of nature in its most general
form.

Here as elsewhere the more recent scholars have tried to
free themselves gradually from the Platonic and Aristotelian

standpoints, keeping as close as possible to the surviving fragments of the philosopher's work.[5] This is what we, too, must do,
though we cannot altogether dispense with the doxographic
reports of later ancient authors when they do not merely express
their own opinions but supplement our fragments with facts.

Let us begin by examining the peculiar stylistic form of the
Heraclitean fragments. There is simply nothing with which
their style can be compared: it resembles neither the didactic
epic of Parmenides nor the *silloi* of Xenophanes, nor even the
didactic philosophical prose style of Anaximander and Anaximenes, so far as we have been able to trace it. Heraclitus is the
creator of a new philosophical style tremendously effective in
its incisiveness and lapidary power of formulation.[6] It is true
that except for the opening passages we possess no extensive
portions of his book, but only isolated sentences. Their terse
and rounded phrasing, however, makes us suspect that it is
not by accident that Heraclitus' teachings have come down
to us in a surprisingly large number of sentences of this sort.
Either his whole book was written in this form, or it must
have been particularly rich in such utterances, so that those
who made use of it later were tempted to convert this capital
into small change. We are reminded of the collection of
Aphorisms in the Hippocratic corpus; but unfortunately there
is nothing original in the form of these as such. Many of them
have been taken from other Hippocratic writings, where they
appear in fuller contexts.[7] Indeed, the author of the collection
of *Aphorisms* may well have been impressed with earlier collec-
tions of individual sentences of this very type and accordingly
was tempted to compile something similar out of Hippocrates.
Perhaps it was Heraclitus himself who served as his model; the
aphorism may indeed have been the form in which he wrote.[8]
One could hardly find a piece of connected writing made up
entirely of mere sentences like the following: 'Character—
man's demon' (B 119),[9] 'Dry flash—wisest and best soul'
(B 118), 'Way up and way down—one and the same' (B 60),
'Invisible harmony—better than visible' (B 54), 'One man—to
me ten thousand, if he be the best' (B 49). The old gnomic wisdom had found its proper literary form in poetry, particularly
in Hesiod's *Works and Days* and the collection of Theognis of
Megara. Here again we meet long rows of apophthegms strung

loosely together. The same device reappears in prose in Democritus' tract *On Tranquillity* (Περὶ εὐθυμίης) and in the exhorta-
tion to Demonicus that has come down to us under the name
of Isocrates. Even the latter hardly succeeds in making a whole
of the numerous specific admonitions it contains (some of which
have been handed down from the earliest times); and it is
equally difficult to imagine how this could have been done with
the remarks of Democritus in the light of our fragments. They
approximate to the Heraclitean form more closely than anything
else, and in many cases can be shown to have made use of his
work.

The tone of Heraclitus' maxims, however, is utterly different
from the rules of life that we find in the older gnomic wisdom.
His style cannot be reduced to any one common denominator,
but includes a number of interconnected elements. We shall
now examine these in the light of the fragments, keeping a close
eye on the content.[10]

The beginning of the work, which fortunately is still preserved, tells of the 'word' that the philosopher proclaims—the
logos. Men fail to understand it, even though it is eternal.[11]
They understand it neither before they hear it nor when they
have heard it first. But even if this *logos* is primarily the word
of Heraclitus himself, it is not merely his word as a man among
men, but one that expresses eternal truth and reality and is
therefore itself eternal.[12]

'For while all things come to pass in accordance with this Word,
men behave as if they had no experience thereof, putting to test such
words and deeds as I set forth when I explain[13] things each by its
own nature and point out the real state of the case. But other men
are just as unaware of the things they do when awake as of those
that they do in their sleep' (B 1).

This is not the language of a teacher and scholar, but that of
a prophet intent on rousing men from their slumber. We can
see how much significance Heraclitus must have attached to
this image of sleeping and waking if we observe how often he
makes use of it. In another passage he speaks of a 'cosmos of
the waking', which presupposes a world of the sleeping as its
opposite.[14] But the waking state he has in mind is intellectual,
not merely physiological, as indeed he has already told us in his

opening sentence: what other men call 'waking', he insists, is
so utterly devoid of any intellectual awareness of the way
things actually happen that it is hardly to be distinguished
from sleep. In this sharp contrast between the speaker who
feels himself to be the sole bearer of the Word, and the whole
body of other men,[15] who fail to understand it even though
everything in the world is ordered in accordance with it, we
again detect the prophetic tone. To be sure, it is not the will
of a god that Heraclitus is proclaiming, but rather a principle
in accordance with which everything occurs. Heraclitus is the
prophet of a truth of which he has intellectual cognizance, but
this truth is not purely theoretical like Parmenides' revelation.
Too little attention has been given the fact that while Parmenides always uses the words νοεῖν and νόημα when he wishes
to designate the activity of the philosophical mind, Heraclitus
favours the word φρονεῖν—the traditional Greek term for 'right
thinking' or 'right intuition', with plain reference to man's
practical conduct.[16] The word is thus particularly appropriate
in connexion with moral and religious cognition. In Aeschylus'
prayer to Zeus in the *Agamemnon* the believer's insight into
the tragic events under divine control is called φρονεῖν, and so
is the conscious human attitude to which that insight gives
rise.[17] Similarly, the Delphic wisdom which calls for self-
restraint in every human endeavour and instils a fear of any
ὕβρις beyond man's province is called φρονεῖν. Heraclitus
teaches men φρονεῖν in the light of his new knowledge of the
universe; he also speaks of the 'words and deeds' that he intends
to set forth,[18] and says that men 'make trial' of these vainly
because they lack insight into the true nature of things. It is
evident, therefore, that his teachings are meant to influence
men's practical conduct as well. This is clear also in other
passages, where he describes wisdom as a speaking and acting
according to the truth.[19] We read elsewhere that men ought
not to 'act and speak' as if they were asleep.[20] Heraclitus is the
first thinker who not only wishes to know the truth but also
holds that this knowledge will renew men's lives. In his image
of the waker and the sleeper he makes quite plain what he
expects his *logos* to contribute. He has no desire to be another
Prometheus, teaching men new and more ingenious methods
of reaching their ultimate goals; he hopes rather to make them

capable of leading their lives fully awake and aware of the *logos* according to which all things occur.[21]

Before we inquire further into the content of the *logos*, which men do not understand though it lies at the basis of everything, let us try to grasp its nature from another of the characteristics which Heraclitus emphasizes: those who are awake have a cosmos in common,[22] while every man who slumbers, one must add, has a cosmos of his own. This distinction may be taken quite literally; but it also has a symbolic meaning, as we have indicated; here we have not merely the symbol of 'those who are awake', but also a more precise determination of their character in that they share a common world (as their intercourse with one another proves), while the world of dreams in which the sleeper finds himself proves inaccessible to others. Another fragment that is relevant here deduces the practical conclusion: 'So we must follow that which is common; . . . for even though the *logos* is common, the many live as if each of them had his own private wisdom.'[23] As soon as the philosopher begins demanding seriously that men be fully awake in the conduct of their lives, he finds the way blocked by the absence of this community of insight, or more accurately, by the presence of that which the crowd mistakes for it. Another fragment, which asserts that 'insight [$\phi\rho o\nu\epsilon\hat{\imath}\nu$] is common to all',[24] does not contradict what we have already found, but means merely that every true insight recognized as such is characterized by the fact that it immediately binds together all who share in it and lays the same obligation upon them all. This is what distinguishes philosophy from the mere private opinions of individual men, although it might seem very similar at first, since philosophy is by no means common property but always some person's special conviction. Parmenides uses the image of a revelation to explain why it is that the philosopher who has known true Being must find himself isolated as a man;[25] and Heraclitus likewise requires a special sanction to justify the lonely stand from which he confronts his fellows. We can now understand why he should have a genuinely religious sense of his own mission. Without his prophetic cognizance he would not have strength enough to withstand the pressure of the overwhelming majority of the unknowing—the 'many'.[26] But he is sustained by knowing that he is the bearer of the *logos*, which is incomprehensible to men when they first hear it, but which will unite them in a common cosmos once they have come to understand it. Thus the self-emancipating thought of the philosopher, which seems at first to be simply one more example of the intellectual decadence of a society already thoroughly individualized, is for Heraclitus the bond by which these same individuals can be bound together in a new community.

It might therefore seem that the content of the *logos* is ethical and political in character; and in a certain sense this is true, as is proved by the repeated emphasis upon its being something common (ξυνόν),[27] quite apart from its connexion with the 'words and deeds' of men. We have no right to construe this unequivocally social conception in Heraclitus as a mere figurative device for expressing logical universality. Heraclitus is actually the first man to approach the problem of philosophical thought with an eye to its social function. The *logos* is not only the universal (*das Allgemeine*) but also the common (*das Gemeinsame*). But while this makes it akin to the law of the State by which all citizens are bound, it is still far more than the law of even the greatest and mightiest commonwealth, for the *logos* is that which is common to all things whatsoever (ξυνὸν πᾶσι).[28] Its organ is the mind or νοῦς. To speak 'with the mind' (ξὺν νῷ) means for Heraclitus nothing else than 'with that which is common' (ξυνῷ).

'Those who speak with the mind', he tells us, 'cannot but strengthen themselves with that which is common to all, just as a city makes itself strong with its law [νόμῳ], and much more strongly than this. For all human laws are nourished by the one divine law; for this holds sway as far as it will, and suffices for all, and prevails in everything (B 114).

This is the first time that the idea of 'law' has appeared in philosophic thought; what is more, it is now regarded as the object of the highest and most universal knowledge; the term is not used in the simple political sense but has been extended to cover the very nature of reality itself.[29] This shift of meaning has already been foreshadowed by the designation of the world as an ordering-together or *kosmos*—a term which we have traced back to the older philosophy of nature,[30] and one which Heraclitus uses freely in an almost technical sense. Anaximander's

symbolic interpretation of the cosmic process as a trial
or legal contest (*diké*) is also a forerunner, to which Heraclitus himself reverts when, for instance, he writes: 'The sun
will not •overstep his measures; for otherwise the Erinyes,
Diké's deputies, will find him out' (B 94). Here Diké serves
as an embodiment of the inviolable order of nature. At first
glance it is rather startling that the Erinyes should be mentioned here; but there is a Homeric precedent for introducing
them in such a context, for it is they who stay the voice of
Xanthos, the horse of Achilles, when he foretells his master's
death.[31] What is new in Heraclitus is the way all this juridical symbolism is summed up in the conception of a single
all-controlling cosmic law. He calls it the 'divine law' as
distinguished from the human. In so doing, he carries the
Anaximandrian identification of the basic principle with the
Divine[32] a step farther. He does not, however, find the Divine in
eternity, imperishability, and omnipotence alone; on the contrary, he connects this idea with that selfsame principle of law
which Anaximander thought he had found in the processes of
nature. This principle has become generalized far beyond that
highest concept of human legalism and morality—the idea of law;
it is now interpreted as the law of all laws whatsoever. We may
assume that Heraclitus' book, which began with the idea of
logos, went on immediately to define the *logos* more precisely
as that which is common to all and as knowledge of the divine
law. Only in these terms can we understand his justification
for introducing himself as a prophet. The *logos* according to
which everything occurs, though it still remains hidden from
mankind, is the divine law itself. And the philosopher now
sounds his reveille, calling on men to awake and to do as this
divine law commands. This theological aspect makes very clear
how profoundly the law of Heraclitus differs from what we
mean when we speak of a 'law of nature'.[33] A 'law of nature'
is merely a general descriptive formula for referring to some
specific complex of observed facts, while Heraclitus' divine law
is something genuinely normative. It is the highest norm of
the cosmic process, and the thing which gives that process its
significance and worth.

The theological elements in Heraclitus' solemn proclamation
of the *logos* raise the question whether and how far his teachings

are in line with his introductory approach. Let us first hear what the ancient tradition has to say. Diogenes Laertius reports that Heraclitus' work was held together by the unifying theme of the theory of nature, from which it acquired its title. He adds, however, that it included 'considerations' (λόγοι) on three subjects—on the All, on politics, and on theology.[34] Though the title is naturally of later origin and there is nothing to guarantee its authenticity, we can infer from it that the groundwork of the whole was a cosmology, as Diogenes seems to intimate. But evidently either he or the writer from whom he got his information was struck by the fact that the title did not represent the contents in full. Our fragments confirm this; on the other hand, they rule out any clean-cut distribution of the cosmological, ethico-political, and theological elements into three distinct sections. When Diogenes refers to these as three *logoi*, it is either a rough way of putting a correct observation, or he merely has in mind three types of statement that can be distinguished in the philosopher's work, even though they are closely intertwined. So we really have no right to regard Heraclitus' theology as a separate part of his teachings. It must rather be thought of as forming with the cosmology an indivisible whole, even if we lay the chief emphasis on the theological side. I have elsewhere compared the relationship of these three aspects with that of three concentric spheres or rings: they are all held together by one and the same principle.[35] If in our discussion of this principle we begin with the cosmological side, we are quite in accord with what our fragments themselves suggest and also with the testimony of Diogenes. But while Diogenes speaks of the naturalistic or physical aspect as the thing that holds Heraclitus' work together, it is still worth mentioning that the grammarian Diodotus, who has likewise given some thought to the relationship of the physical and political elements in Heraclitus, stands for the view that in general the work does not deal with nature but rather with state and society, and that the physical element had merely a paradigmatic function. Evidently this struck Diodotus not as the main topic of the work but merely as a pattern for what he calls the 'political' factor.[36]

Central in Heraclitus' thought is his doctrine of the unity of opposites. Here the relations between the different sides of

his philosophy become particularly plain. On the one hand,
cosmological examples are employed to illustrate this basic
truth and show how the principle of opposites operates.[37] But
this principle reaches much farther than the realm of physics,
and its application to human life seems almost more important
than its role in natural philosophy. On the other hand, Heraclitus also explains the cosmic process in terms of essentially
human experiences, which thereby acquire symbolic significance.[38] 'War is father of all and king of all. Some he makes
gods, others men. Some he makes slaves, others free' (B 53).
The hostile clash of opposing forces—one of the major experiences of human life—is here found to be the universal principle
by which all the realms of being are ruled. War thus becomes,
in a way, Heraclitus' primary philosophical experience. This
utterance is no mere sober exposition of a well-known state of
affairs, but also, as the impassioned tone indicates, a startling
reinterpretation and revaluation of it. In calling attention to
the general phenomenon of opposition as involved in the partial
phenomenon of war, Heraclitus enhances the bold paradoxical-
ity with which he affirms and accepts this basic fact of the cosmic
process. To the man of normal sensibility there is nothing more
horrible than war. What is one to think of a world where this
evil prevails universally! When Heraclitus declares that even
the division of the world into gods and men, slaves and free,
which according to Greek ideas is the foundation of all order,
is based upon war, he aims at nothing less than revolutionizing
our normal habits of thinking. We must remember his suggestion elsewhere that man can enter the sphere of the Divine by
the heroization of those who have fallen in war.[39] This belief,
which is common among the Greeks, becomes especially significant in Heraclitus because he thinks of men and gods as
opposites. The 'men' of whom he speaks[40] are obviously those
who survive; victory makes some of them slaves and some of
them free. The fragment on war also shows us how the struggle
of opposites has been generalized until it becomes the supreme
principle of the world. In proclaiming this, Heraclitus' style of
predication becomes quite hymn-like: when he describes war
as 'father of all and king of all', he enthrones it as the very lord
of the universe.[41]

In the statement that 'War is father and king of all' we have

discovered the content of that divine law which, according to
Heraclitus, is the foundation of all human laws and of the
community that rests upon them.[42]   In another sentence he
identifies this principle with God himself: 'God is day—night;
winter—summer; war—peace; surfeit—hunger. He changes
himself like fire, which, when mingled with various kinds of
incense, is named from the fragrance of each' (B 67). He contrasts war with peace in an array of typical pairs of opposites
from the cosmic, social, and somatic spheres; so it can hardly
have the same comprehensive, symbolic meaning as in the
sentence in which it is declared to be the father of all things.
But this makes all the clearer what we are to understand by
'war' in the higher, symbolic sense: it is the constant interchange
and struggle of opposites in the world, including even war and
peace. In all these pairs there is a single something which underlies them, though it appears each time in a different guise and
so receives different names among men. This one thing that
keeps asserting itself in struggle and in change is what Heraclitus calls God. This God is to be found no less in night than in
day, in winter than in summer, in war than in peace, in hunger
than in surfeit—or, as we read in another passage, in poverty
than in surfeit.[43] He is not to be thought of as merely the positive member of some pair of opposites with positive and negative values respectively, nor even as the common denominator
of all positive members of all pairs of opposites. 'There is
always one and the same herein: living and dead, the awake
and the sleeping, young and old. For these by their changes
are those, and those, changing back again, these' (B 88). This
figure of reciprocal transformation is a device for showing how
unity maintains itself in opposites which, since they follow each
other in immediate temporal succession, seem distinct states
to us. Heraclitus is tireless in finding new concrete images for
expressing the unity of opposites. It is for this purpose that
he coins the words σύναψις—a 'contiguity' or 'nexus', and
ἁρμονία or 'harmony'—a fitting-together. When he speaks of
'contiguity' he is thinking of the unity as simply mechanical;
'harmony' is more dynamic. In one fragment he writes:
'Wholes and non-wholes, drawing together and drawing apart,
concord and discord—these are contiguities. From all one, and
from one all' (B 10). And in another fragment: 'They do not

understand how that which draws apart agrees with itself: a fitting-together with counter-tension, as of the bow and the lyre' (B 51).

In these two passages the new and fruitful idea of tension is clearly expressed. The *tertium comparationis* between the bow and the lyre lies in the dynamics of two opposing forces stretched together so that they work in unison; in each case these forces naturally tend apart, but now that they are joined together a third force emerges with a significance of its own. The Greeks call this joining-together a 'harmony'. In Greek this term, especially in early times, has a much wider range of application than to the realm of music, with which we associate it. It signifies anything that is tectonically or technically joined together; even in music the original conception is similar. While the reference to the lyre reminds us of musical harmony, our passage is primarily concerned with something else, namely the tension. But I cannot think it likely that Heraclitus has altogether missed the musical analogy, even though this has been claimed in the light of his comparison of the lyre and the bow.[44] It is surely precarious to try to find a reason here for distrusting Aristotle when he credits Heraclitus with saying that that which tends apart (ἀντίξουν) comes together, and that the most beautiful harmony arises from things that are different. Naturally this cannot refer to anything but musical harmony.[45] Moreover, another Aristotelian passage tells us expressly that Heraclitus adduced the 'harmony of the high and the low' as an argument against Homer, who had wrongfully cursed the strife prevailing among gods and among men.[46] It must also have been Heraclitus who cited as a further example the harmony of the sexes, which Aristotle mentions in the same passage. The doubts raised against this are likewise unconvincing.[47] Heraclitus' idea of the unity of opposites is by no means to be limited to any single meaning. We cannot tie it down to contiguity or connectivity any more than to tension or harmony or fusion. Heraclitus often has recourse to examples; but his use of them is symbolic, not inductive. What he expresses with them is not so much a clearly definable logical abstraction as a profound intuition revealing itself in the most various colours.

At bottom Heraclitus' unity cannot strictly be perceived in

any of the visual forms he uses for illustration. It is not without cause that he says of it: 'Invisible harmony—better than
visible' (B 54). Because it is invisible it is hidden from the eye
of man, even though it is actually the supreme power in accordance with which everything in the world proceeds. 'Nature
likes to hide' (B 123). Heraclitus remarks elsewhere that 'In
their knowledge of visible things, men are as easily fooled as
Homer, though he was wiser than all the Greeks. For he was
taken in by the boys who were killing lice and who told him,
"The ones we have seen and caught, we leave behind; but the
ones we didn't see and didn't catch, we take along"' (B 56).
Here we have a genuine riddle, symbolizing our own situation
with respect to reality itself. To Heraclitus this is the greatest
riddle of all. He thinks of the philosopher neither as the man
who sets forth the nature of the physical world, nor as the dis-
coverer of a new reality behind sense-appearance, but as the
solver of riddles, the man who interprets the hidden meaning
of all that happens in our lives and in the world as a whole:

> Hier ergreifet ohne Säumnis
> Heilig öffentlich Geheimnis.

Hence comes the fondness of the 'dark' Heraclitus for a style
which, like nature itself, does not reveal its inmost meaning
at once, but often resorts to riddles; it is like the Delphic oracle,
whose lord, he remarks, 'neither speaks nor conceals, but indicates' (B 93). Heraclitus also is struck with the philosophical
significance in the language of the Sibyl: 'With her raving lips
she utters things unlaughing, unadorned, unperfumed' (B 92).
Do we not seem to hear in these words a most pregnant characterization of the philosopher's own language? This leaning
towards the oracular, mystical, and enigmatic is in line with
his whole prophetic bearing. 'Men contradict the *logos*, though
they are dealing with it constantly; and the things which they
encounter every day are strange to them' (B 72). Therefore
a mediator and interpreter must appear. 'Wise it is for those
who have listened not to me but to the *logos* [as I have proclaimed it] to agree that all things are one' (B 50).

Heraclitus always keeps coming back to this one point. The
unity of all things is his alpha and omega. We have already
observed the seriousness he attaches to his message, the high

value he sets upon himself as the man who brings it to mankind, and the lengths to which he has gone to present it as true knowledge of the Divine and to surround it with an air of deep mystery. It now becomes all the more pressing to ask where the novelty of this doctrine lies and how it is related to the thought of his predecessors. The natural philosophers have already spoken of the primal ground of all things; Xenophanes has proclaimed the one world-God; Parmenides has taught the unity and uniqueness of the Existent and striven to show the multiplicity of the sense-world to be mere appearance. At first glance it seems rather hard to say in what particular modification of the theory of unity the originality of Heraclitus' achievement consists.

The Milesians' principle of unity stood at the beginning of a rectilinear process of cosmic development, as its material ἀρχή. Their ambition was to find out how and where all things had originated and what had been present at the first. Heraclitus sees the process of coming-to-be and passing-away as a constant intertransformation of opposites, one into the other. He experiences it as 'the way up and down', along which things wander unceasingly.[48] He even applies this principle to cosmology, and here we encounter his peculiar doctrine of fire as the imperishable basis of the universe. Of course, his fragments do not exhibit a completely developed physics, and it is more than doubtful whether Heraclitus ever felt that his primary achievement lay in improving on the doctrines of his Milesian predecessors. It almost seems that even his choice of fire is to be explained entirely by his dominant idea of the intertransformation of opposites and their constant changes; and it is questionable whether fire is really to be described as the first principle or ἀρχή at all. 'This cosmos, the same for all, was made by neither a god nor a man; but it always has been and is and will be fire ever-living, kindling itself in measures, and quenching itself in measures' (B 30). We need not stop to discuss the more precise interpretation of these words, which involves a number of difficulties; nor need we embark on the vexed question of whether Heraclitus taught the theory of a universal conflagration (ἐκπύρωσις) ascribed to him by the Stoics. To me it seems plain that even in ancient times there were no clean-cut Heraclitean statements about a period in the world's history when

everything would be destroyed by fire,[49] but that this theory
was inferred from such sentences as: 'All things are exchanges
for fire, and fire for all things, just as wares for gold and gold
for wares' (B 90). This exchange, however, is always occurring
in the world, as is clear from the following fragment: 'Fire's
transformations: first sea; and half of sea is earth, half whirl-
wind' (B 31). Here the writer must be referring to the constant
cycle of the elements. These fragments indicate that Heraclitus
had given his theory of opposites a particularly conspicuous
position even in his cosmology. While the older philosophers
of nature, in line with their basic assumptions, tried to explain
the emergence of the world from the one primal ground by
resorting to purely physical hypotheses such as separating-out
or rarefaction and condensation,[50] Heraclitus obviously is little
concerned with the physical how, but is far more intent upon
finding support for his fundamental notion that everything
which occurs involves opposites, and that in these very opposites unity perpetually renews itself.[51] Unity thus becomes the
central fact; it is always fully present, even if the events themselves have all the impetuosity of a river that is no longer the
same when one steps into it for the second time. 'In changing,
it takes its rest' (B 84). The whole world itself is likewise subject to change, and fire is the opposite into which it transforms
itself. Thus we can understand why Heraclitus is not satisfied
with such formulae as 'All things have come from one', but
declares: 'All is one', and 'From all one, and from one all'.[52]
The most important thing for him is that the order is always
reversible.[53]

Unlike Parmenides, Heraclitus makes no attempt to anchor
unity to any rigid Being, but finds it in the incessant change
itself. Thus with the same goal in view, he follows the opposite
road. It has recently been suggested that this solution of the
problem of unity is the more complex of the two and presupposes a knowledge of Parmenides—as if Heraclitus were
frankly trying to save unity as an eternal principle without
positing any immobile Being and without rejecting the apparent
multiplicity of things.[54] To me this hypothesis seems improbable. To fixate unity in the Eleatic conception of the Existent
was one possible course to pursue; but the way chosen by Heraclitus, which permitted unity to maintain itself even in the

world of change, was more plausible from the standpoint of the
natural science of the Ionians and much more in accord with
the spirit of it. The thing that is new is the mystical approach
to the concept of unity, which makes us realize how the
naturalistic world-view has stirred man's religious powers to
more and more vigorous response and roused them to extort
from it, with the help of its own methods, a new interpretation
of existence. This is what Heraclitus has achieved. He does
not stand on quite the same ground as the older philosophers
of nature, but his outlook has been profoundly revolutionized
by the truths which they proclaimed—discoveries so great and
overwhelming that they were still expounded with little regard
for their inevitable influence upon man's inner life and his own
place in the world. Heraclitus is the first thinker to expose
himself unreservedly to this influence, which threatens to
annihilate man as a human being and to make any rational
individual life quite impossible. The conception of the cosmos
as a revelation of the one divine law to which all things are
subject, and for which man, like everything else that exists,
must serve as executor, becomes for Heraclitus the point of
departure for a new interpretation of the world and of human
existence. He hopes to lead his fellows to take the law unto
themselves with full consciousness and accept it heroically in
every 'word and act.'

It might seem that our interpretation of Heraclitus brings
him farther away from the philosophers proper and closer to
Xenophanes, who is also strongly influenced by the philosophers
of nature, but still stands somewhat apart from them—a
teacher of the people in his own right, a man of enlightenment,
working out the bearings of the new knowledge upon the old
gods and the whole mythical scheme of the world. But this
comparison, which has recently been suggested, is only super-
ficially appropriate and—if anything—leads us off the track.[55]
Heraclitus is not a man of the open market-place like the poet
of the *silloi*: he is a solitary. The many and vehement interests
of the Colophonian (who never reaches a sufficient pitch of
intellectual concentration to create a fully original thought),
the restless variety of his production, and the number of posi-
tions that he is willing to assume—all these are the very antithesis of the firm and solid vigour with which Heraclitus rouses

himself for a single magnificent venture. Heraclitus thinks for himself as do very few others. He is no mere herald of enlightenment, despite his sharp and often cynical attacks on the popular religion.[56] Behind these is a world-view that is complete in itself and utterly his own—one that not only overturns the ideas of the past, but makes life subject to a new divine law. In Xenophanes we find no trace of this power of pervading life from a single centre and giving it form. There is, of course, one passage where he claims that he and the intellectual culture for which he stands promote the order of the state; but there he is fighting to maintain his place in society and contrasting his own wide knowledge with the athletic prowess which the Greeks of his time rated higher than intellectual achievement.[57] All this is a far cry from the rigour of the Heraclitean φρονεῖν. Heraclitus himself has shown us what he thinks of Xenophanes: 'Great learning does not teach insight. Otherwise it would have taught Hesiod, Pythagoras, Xenophanes, and Hecataeus' (B 40).

'Of all those whose teachings I have heard, no one has gone far enough to learn that the Wise is something apart from all things' (B 108). It is regrettable that this sentence, in which Heraclitus explains how he has outstripped all his predecessors, is not entirely clear. Just what is 'the Wise' that it should be 'apart from all things'? 'Apart from all things' can refer only to the things of the world of experience. The Wise, therefore, is something that is identical with none of them and present in none of them. It transcends them all. Man in particular is not entitled to this predicate. 'Human nature [ἦθος] has no insights',[58] we read elsewhere, 'but the Divine has them' (B 78). And again: 'One thing, the Wise alone, is unwilling and yet willing to be called by the name of Zeus' (B 32). Nowhere does Heraclitus make his attitude towards the popular religion clearer than he does here. On the one hand, he finds a number of customs and ideas that strike him as unworthy and shameful and stir him to merciless ridicule; on the other, he sees the religious idea of the highest God, whose name—Zeus—he regards as sacred because of the pure and lofty ideas it awakens.[59] Of course, his own idea of God is not to be equated with this anthropomorphized form of Zeus; but he feels that this name points in the same direction as that towards which his own

discoveries have led him.[60] All Heraclitus' remarks about man's
relation to God seek assiduously to keep God free from any
human features. 'A man is called childish by God, just as a boy
is called childish by a man' (B 79). Heraclitus also touches
upon the problem of the form of God, just as Xenophanes has
done, and as was only natural in a land where the gods were
honoured in paintings and statues. 'Compared with God, the
wisest of men seems like an ape in wisdom, beauty, and everything else' (B 83). Even the achievements of man's intellect
are mere 'child's play' (B 70). 'For the things that the most
trustworthy man knows and holds fast are merely matters of
opinion. But of course Diké will catch the fashioners of lies
and those who support their testimony' (B 28). 'There is only
one wisdom: to know that insight which governs all through
all' (B 41). The word 'govern' (or 'steer') calls to mind the
sentence in which Anaximander identifies the *apeiron* with the
Divine.[61] Ever since Anaximander's time this has evidently
been the conventional expression for that activity of the divine
principle by which the world is guided. Heraclitus uses the
same idea again in connexion with his doctrine of the universal
fire, when he writes: 'The thunderbolt steers all things' (B 64).
The thunderbolt, traditional weapon of Zeus, is here again the
weapon of the supreme god: it is the angry flash of the primal
fire as it forces its way out of the universe. The fact that Heraclitus' fire has the power of governing or steering[62] makes it
closely related to the highest wisdom, even if not quite the same
as God. When Anaximander speaks of his first principle as
governing all things, it is hard to think of it as having no
intelligence. Both Xenophanes and Heraclitus go so far as to
endow their first principle with supreme wisdom and a mind
that moves the world; only in Heraclitus, however, do we find
God's mental activity determined more specifically by the
unity of opposites, which is the content of the divine law. But
can any law prescribed by a single power rightly be called a law
at all? The idea of law, which comes from the sphere of juris-
prudence, means to a Greek the universal norm obeyed by all.
In Heraclitus' time this would ordinarily be decided by majority
vote, for his is a democratic age. He feels, however, that he
must connect this universal norm, which he regards as an
expression of the cosmos itself, with the idea of the oneness of

the supreme principle, which his conception of a single divine ruler implies. And he solves this dilemma by declaring that 'There is also law in obeying the will of one' (B 33). When God himself, in all his absolute perfection, is the ruler, then his will is actually the most salutary law for all.[63]

CHAPTER VIII

EMPEDOCLES

AT the time when the Greeks of the mother country were making history in the battles of Salamis and Plataeae by repelling the advance of the Persian hosts across the Aegean, and concentrating all their energies upon the inner and outward development of their states for decades after the victory, the philosophical movement begun in Ionia remained, no less than in the preceding sixth century, chiefly confined to the outlying regions of Greek culture. In its turn the movement was unaffected by the creative renascence which the mainland of Greece was enjoying in the great poetry of Pindar and the Attic tragedians. The men of the mother country, apparently more than a century behind the times in comparison with the enlightened cosmological thought of the Ionians, continued to draw from the still unexhausted depths of their own native powers the ability to bring about this great poetic transformation of their universe, even when the rationalistic movement had already largely taken hold of the more outlying territory. Their point of departure was altogether different from that of the philosophers. The world-view of the poets centred in their experience of human destiny itself and of the way in which it could be overcome through that spirit of heroism in the midst of tragedy which had grown to maturity in the hard struggles of a century filled with inward upheaval and threatened with constant danger from without.

In the poetry of the Greek mainland, which was the passionate expression of a new closeness to life, the urge for sober and rational thinking seemed to have come to a standstill; and the trend of the times took a decidedly anthropocentric turn in manifest reaction to the sovereignty of the inquiring reason. But in the periphery of colonial Greece, both in the east and in the west, philosophy still followed with remarkable persistence the path it had originally struck out. For an entire century its development had been glorious and unhampered; retrogression was here no longer possible; even the new emergence of ethical and religious problems served merely as an occasion for philosophy to strengthen and enrich itself. Xenophanes

had begun the process of liberating the religious consciousness
from the anthropomorphism of the old beliefs. Since his time
the germs of a metaphysical and religious interpretation of the
new naturalistic picture of the world, already latent in the work
of the Milesians, had developed more and more vigorously under
the influence of the religious currents of the age. Over against
the appearance of incessant coming-to-be and passing-away
Parmenides had tendered his conception of a single, immovable
Being, in which all the meaning of existence would be preserved;
and virtually at the same time, but quite independently, Heraclitus had found in the unity of opposites the divine core at the
heart of the world of Becoming.

Neither of these thinkers had either the desire or the competence to give a genuine explanation of nature after the
Milesian pattern in the form of a complete cosmogony. But
this side of the Ionian philosophy of nature—from which, indeed, all later natural science sprang—comes to life again in
Empedocles, who takes a long stride forward in this direction.
Hence it is quite natural for the later Greek philosophers after
the time of Plato and Aristotle to refer to him repeatedly, and
to think of him as the creator of the theory of the elements and
therefore of physics itself in their sense of the word. From our
point of view, however, it is more important that in Empedocles
this physical type of thinking does not appear in its purest
form, but is complicated by his efforts to interpret the natural
facts of our existence in this world in metaphysical terms. This
pronounced religious element in Empedocles, which could not
help being echoed by the Neoplatonic mystics of the later
ancient period, inevitably made serious difficulties for his modern
expositors as long as they looked at him through the eyes of
his enthusiastic admirer Lucretius[1] and thought of him chiefly
as the materialist and student of nature. Even when they have
not tried to eliminate the religious element as a disturbing
feature alien to the real spirit of his work, they have at least
cavilled at it as an inconsistency in his intellectual attitude.
But the more striking the contrast between Empedocles the
scientist and Empedocles the man of religion, the more remarkable a phenomenon he becomes for a history of the theology of
the Greek philosophers.

On the surface the religious problem is by no means the same for him as it was for his predecessors. It does not lie hidden behind a strict and universal conception of pure Being like that of Parmenides, which hints at metaphysical significance only in that it is proclaimed in the form of a divine revelation; nor is it at all comparable to Heraclitus' cosmic vision, in which a logical insight into the dialectic of the physical process—the unity of opposites—is at the same time experienced as a revelation of the divine secret at the heart of the world. We possess fragments from two independent epic poems by Empedocles, in which a naturalistic cosmology and a religious conception of human existence are separately exhibited: the poem *On Nature* and the *Katharmoi* or *Purifications*. In the poem *On Nature*, as far as matters of form are concerned, Empedocles, the native Sicilian from Akragas, is obviously following in the footsteps of his south Italian compatriot Parmenides, apart from whose influence the very idea of the Empedoclean theory of elements would have been unthinkable. The *Katharmoi* is the only surviving work of early Greek poetry in which we come face to face with the Orphic pietism, though in a somewhat refined form, refracted through the medium of a remarkable individuality. How both these works can be understood as expressions of one and the same personality has recently been a much-mooted problem, which has called forth many different attempts at solution.

For a long time the prevailing opinion was that in the poem on *Purifications* Empedocles had combined certain religious ideas like those of pre-existence and metempsychosis and even taboos on the eating of meat with the so-called 'mechanical physics' of his naturalistic masterpiece, with which, as Eduard Zeller remarked,[2] they not only had no obvious scientific connexions but even seemed contradictory. Others, like Diels and Bidez, tried to assign the two poems to successive periods of the author's life, regarding their inner divergence of outlook as indicative of distinct developmental stages.[3] Here two solutions have been suggested: either Empedocles may have started with fusty religious beginnings and advanced to strictly rational thinking and research, or he may in later years have become so dissatisfied with explaining the world in mechanical terms that he threw himself into the arms of the irrational Orphic faith in salvation and expiation. Such attempts to solve the problem of the two poems were a definite step forward in that they recognized the necessity of giving more attention to Empedocles' personality in its concern with both these worlds; for evidently this is where one must look to discover how two approaches so contrary can have been combined. Naturally this fact is of more than mere biographical significance. On the other hand, the problem of whether these two intellectual attitudes, which seem so antagonistic, can somehow have been reconciled in the philosopher's own mind is not really solved by assigning them to two successive periods in his life; the idea of temporal development merely parries the problem and serves to dull its edge. Indeed, the whole intellectual unity of Empedocles' personality has hereby been jettisoned without sufficient effort to see whether there is anything to justify thus breaking up his inner life into disconnected episodes. Perhaps the fault may lie, in part at least, in our very conception of religious experience, which modern psychology of religion often regards as including something temperamental, incalculable, and sudden. But even if this really were the nature of Empedocles' Orphic *katharsis*, can one seriously suppose that the firmly rooted physical conceptions of the poem *On Nature*, which served for so many centuries as the foundation for all scientific study of the natural world, should so soon have lost significance for their creator as to make him toss them lightly aside and abandon himself to new fervours of a radically different type? The first step towards a real understanding must be to restore the original antinomy in the problem of the juxtaposition and contraposition of Empedocles the student of nature and Empedocles the religious mystic, as Ettore Bignone has tried to do in his book on Empedocles[4] (which is equally fascinating from the point of view of psychology and from that of intellectual history), and to reveal the unity behind this opposition.

Even in ancient times the importance of the philosopher's human personality for the understanding of his teachings was recognized, at least indirectly. There is no other pre-Socratic about whom such abundant biographical material is still available. In the ancient period Empedocles was decidedly more prominent than he is in our present-day histories of philosophy. Nowadays we are inclined to treat him as a straddler and compromiser, and, indeed, he does not seem to have the full integration

and sheer intellectual momentum that we find in Parmenides
or Heraclitus. Despite all this he remains one of the most
arresting figures of the pre-Socratic Olympus, if only for his
historical interest, for he has given us a better idea of the intellectual culture of the Greek west than anyone else has done.
Its strongly distinctive quality shines forth in him with peculiar
richness of colour.[5] The complexity of Empedocles' inner world
is obviously more than a purely individual affair: it reflects
with particular impressiveness the many inner stratifications
of culture in Sicily and Magna Graecia, and at the same time
proves the intellectual and spiritual solidarity of these two
neighbouring centres of Hellenic colonization in the West. The
two disparate elements that we meet in Empedocles were here
already traditional. The naturalistic enlightenment from Ionia,
of which Xenophanes was the first pioneer, had already left
its mark on a personage no less indigenous than the Syracusan
Epicharmus,[6] whose poetical comedies had reached their peak
in the days of Empedocles' youth. On the other hand, the
Orphic pietism had nowhere been more profoundly effective
than here in the West—not even in Athens, where, under the
protecting wing of the Pisistratidae, the active circle of Onomacritus had embraced it very seriously for a while. When we
look to the Greek literature and culture of this and the preceding
period for traces of Orphic influence, it is not only in the Pythagoreans of southern Italy that we find them, but also—and this
is significant—in an ode of Pindar addressed to Theron, tyrant
of the Sicilian city of Akragas,[7] and in the work of Theron's
fellow-townsman Empedocles. Moreover, our most important
Hellenistic evidences of similar religious developments also
come from Magna Graecia.[8] Hence, when we find in the person
of Empedocles Orphic ideas running hand in hand with the
more precise concepts of the natural philosophy of his day,
we ought to be no more surprised than when we come upon
a purely scientific rationalism combined with the religious spirit
of Christianity in a man of our own times.

The fact that such various intellectual elements were already
traditionally available and ready to become fused with one
another in the same individual could not help giving rise to a
new synthesizing type of philosophical personality. It is not
surprising, therefore, that the mind of Empedocles is one of

extraordinary breadth and inner tension. It shares with the imagination of the poet the plastic flexibility of response. Aristotle has expressed some doubt whether Empedocles' verse has anything but the metre in common with the epic of Homer,[9] but we have no right to apply this rigid yardstick of perfection to his poems if we wish to treat them fairly.[10] Only a true poetical genius could embrace the astonishing contrasts that appear in the thought of Empedocles, and only a born poet could possess an imagination ardent enough and versatile enough to entertain truths of such different orders, preserving each of them in all its absoluteness despite their basic incompatibility. In the poem *On Nature* every detail seems to be fitted into the frame of a single structure with the logical consistency of the true philosopher. But as soon as the first lines of the *Katharmoi* strike our ear, we find ourselves in a realm where a completely different, mystico-theological style and type of thought prevail. Neither of these two forms of thought seems to weaken the other in any way or to encroach upon its domain, and each of the two realms embraces the whole of reality in its own manner. The one thing they have in common is the fact that they are both poetical reality and take the form of poetry, which means for the Greeks that they appear in the form of myth.

From the very beginning we have stressed the fact that there is no unbridgeable gulf between early Greek poetry and the rational sphere of philosophy.[11] The rationalization of reality began even in the mythical world of Homer and Hesiod, and there is still a germ of productive mythopoeic power in the Milesians' fundamentally rational explanation of nature. In Empedocles this power is by no means diminished by the increasingly complex apparatus of his rational thought, but seems to increase proportionally, as if striving to counteract the force of rationalism and redress the balance. It is also the source of that inner compulsion which leads him to put his thoughts in poetical form and take Hesiod and Parmenides as his models. Empedocles' philosophy of nature is presented as a genuine theogony; and the mythical imagination of the philosopher-poet draws new vitality from the rich, sensuous content of the physical forces out of which he constructs his cosmos. The Greek consciousness requires no rational proof

that the Divine is everywhere alive and active in this world;
and like the song of atonement in the *Katharmoi*, the epic *On
Nature* will show us how this divine activity really operates
and will teach us to recognize it in a form now descried for the
first time. In the mythical space of a world pervaded with
divine figures, the two attitudes so irreconcilable from our
abstract point of view will be seen to fit together as two distinct, but in the last analysis basically homogeneous, spheres
for the interplay of divine forces.

It is not our aim to discuss the fragments of the poem *On
Nature* exhaustively and consider all the particular questions
they involve; but we need some idea of Empedocles' philosophy
of nature by way of contrast and as a background for further
discussion, and must therefore examine it here. We are reminded of Parmenides when our poet calls upon his Muse to
give him knowledge,[12] for she, like Parmenides' goddess, is an
embodiment of wisdom. But there is no hint that Empedocles
is following any one special road to the truth. Unlike his predecessor, he does not knock at the door of the divine realm of
light in person, but begs the goddess to come to him and bestow
on him the gift of reverent song. This awe is present in the
feelings of the poet himself,[13] and when he beseeches the Muse
to tell him 'as much as it is permitted ephemeral beings to
hear',[14] it is quite evident that he is deliberately contrasting
himself with Parmenides' bold entrance into the hidden realm.
Parmenides had told how he had been greeted by Truth herself
and had received from her a revelation of Being such as no
mortal either before or after him could ever enjoy.[15] He had
hoped to deduce its essence and characteristic properties by
steeping himself in the concept of Being as such[16] and had dared
to reveal its form, which resembled nothing on earth and was
not to be grasped by the senses. Scorning the testimony of eyes
and ears, he had put all his trust in rational thought,[17] and this
had shown him a road leading 'far from the path of men'.[18]
Then, with boldness amounting almost to rashness, he had con-
tested the reality of this our world, which up to that time had
provided the entire content of the ideas of φύσις and ὄντα.[19]
To a man with the reverence of Empedocles, this is sheer
hybris, no true mystery.[20] Accordingly he addresses his Muse
as follows:[21]

And may not the flowers of glory and honour
Given by mortals induce you to gather them
At the price of making so bold as to utter far more
Than is holy, and throning yourself on wisdom's peak.

We must be careful not to interpret as a mere poetic metaphor this expression of the piety that keeps him from following the path of his all-too-confident predecessor. It comes rather from the man's own innermost nature, which impels him to devote himself with understanding and reverence to the world about him and the interplay of its forces. Every word is a protest against that adamantine logical consistency which would draw this foundation from under his feet; and so he begins with an admonition comparable to that with which Goethe counterbalances his own idealistic conviction that for man the centre lies within himself:[22]

Den Sinnen hast du dann zu trauen,
Kein Falsches lassen sie dich schauen,
Wenn dein Verstand dich wach erhält.

It is true, of course, that in Empedocles' poem *On Nature* we find no contrast of the experience of the senses with the inwardness of man's moral world such as provides the point of departure for Goethe's admonition. When Empedocles urges us to trust our senses,[23] he does so merely to repudiate the distrust with which Parmenides regards them.[24] Nevertheless, the complexity of Goethe's feelings in contemplating the world with concern for both the inner and the outer is already present in Empedocles. He is well aware of the moral reality of man's inner daemon, as he reveals in his song of expiation. He might easily have combined this belief with the Eleatic denial of the sense-world. But the same inner sensitivity and readiness which enable him to experience all the anguish and turmoil of his inner soul as a world in itself and to recognize it as such, compel Empedocles to resign himself willingly to his senses and the impressions derived from them, and give them their just due. But each of them is to be trusted only so far as it makes clear assertions about its own specific field;[25] so in Empedocles, as in Goethe, the senses are subject to the examining check of the understanding. On the other hand, to be 'kept awake by the understanding' in this manner is something quite different from Parmenides' *elenchos*, which is for the *logos* alone to decide.[26]

But how does Empedocles escape the bewildering multiplicity of sense-impressions and find his way to a unified explanation of the world? How does he deal with Parmenides' argument that since the Existent is, no coming-to-be or passing-away is possible?[27] Now that the logical incompatibility of Being and coming-to-be has been disclosed, Empedocles' instinctive trust in the senses will never be strong enough to make him return simply to the naive assumption of the Milesians that in perceiving these very phenomena of coming-to-be and passing-away we are perceiving something that really 'is'. On the other hand, in exhorting us to trust our senses he takes a positive stand towards empirical reality that is utterly different from that of Parmenides. Therefore, even if Empedocles feels that he must accept those conclusions about Being which his predecessor has deduced from that concept, this fact is not enough to make him sacrifice the whole world of Becoming as mere illusion. He finds his way out of this dilemma in a manner approaching genius. Parmenides is right: true Being must persist in itself unchangeably; therefore we cannot say that our world 'is' in the strict sense; on the contrary, that which 'is' must lie hidden somewhere beneath the surface of coming-to-be and passing-away. In our world there is obviously no absolute coming-to-be or passing-away, but only mingling and separating of certain things that are fundamental and unchanging.[28] This doctrine presupposes, to be sure, that there is not merely one single principle of this sort, as the older physics assumed, but several. But was it ever really possible for the Milesian physics to explain the whole multiplicity of things in terms of one primal ground alone? Was not Anaximander's hypothesis of the 'separating-out' of certain basic opposites in nature[29] like heat and cold, dryness and moisture, from a single principle, a mere tautology, inasmuch as the very idea of separating-out presupposes that the opposites are already contained in the primal ground? And did Anaximenes fare any better with his hypothesis of the origin of these fundamental opposites by mechanical condensation or rarefaction of the basic stuff?[30] The fact that he felt the need of a correction at this point shows rather that this was where the real difficulty lay, and that it was not to be evaded. Accordingly, since the opposites themselves must have been present from the first, Empedocles now makes them the immutable substratum of all coming-to-be and passing-away as the only true Existents in the process of nature, and concludes first—as against the Milesians—that there is not one primal stuff but several, and second—as against Parmenides—that Being is not monistic but a plurality. In this way multiplicity and movement, which had been declared as unreal by the Eleatic school, have been saved; the world as a whole becomes a vast process in which the intermingling of a certain number of primal stuffs gives way in turn to the dissolution of the mixture thus achieved. Empedocles limits the number of these stuffs to four, corresponding to the primary opposites—wet, dry, cold, and warm—which he has doubtless met as basic categories in the physics of his predecessors. He maintains that each of the substances these men have put forward as basic—water, fire, air, and earth—represents in truth one and one only of the four primary opposing qualities; and he accordingly identifies the four primary qualities with the four substances respectively.[31] In this peculiar theory of the elements the enduring truth of the older natural philosophy is ingeniously crossed with Parmenides' logic of Being. A number of verses directed against the older physical conception that 'something existent can come from something non-existent'[32] betray Parmenides' influence in their dialectical sharpness. Even his words are echoed in the following sentence:[33]

> For in no way can anything come into being from that
> Which is not; and for that which is, to become destroyed
> Is impossible, not to be heard of . . .

Empedocles refers to the four principles or roots of all things as gods, and names them Zeus, Hera, Aidoneus, and Nestis.[34] This allegorical personification brings out very clearly the qualitative character of his pluralism as opposed to Democritus' purely quantitative theory of atoms. Empedocles' elemental principles are imbued with the very life-breath and essence of divine powers. The theogonical has here invaded the rational; but in this process the Hesiodic genealogical approach is now reduced to the construction of physical principles.[35] Only in the way the four primal beings are paired as Zeus and Hera, Aidoneus and Nestis, does it still operate as before.

But in those things which Empedocles calls ever-existent and unmoved[36]—namely, the four eternal roots of things—one basic metaphysical quality of the Parmenidean ὄν is abandoned: the quality of completeness, unity, wholeness.[37] We shall see that in Empedocles these essential properties of the Divine are not regarded as attributes of the four elemental gods, but pertain only to a certain state in which the world sometimes finds itself. The four material principles are not sufficient in themselves to bring this state to pass: they must be supplemented with the activity of two additional formative powers, which accomplish the mixing and unmixing of the basic substances. Empedocles gives mythical names to these two powers as well, and declares them to be gods of equal rank with the four material principles, calling them *Philia* and *Neikos*—Love and Strife.[38] In accord with the general tendency to translate Greek philosophy into the categories of modern mechanical physics, it has been tempting to speak of 'Attraction' and 'Repulsion' instead; but Empedocles' names stand for something quite different—two powers that reign throughout the inorganic and organic worlds alike. Empedocles seeks to understand the inorganic processes in terms of organic life rather than vice versa. He also speaks of Love as Aphrodite,[39] whose nature he has thus expanded and generalized into a divine life-giving power by which all things are made one. Empedocles not only endows her with many of the characteristics of Hesiod's cosmogonic Eros,[40] but makes her the cause of all pairing, both in the realm where we are accustomed to distinguish male and female and far beyond this in the whole structure of nature, which he holds to be organized in the same way throughout.[41] Under her influence things disjoined become united, and in this way she brings about an order based entirely on Love. But when this unity has been reached, it always becomes split into multiplicity by the destructive power of Hate.[42] This process is not perceptible to the senses but only to the eye of the mind.[43] None of these gods is more primordial or more revered than the others: they are all equal, but each has its own ethos, and in the cycle of time each prevails in its turn,[44] in the bodies and lives of individual plants, animals, and men, no less than in the life of the cosmos itself.[45] For even the parts of the cosmos— Sun and Earth, Heaven and Sea—are bound together in Love.[46] Nature is like the painter who mixes his colours to bring forth manifold forms—trees, men and women, wild beasts, birds and fishes, and the long-lived gods.[47]

The cosmology of Empedocles shares with its predecessors, the cosmologies of Anaximander or Heraclitus, a feature characteristic of all Greek cosmological thought: the interpretation of natural processes by means of analogies taken from man's political and social life. In Anaximander it was the concept of a *diké* or *tisis* ruling the process of coming-to-be and passing-away which made the *physis* a true *cosmos* (i.e. a legal order). Heraclitus took over this conception; but he varied and expanded its application to nature by proclaiming a 'law' (*nomos*) of the universe corresponding but superior to all human law. In Empedocles we discover similar forms of interpretation of physical phenomena. When he places much emphasis on the fact that the primordial gods of his cosmogony are all equal (ἴσα) and of the same age (ἥλικα γένναν), though their honour (τιμή = γέρας, 'function') and character (ἦθος) differ individually, he is obviously attacking the tradition of the earlier Greek theogonies, most of all that of Hesiod. Hesiod had taught that when the oldest gods began to emerge from the yawning Chaos, Earth and Eros appeared first. Plato quotes this passage in his *Symposium* in the speech which Phaedrus makes on the nature of Eros, in order to prove that Eros was the oldest of all gods (πρεσβύτατος). In the religious and political language of the Greeks that meant that he was also the most honoured (τιμιώτατος). The words for 'old' and 'honoured' were used as synonymous throughout the history of Greek thought. The attempt to break up this divine hierarchy of age and honour is condemned as revolutionary in Aeschylus' *Eumenides*, in which the Furies complain of being denied by the younger deities the honour due to gods of the older generation.

Thus when Empedocles proclaims that all his gods are 'equal and of the same age' he is not speaking of the equal quantity of his four elements existing in the universe, as has been assumed by some who try to understand the Greek philosophy of nature in terms of modern physics or chemistry. His words should not be referred to the four elements alone, as in Diels's translation of the fragment; they seem also to include Love and Strife.[48] The plea for the equality of the gods refers not only to the monistic cosmogonies of Thales, Anaximenes, or

Heraclitus, but also to Hesiod's *Theogony*, in which, as we pointed out before, Earth and Love represent the earliest stage of the cosmogonic process. These oldest gods are now deprived of their privileges and absolute power, and they are all (ταῦτα πάντα) declared equals. They are all the same age, i.e. have existed from the beginning. Fire, Water, and Air are as essential to the world as is Earth. Hate is as necessary as Love to maintain its dynamic structure, even though Empedocles loves Love and hates Hate. Love and Hate are not above the four elemental gods, as Aristotle might make us believe in distinguishing them as *causa movens* and *causa materialis*. In other words, the aristocratic order of the older theogonic thought which was all based on difference of rank, age, and genealogy, is superseded now by the democratic equality of all the elementary and moving forces which make up Empedocles' cosmos. They are, however, bound together by the law of a higher unity to which their individual functions and characters are subordinate. This view suits perfectly Empedocles' social ideal; for tradition represents him as a passionate champion of democracy in the political struggle of his home town Akragas. But the relationship of the social element in Greek thought to the cosmological was always a reciprocal one: as the universe was understood in terms of political ideas such as *diké, nomos, moira, kosmos,* equality, so the political structure was derived throughout from the eternal order of the cosmos. It is of deep interest to the historian of the Greek mind to trace the changing social ideals in the development of this mutual relation, and to appreciate the importance for the democratic age, in the second half of the fifth century, of a new cosmo-theogony which expressed the trend of the time to discover the origin of its favourite ideas in the divine nature of the world.

In the system of Empedocles the parts of the world and its elements grow together in love for long periods of time until they unite in complete harmony in that perfect crowning state which Empedocles calls the *Sphairos*. Following Diels's interpretation, we may render the verses dealing with this as follows:[49]

> . . . And there the swift limbs of the Sun
> Are no longer descried, nor even the rough strength of Earth,
> Nor the Sea; so firmly is circular Sphairos held fast
> In the solitude round about . . .

The *Sphairos* is so called because of its spherical shape.[50] This concept is a conscious reminiscence of the Being of Parmenides, which was described as 'like to the volume of a well-rounded sphere'.[51] In this form the four elements are held fast by 'Harmony', who prevents their distinctive features from appearing, just as Parmenides' Diké holds Being chained in her bonds and keeps it far remote from coming-to-be and passing-away.[52] Empedocles also gives us a description of the *Sphairos* as 'equal on all sides', which is likewise appropriate to Parmenides' Being;[53] on the other hand, his emphasis on its infinitude is clearly a polemic against the finite Being of Parmenides.[54] Only the delight of the *Sphairos* in his solitude is out of keeping with this conception of the god—for that is what he is to Empedocles.[55] The word μονίη,[56] which Diels would translate as 'solitude', must rather mean 'rest' or 'repose'. We find such an interpretation as early as Eudemus, who understood this line as indicating immobility;[57] nothing but the word μονίη could have suggested such an idea. This derivation from μένω, 'to remain'—rather than from μόνος, 'alone'—seems to be further confirmed by a papyrus containing a new elegy by Tyrtaeus, where the word is used for the soldierly virtue of sticking to one's post.[58] Thus in the cycle of the Empedoclean universe the *Sphairos* assumes both the function of Xenophanes' God, who 'remains at rest in the selfsame place', and that of the Parmenidean ὄν.[59] But while the four primal elements or 'roots', despite their mixture and separation, remain really 'unmoved' in that they each persevere in themselves forever,[60] the repose of the *Sphairos* is confined to a specific phase of the cosmic process. In this way Empedocles retains the Eleatic Being as one stage in the cycle: it is the stage when the divine Love which keeps the world going has realized its dominion and become fully achieved.[61] In the description of the blessed god *Sphairos*, the philosopher again follows Xenophanes' example and protests against anthropomorphic representation:[62]

. . . For no pair of branches shoots up from his back;
No feet, no swift-moving knees, no engendering parts.
But he was a sphere, and everywhere like to himself.

 . . . .

. . . But when mighty Strife had grown great in his limbs
And had risen to honours, then, when that time should come round

Which alternately is fixed for them [Love and Strife] by an ample
  oath, . . .

a new phase of the world-cycle would begin.[63] The change is not
sudden but quite gradual. Love can maintain its dominion only
as long as it stays in the midst of the whirl, where it can still
keep control, and as long as Strife remains in the lowest depths
and cannot succeed in developing its power.[64]

In the doctrine of the four elements, therefore, Empedocles'
cosmos embraces with antinomic tension both the Milesian
physics—with its theory of the primal source of all becoming—
and Parmenides' idea of Being. In the doctrine of the *Sphairos*
it also embraces the Heraclitean metaphysics of the eternal
coming-to-be of Harmony out of Strife and War, but is combined with Parmenides' vision of a single, reposeful, complete,
and spherical Being. Mixture and dissolution are the work of
two separate forces; Empedocles does not think of Harmony as
produced by Strife itself but by a rival divine power instead.
In the figure of Love, from which all the constructive forces of
reality arise, the world possesses a unifying and monistic tendency, though the world itself cannot be entirely understood
except in terms of a fundamental dualism permanently effective
within it, which does not permit the redeeming work of Love
to endure but is constantly bringing about its destruction.
Unlike Heraclitus, Empedocles does not predicate Strife as 'the
father and king of all things',[65] but as the evil and sinister
element in the world.[66] And his enthusiastic conception of
Love shows that the emotional basis determining his entire
evaluation of reality is utterly different. To feel this difference
it is enough to compare some of his lines with Heraclitus'
rugged and masterful language: there hardness and harshness,
here softness and flexibility; there triumphant affirmation of
significance in what seems contrary to all significance, here the
sense of being violently tossed back and forth between Love
and Hate, construction and destruction; there the heartening
consciousness that in the very midst of all the fearsome discord
of existence the victory of Harmony is secure, here the painful
certainty that individual life is dependent upon a mere stage in
the cosmic process when the pendulum is swinging back from
the consummation of Love's dominion to the dominion of
Strife and of Hatred. The old Hesiodic speculation about the

several ages through which the world has passed is here revived :
in the light of the doctrine of perpetual recurrence, Hesiod's
conviction that he lives in the decadent Iron Age now becomes
in Empedocles the belief that his own human existence is wedged
in between a Golden Age of the past, when Love prevailed, and
a brighter future when that Age shall come again, only to be
vanquished by the reign of Hate.

This is what we must bear in mind if we are to understand
why the Orphic beliefs are significant for Empedocles. His view
of nature is by no means purely physical. It contains an element of eschatology such as always accompanies the idea of a
paradise lost or divine primal state. It has already been correctly observed that the theory of the four elements, as it is
generally called, is presupposed in the *Katharmoi* as well.[67]
This is true also of the two powers, Love and Hate, which
alternately rule the world.[68] In the religious poem, of course,
the impassioned tone of proclamation does not spring from the
discovery of these forces as such, as it does in the hymns on
nature.[69] But their activity is fundamental even for this Orphic
drama of the soul's destiny.

O friends of mine, who dwell in the mighty town
That slopes from the yellow Akragas up to the heights
Of the citadel, you who are busied with excellent works,
A haven to strangers, duly aware of their rights
And unwitting of evil, hail!
But I—I now walk among you, a god free from death,
No longer a mortal, and honoured by all, as you see,
With garlands and fillets and flowery crowns. When I come
Into flourishing towns with these people, both women and men,
I am revered as a god. And in myriad throngs
They pursue me, inquiring the path to their gain; and while some

Are hungry for oracles, others beg but to hear
In their manifold illnesses, too long pierced with distress,
A word that will bring them health . . .

In these words of his proem the philosopher presents himself[70]
to his fellow-countrymen as a religious teacher and medical
man surrounded by a crowd of faithful votaries seeking his aid.
We have definite accounts of his achievements as physician;[71]
and the later histories of Sicily testify to his influence with the
populace, telling how he overthrew the tyranny in Akragas as

a friend of the people and refused the honour of the kingship
when they offered it to him.[72] Obviously his high reputation
was more than just political: he was something of a saviour,
and for the peculiar religious sensibility of the Greeks it would
not take much more to speak of him as a god or at least as
divine. If he felt fairly sure of himself, that was because the
people had faith in him. Nevertheless, the way he depicts
himself as an 'immortal god' is something unique in our historical records of the older Greek religion.[73] This representation
has been very disturbing to modern critics and has led to
Empedocles' being called a charlatan or medicine-man. And
certainly he is no scholar of the type of an Anaxagoras or
Democritus. The fanciful exuberance which we find in the
language of his poem *On Nature*, with its peculiarly dynamic
creativity of phrase, sets him well apart from the rationalistic
sobriety of those writers; indeed, he has no sooner boasted of
his own astonishing achievements than he promptly recalls his
true eminence and takes himself to task for suggesting that
there should be anything at all remarkable in his superiority
to mere men destined to perish.[74] Such exaggerated self-
assurance must have a religious root. It comes from his certainty of a divine salvation which he proclaims and expects
for himself—the salvation that comes when the soul is reunited
with its divine source. He demands men's faith in this gospel.
He asseverates its truth, though he admits that only with
difficulty does it work its way into the hearts of those who give
ear to it.[75] We must not assume that Empedocles is entirely
clear about the difference between this πίστις and that which
he repeatedly demands for his theories of nature; indeed, the
very fact that he uses the same word for both kinds of inner
certainty indicates the contrary.[76] He regards the religious
avowals of the *Katharmoi* as something that he has himself
indubitably experienced, like the forces of Love and Hate;[77]
but these are experiences of an inner world for which he would
not have had so keen an eye had it not been for the Orphic
soul-theory.

Empedocles' confidence in his own divinity seems sharply in
conflict with the sense of wretchedness that emerges in the
longest of the surviving fragments of the *Katharmoi*. This is
the dramatic description of the fate of the soul—which he calls

the demon—when it becomes exiled from its divine home to this world of the corporeal and the corruptible:[78]

> There is a decree of Necessity, long since ordained
> By the gods, eternal, and sealed with extensive oaths,
> That whenever a demon who draws a long life for his lot
> Shall sinfully soil his hands with murderous blood
> Or forswear himself [in the service of Strife], he thrice
> Must stray from the homes of the blest for a myriad years
> And be born in time in all manner of mortal forms,
> Changing the arduous paths of life. For the Air
> By its might drives him into the Sea, and the Sea in turn
> Spews him forth to the floor of the Earth; Earth tosses him up
> To the rays of the glittering Sun; Sun pitches him back
> Into the eddies of Air. One passes him on to another,
> And all despise him. Now I am, too, one of these,
> An exile from God and a roamer, putting my trust
> In furious Strife . . .

We possess no other fragment of the *Katharmoi* revealing so clearly in what dimension of reality the mystical events described in the poem occur. That the soul here appears as a demon is more than mere poetical colouring. The Orphic conception is closely connected with Hesiod's old Greek belief that the spirits of the dead continue their existence as bands of demons roving unseen through the world.[79] In the Orphic myth of the soul this conception is bound up with the idea of the soul's pre-existence and transmigration through various mortal forms. The demon becomes involved in the same universal cycle which we have met in the philosophy of nature. He, too, undergoes a cosmic sequence comparable to that of the elements: from the Divine he sets forth on his wanderings through manifold forms, and to the Divine he returns. This theory has a twofold basis: first, a mystical certainty of the soul's essential kinship with the Divine; secondly, a consciousness that through some great transgression it is weighed down and kept far removed from its divine origin. All the other factors—the cycle, the purification, the return—follow from these assumptions. Empedocles sees in pollution of the hands with murderous blood the primal sin that has led to the demon's exile from the divine realm; hence his vigorous admonitions against the eating of animal flesh and his prohibition of blood-sacrifice:[80]

> . . . Will you not cease
> From this harsh-sounding murder? Do you not see that you rend
> One another apart in the heedlessness of your minds?

This fragment, which obviously comes from the *Katharmoi*, is quoted by Sextus Empiricus as evidence for the asceticism of the Pythagoreans and Empedocles and their abstention from animal food.[81] This abstention is not so much a consequence of generalizing the universal horror of any human bloodshed to the whole animal kingdom as it is an implication from the theory of metempsychosis with its sense of the presence of embodied spirits even in the animals. We have here the same theory that Xenophanes once ridiculed[82] in the name of the rational conception of nature which he had learned from the Ionian philosophy; in Empedocles the two conceptions now lie side by side. Empedocles cannot do enough to show the grisliness of the guilt in which one unwittingly entangles himself by sacrificing an animal to the gods:[83]

> . . . And the father lifts up his own dear son,
> Who has altered his shape, and slaughters him, adding a prayer,
> The monstrous fool! And those who assist at the rites
> Are distraught by the victim's pleading. Yet the father is deaf
> To his outcry, and slays him, and then proceeds to prepare
> An infamous feast in his dwelling. And likewise the son
> Lays hands on his father, and children their mother, to tear
> Their lives from their bodies and devour their dear-loved flesh.

The most appalling abominations known to Greek myth—whether committed quite unawares, as in Atreus' banquet, where the father consumes the flesh of his own son, or tremblingly performed in fear of a threatening divine command, as in Orestes' matricide—these are unwittingly perpetrated every day whenever men lay blood-sacrifices on the divine altars and fancy that what they do will be pleasing to God. How great a transformation the divine nature must have undergone to appear so incompatible with the old Hellenic cult of sacrifice! The demand for purity which we find in Orphic asceticism must have made a profound change in the relationship between body and soul. The force by which the world is formed clothes the soul 'in the strange garment of alien flesh',[84] as we read elsewhere in the *Katharmoi*. In this image we see corporeality regarded as a mere transient, non-essential wrapping—a conception just as strange to the Greek of Homer's time as it is to the Ionian philosopher, his intellectual kin. The soul puts its bodies on and off as a man changes his shirt. Empedocles envisages the soul as having to choose between bodies of many sorts, and he reflects upon the advantages of the various habitations it may consider:[85]

> ... The best of all beasts [that souls may become]
> Are lions that couch on the hills and rest on the ground;
> And best of all fair-tressed trees are the laurels . . .

All this is no dispassionate dogmatic theory expounded with suitable detachment, but is described by Empedocles as his own personal fate. Statements in the I- and we-forms are common in the fragments of the *Katharmoi*. Among those fallen spirits tossed back and forth by the elements and then expelled again he includes himself:[86]

> ... And I, too, am now one of these,
> An exile from God and a roamer . . .

Earthly life loses all value to anyone who sees in it merely the rootless and unstable existence of the refugee driven from home. In the depth of passion with which Empedocles describes the fate of the soul flung hither and yon, the 'arduous paths of life', and the length of those endless periods for which 'it must wander far from the homes of the blest',[87] we see that the world of these conceptions, bizarre as it sometimes appears, has its source in profound human suffering. How much difference there is between the way a natural philosopher like Anaximander approaches reality when he depicts the emergence of living creatures out of a primordial principle objectively conceived, and the attitude of the man who shudders within as he tells us:[88]

> I have already been a boy and a girl, and a bush,
> And a bird, and a dumb fish out of the sea . . .

Empedocles speaks of all these various forms of life with the loving inflexion of one who has felt their existence from within, and to whom none of these is any more remote than he is remote from himself. The universal animization taught by the Orphics[89] here includes something all-embracing, something that understands all things and is akin to all things. We discern it everywhere in the way Empedocles describes things themselves; it gives his verses their peculiar warmth. He knows no mere things as such, but only creatures like himself, and takes them to his heart with a grave sympathy and even a touch of sadness. His sympathy is not a feeling of whimsical regard for comrades of another species like that of the horseman for his horse or the hunter for his dog; it is a metaphysical sympathy, genuinely compassionate with every creature, feeling its own sufferings in each.

From the conception of an infinitely long process in which the demon of the soul passes through all possible phases of vegetable and animal existence, a whole new myth arises. The soul of short-lived man now acquires a history. It looks back on a previous existence that has endured for aeons. The fancy of the religious poet paints in boldly contrasting colours the descent of the divine stranger from his heavenly home of light into the darkness of terrestrial space. We learn from how high a rank and from what immeasurable fullness of happiness long since left behind the soul has arrived here at last, where it now has converse with mortals.[90] The sense of having come down from above and of being here below is the spatial expression of that fundamental inner contradiction which this faith discerns in human life and which furnishes its real point of departure: the contradiction between actual experience with all the disheartening woes that attend it on the one hand, and, on the other, that inexplicably high pitch of attunement which every truly vigorous soul still cherishes as something to be claimed and looked forward to and never to be relinquished, just as it cherishes the memory of its derivation from a higher world. In this conception the moment of man's entrance into the earthly sphere demands particular attention; for this is the first time that the soul crosses the threshold of the world of evils into which it is now to be exiled. Of this moment we have no conscious memory; but once the soul recognizes its connexion with an earlier, better existence, it sees far beyond the short range of individual consciousness. The piteous cry of the newborn child rouses in Empedocles the clear recollection: 'I wept and I wailed at the sight of the unaccustomed place.'[91] Pain is the first-fruit of man's contact with our world. The philosopher's symbolism compresses this unfamiliar, comfortless

place (ἀσυνήθεα χῶρον) into a dark cavern; for there is undoubtedly a reference to the terrestrial world in the words 'We
arrived in this roofed-in cave',[92] which have come down to us
torn from their context. We have strong evidence elsewhere
that the conception of the world as a cave is Orphic. It is
interesting that here, too, just as in the great fragment where the
soul-demon is tossed back and forth by the elements,[93] the poet
sees himself as one among many such spirits, and his own
downward journey as one that all of them have made. His
sense of solidarity with those who share this common lot is
clearly expressed in his use of the first person plural.

The image of the 'joyless place' is also found in another
fragment,[94] which describes it in greater detail. We learn from
this that in the *Katharmoi* no less than in the poem *On Nature*
Empedocles is a great mythologist, who understands how to give
shape and body to the forces of his religious world. Following
the allegorical style of the epic theogonies, he makes the demons
of disaster here appear as a multitude of Hesiodic or Epimeni-
dean gods peopling

> . . . that joyless place
> Where Murder and Rancour and hordes of calamitous sprites,
> And parching Ills and Putrescence and Floods, rove here
> And there in the darkness, over the meadow of Bane.

As soon as the soul arrives here below, it encounters these
spirits, who receive it like those formidable demons who greet
Aeneas at the gates of the lower world.[95] Empedocles, too, must
have depicted the soul's descent into the terrestrial cave as a
sort of journey to Hades. Whether he had any model for this
besides the *Nekyia* of the *Odyssey*, we cannot say; but it is
tempting to think of Orpheus' journey to Hades in this connexion.[96] A *katabasis* of Orpheus would fit the Orphic religion
very well; and, what is more, such a legend undoubtedly existed.
If Empedocles was already familiar with this, its description
of the underworld must have seemed particularly rich in
allegorical figures as compared with the Homeric version, and
in this respect it could very easily have stimulated his fancy.

Nevertheless, his description of the soul-demon's downward
journey into the dark cave of the world is decidedly different
from a mere journey to Hades, and is of far deeper import and
inner reality. The peopling of this world with the hordes of

spirits who fill it must, moreover, have been the work of Empedocles himself; for they bear the unmistakable stamp of his
basic naturalistic outlook. Here we find the demons of mischief
and discord, as becomes clear in another passage, where they
are enumerated pair by pair:[97]

> Mother Earth was there with the far-glancing maid of the Sun,
> And bloody Dissension with Harmony, sober of face;
> Lady Fair and Dame Ugly, Dame Haste with Lady Delay,
> Lovely Truth and dark-eyed Obscurity.

This catalogue of allegorical divinities is most appropriate to
the *Katharmoi*. They are all embodiments of that same primordial opposition which holds sway throughout all reality;
accordingly the examples are taken from realms as different
as possible—the physical and the ethical, the aesthetic and the
intellectual. The soul encounters these oppositions as soon as
it enters this world, which but for them would never exist. That
the soul is pent up here at all Empedocles explicitly explains as
a result of 'trusting in furious Strife'[98]—a mythical way of
expressing its entanglement in the cosmic machinery under the
rule of Hate. In this way the philosopher tries to interpret the
fundamental religious facts of the Orphic theory in accordance
with the supreme principle of his natural philosophy. Bloodshed
itself, which the Orphic rules of purity forbid, is a consequence
of Strife. Empedocles raises a prophet's despairing cry for
humanity:[99]

> . . . Alas, O pitiful mortal race,
> Devoid of blessings, such are the strifes and the groans
> That have given you birth . . .

This unhappy state, from which man is to be released by religion,
is implicit in that whole phase of the cosmic process in which
we now find ourselves. The will to free the demon in us from
its pollution and return to the felicity of God is the eternal
longing which the divine Love has implanted in all creatures
as their inborn natural law.

In bright contrast to the dark nocturne of the world of Strife,
Empedocles also depicts in the *Katharmoi* the state of paradise
that is his analogue for the Golden Age—the period when
Love's dominion was at its height. The vision of the blissful
past brings with it an expectation of future salvation. Among
the men of that age, he tells us,[100]

> ... there was no god War, no Battle-din,
> No kingly Zeus, no Kronos, nor any Poseidon,
> But Love alone was queen ...

When the further details of this picture are filled in, we can see what decisive significance Empedocles attaches to the problem of pure, bloodless sacrifice as the one true way of honouring the gods. In the right kind of devotion, indeed, he sees the chief yardstick by which the attainments of human culture are to be measured. The *Katharmoi* has much to say about sacrifice and other aspects of the cult, all which material is closely connected with the fundamental idea of the poem—the realization of the dominion of divine Love. The men of the Golden Age, he goes on,[101]

> Sought to please her with reverent gifts, with paintings of beasts,
> With daintily fragrant salves, and oblations of myrrh
> Unmixed, and sweet-smelling frankincense; they poured
> Libations from golden-brown honeycombs over the ground.
> And yet with the pure blood of bulls no altar was wet;
> But to tear out the life and eat of the goodly limbs
> Was considered man's greatest defilement. . . .

> Then all creatures were tame and kindly disposed
> To mankind, the beasts and the birds alike; and the flame
> Of good-fellowship glowed.[102]

> . . . And among them there lived
> A man of rare knowledge, possessing the utmost riches of mind,
> And master of every sort of ingenious skill;
> For whenever he put all his wits to the stretch, he could look
> With ease upon everything that exists, having lived
> Ten and twenty lifetimes of men.[103]

These lines have often been supposed to refer to Pythagoras. Such a presumption was especially congenial to the Neoplatonists, who revered Pythagoras as the divine founder of their religion and were always on the watch for ancient accounts of his personality. But despite the authority of Iamblichus, who presumably took this interpretation of the passage as one already accepted, we can hardly consider the reference to Pythagoras well established. On the other hand, the question of how Empedocles' ascetic doctrine is connected with that of the Pythagoreans is not to be evaded. Even in ancient times he was made a pupil of Pythagoras; and while there are chronological reasons that make this hardly possible, his precepts are so strikingly akin to the Pythagorean rule of life that some connexion must be assumed.[104] Whether we should infer that Empedocles was directly influenced by the Pythagoreans, or should rather attempt to explain these resemblances by their common relationship with the Orphic religion, cannot be decided with the means at our command. It would be good to know what role this primitive superman originally played in Empedocles' poem, for he can hardly have been a mere supernumerary. The wisdom that he has obtained in ten and twenty human lifetimes is obviously to be contrasted with the resigned recognition of men's short-sightedness that we find in the prooemium of the poem *On Nature*. Men make judgements about everything in terms of their own experience, even though they have seen only a small fragment of the whole.[105]

> They have hardly looked over a meagre part of their lives,
> When swift Fate snatches them off, and they flutter away
> Like smoke, believing only those things which each
> Has singly encountered, driven from place to place,
> Each of them vowing that he has discovered the whole.
> But not in this way are such things to be witnessed by men,
> Or heard, or grasped by the mind . . .

If the normal extent of human insight goes no farther than this, the philosopher must be speaking with a longer range of experience than other men; and this well expresses Empedocles' own attitude. The superman accordingly embodies his ideal of the sage. This is important, for it shows the connexion between Empedocles' consciousness of his own mission and his faith in the possibility of extending the human consciousness for many aeons beyond the confines of man's short life.[106] Such faith brings the philosophical spirit nearer to the eternal. Empedocles himself would have been like the superman of the Golden Age if it had not been his unhappy lot to live in the reign of Hate;[107] but perhaps he may return at some future time in just as perfect a form. Even if he is not referring to Pythagoras in this description, it is very likely that the characteristic feature of the superman's knowledge of his own earlier existence has been borrowed from the Pythagoreans' traditional tales of their master, for something very similar was told about him.

Let us conclude by recapitulating Empedocles' theological position. On one side stands his philosophy of nature with its new vision of the cosmic cycle and the powers that there hold sway. Empedocles feels that he has revealed the true character of the divine powers active in nature, as we have shown. He is no more interested in giving a genuine proof of God's existence than any of his predecessors have been, for to all of them the presence of the Divine in the world is an immediate and absolute certainty. The problem of God for Empedocles is simply the problem of the divine form. And this is the angle from which he approaches it as a student of nature. What he finds in nature is no single form but a manifold revelation of the Divine, such as the Greek mind has found there all along. Empedocles discovers the Divine in three aspects of nature: first, in the imperishable primary forms of corporeal existence; second, in the forces of Love and Hate by which the corporeal world is moved, though their innermost nature can be grasped only with the eye of the spirit; third, in that all-embracing state of the world which arises when goodness and perfection reach their consummation in the cycle of these cosmic forces. Empedocles' ontological pluralism thus becomes in his theology a philosophical polytheism. The gods are here transformed into universal principles of natural existence and natural processes; to put it more correctly, they are like what Heraclitus calls 'the wise-alone'—'which is both willing and unwilling to be called by the name of Zeus'—standing somewhere in the no-man's-land between individual personal beings that can be called by name and pure universal potencies. This shows that they still belong to the stage of allegorical theogony.[108] But the idea of unity, which we have met in Xenophanes and the Eleatics, has not failed to leave its mark on Empedocles. In the form of the *Sphairos* it asserts its claims as against the polytheism of the four gods of the elements; and this highest God is essentially akin to the single world-controlling intellectual God of Xenophanes, except in the fact that it never remains fully realized in the world. But the unrestricted dominion of the *Sphairos* shall return. Thus the theology of Empedocles' philosophy of nature is a synthesis of the monism of Xenophanes and the Eleatics with a polytheism that draws the consequences from his own physical pluralism. On the other side, in the doctrines of the *Katharmoi*, the Divine is found within man himself as his very soul, and the sway of the same eternal divine forces which nature herself obeys—Love and Strife and their law—is traced in the soul's life. The normative, ethico-religious intuition of this dual control of nature must really be derived from the inner regions of the self. Empedocles, indeed, reveals it first in his great description of nature; but this very description already reflects the dualistic inner experience implicit in the Orphic view of life as revealed in the *Katharmoi*.

CHAPTER IX

THE TELEOLOGICAL THINKERS: ANAXAGORAS AND DIOGENES

Not all the men who carry on the Milesian tradition come from regions outside Ionia; several come from Ionia itself, though not from Miletus. By far the most important of these is Anaxagoras of Clazomenae. He is more closely akin to the original spirit of the philosophy of nature than Empedocles; he has preserved its rational character in a purer form and has not contaminated it with alien elements drawn from religion. Anaxagoras is the pure scholar; there is nothing of the fiery soul of the poet and prophet in his more limited nature. Empedocles is said to have ended his life by leaping into the crater of Mount Etna; one can hardly imagine any such legend growing up about Anaxagoras. But in its very limitations his mind is more unified and consistent, and reaches full flower in his theoretical explanations of natural phenomena. Empedocles was constantly involved in the religious and political public life of his native Sicilian town. Anaxagoras spent his critical decades as a resident alien in Athens, far from his home in Asia Minor. There is even an anecdote which presents him as one of the first cosmopolitans.[1] On being reproached with neglecting his duties to his country and fellow-citizens he is reputed to have said, 'Watch your tongue, for I care very much for my country', pointing up to the sky. At the time of Euripides there is no reason why such an incident should not actually have occurred. Of course, this cannot mean that Anaxagoras was trying to say that the abode of the soul is in God, as Empedocles might have done.[2] Any such religious sense of being a stranger in this world is utterly remote from his sober turn of mind. When the man who holds the sun to be a mere glowing stone feels more at home in the heavens than in his own normal earthly surroundings, it is because he has found the real content of his life and all his satisfaction in dealing constantly with nature, particularly with the heavenly phenomena.

It is not easy to form an idea of Anaxagoras' views on nature in general; for the remaining fragments of his prose work, which at the time of his Athenian sojourn was an inexpensive and widely read book comprehensible even to the layman,[3] must obviously have been culled from the whole with the intention of demonstrating the theoretical basis of his doctrine of elements and explaining it in the philosopher's own words. If we disregard his theory of the so-called homoeomeries and consult the more indirect evidence of what later writers have to say about Anaxagoras' activity and his teachings, we are struck with the fact that he often receives mention because of his remarkable meteorological observations.[4] Undoubtedly the older Ionian philosophers of nature had done similar work; but in general they seem to have started with more familiar material and tried to make the most of it in their inferences about the cosmos, while Anaxagoras is interested in investigating certain comparatively rare phenomena. When he suggests that the sun is a glowing stone—a hypothesis extremely revolutionary for his time—this theory is obviously connected with his celebrated observation of the falling meteoric stone of Aegospotami.[5] There is a fair likelihood that similar observations underlie some of his other explanations of natural phenomena. This empirical feature is characteristic of the fifth-century Ionians not only in their medicine, where it is best known to us, but also in other realms, such as ethnography, geography, and history. Herodotus and the school of Hippocrates are particularly good examples.[6] Sober-minded empiricism was the new and interesting thing, as opposed to the bold thinking of the older natural philosophers, which was still largely constructive and hence often revealed a schematizing tendency.[7] Apparently medicine was the earliest field of scientific research to develop this spirit from entirely independent motives—a fruit of that self-education in careful methods of testing things thoroughly step by step which springs from a strong sense of responsibility for human life.[8] That Anaxagoras occupied himself with medicine, particularly with dietetics and the theory of nutrition, is revealed by his theory of elements, which grew out of attempts to deal with the problem of bodily maintenance and development through the assimilation of specific foodstuffs and to examine the bearing of this study upon the nature and composition of the matter taken into the body.[9] In this respect his theory of the basic stuffs is directly connected with medical observations. We find a similar interest in medical science in other contemporary philosophers like Empedocles and Diogenes of Apollonia. But Empedocles' teachings are repudiated by some of the medical writers on the ground that in his effort to make medicine a genuine science he has introduced certain general theories more appropriate to natural philosophy; the situation with regard to Empedocles is just the reverse of that which we find in Anaxagoras.[10] What the two men have in common is the fact that they both make their doctrines of basic elements and qualities the connecting link between medicine and the explanation of nature. In contrast to the quantitative atomism of Democritus, they hold that the ultimate underlying basis of nature consists in a number of qualities that cannot be traced back to anything simpler. Anaxagoras and Empedocles are both more decidedly oriented toward the organic world than are their predecessors. Now that Parmenides has shown the impossibility of an absolute coming-to-be and passing-away,[11] they both seek another means of explaining the phenomena hitherto designated by these words, by resorting to the idea of mixing and unmixing.[12] This conception is one that played a role in medicine even before their time. We find it first in the important physician Alcmaeon of Crotona,[13] who was earlier than either of them; and our chief source for the history of this notion in later years is still found in the medical literature. From here it was taken over by philosophy.[14] And there, if anywhere, we can grasp the significance of medical experience for the new philosophical study of nature.

Now that our attention has been called to the profound and fruitful unity of the investigations of natural philosophy and medicine during the fifth century, it is perhaps not out of place to raise the question of how far the theological inquiries of the natural philosophers have reverberated in the medical literature. The medical students of the Coan school whose own contributions have come down to us under the name of Hippocrates, were thoroughly familiar with the work of the natural philosophers.[15] Even their practical thinking was affected, particularly in matters where the empiricism of the new medicine, based as it was on pure observation without any preconceived assumptions, had to come to terms with old religious conceptions such as that of the 'sacred disease', as epilepsy was then called. The author of the Hippocratic treatise *On the*

Sacred Disease, a man of high intellectual attainments, has a number of interesting things to say about the peculiarly 'divine' nature alleged to belong to this ailment. The problem gives him an occasion to ask himself what the Divine really is, and whether and how it manifests itself in nature.[16] His remarks are all the more important for us inasmuch as we find the notion of the sacred disease still enjoying undiminished prestige in the contemporary Herodotus, who otherwise shows a more empirical frame of mind in his own approach to the problem of historical and geographical truth. Herodotus speaks of the sacred disease in connexion with the epileptic fits of King Cambyses of Persia, which he associates with his views of the levelling power of Nemesis in human affairs and in the world of nature alike.[17] His theology of history finds it very appropriate that this brutal despot should have been stricken with the sacred disease, and he accepts this idea with all that it implies: the gods send down a special affliction as punishment for the special crimes of a certain man, just as in Hesiod pestilence, destruction of city and of ships, crop shortages, and miscarriages are regarded as god-sent punishments to avenge the unjust deeds of individual men.[18] To the medical author of the treatise *On the Sacred Disease* this conception of a divine causality essentially moral at bottom, manifesting itself in cases of illness of a special sort, is completely foreign, and he reiterates his attack on any such hypothesis in very general terms. He writes:

'This so-called sacred disease arises from the same causes as any others: from the things that enter the body and those that leave it: from cold, and sunshine, and winds, which are always changing and are never still. These things are divine; and so there is no need of setting this disease apart and considering it more divine than the others: they are all divine and they are all human.'[19]

This polemic cannot be understood except against the background of the profoundly altered conception of the nature of the Divine for which philosophy had been preparing the way for a hundred years.[20] Of course, the words of our author add nothing new to what the philosophers themselves proclaimed; but they have the importance of confirming the increasing prestige of the new idea of the Divine throughout that far-flung group of scientists and thinkers who based their thinking on

the concept of nature, and they also show the effects of this idea
on the realm of religious faith and practical activity.

Let us now return to Anaxagoras and examine his theory of
the elements, with which his theological views are closely connected. It is at this point, as we have remarked, that medical
studies become of immediate significance for his philosophy;
for it is from them that he borrows the concept of mixture, to
supplant the older conception of becoming.[21] For Anaxagoras
there is no absolute coming-to-be or passing-away of things, but
only mixture or separation of the stuffs which underlie natural
changes. He assumes that in the beginning all things were
together, infinite in number and infinitely small. As long as this
state of affairs prevailed, none of these things could be clearly
distinguished because of their tiny size. We must imagine that
in this state everything was held down by vapour and ether,
for these two are both infinite, and they predominate in the
total mass both in size and in number.[22] Anaxagoras now
assumes that vapour and ether have separated themselves from
the surrounding mass, and that in general the process by which
the world originates is one of separating-out, which the rapid
motion of the primal mass has occasioned. It is through this
process that the things of our world arise.[23] These, like the
primal mass itself, contain all stuffs and properties, though in
such a way that in each of them certain stuffs and properties
preponderate and impress their stamp on the object as a whole.[24]
In saying this, the philosopher is attacking the view of Empedocles that there are only a certain few sharply distinguished
basic qualities and stuffs underlying the whole of nature.
Anaxagoras starts with the observation that the food we take
into the body contains the germs of growth for all the stuffs
and qualities it requires: no hair, he maintains, can come from
that which is not hair, no flesh from that which is not flesh; on
the contrary, hair and flesh must be contained in the bread
we eat, and so must bones, sinews, veins, sperm, and so on.[25]
In this way he arrives at the notion that everything consists
of an infinite number of tiny portions of an infinite number of
stuffs differing qualitatively among themselves, though bound
together in various things by the most various types of mixture.
And all these countless qualitative differences must have been
contained in the primal mass at the outset.

The hardest problem for Anaxagoras in connexion with this theory is to handle the reality of the mind. For man is not made entirely of flesh, hair, bones, nails, and sinews;[26] he also has within him that which we call his mind. The problem is to decide in what way this is present in him. Here for the first time the philosophy of nature consciously reaches the limits of its physical mode of thought, which knows only stuffs and qualities, mixture and separation. We cannot say whence came this consciousness of the problem of the mind in the time of Anaxagoras, or what factors contributed to its emergence.[27] We may recall that while his contemporary Empedocles built up a physical system operating with different kinds of matter alone, he also tried to comprehend the soul as a reality *sui generis* in terms of the categories of the Orphic religion and dealt with it in a special poem.[28] Anaxagoras, however, tries to find a place for the reality of mind in the frame of his physical scheme of the world—an attempt which leads him to ask whether the mind is a reality of the same kind as the other constituents of things, and if so, why it is not present in all things as they are, but merely in some.[29] He thinks of the mind, too, in terms of the concept of mixture which dominates his physics.[30] Hence he comes, understandably enough, to the negative conclusion that the mind can have nothing to do with the other infinitely many materials and qualities that are mingled in the things of nature. Mind is the one thing that obviously is not mixed with everything, for it appears only in certain creatures 'in greater or lesser amount'.[31] But to Anaxagoras this fact seems inexplicable except on the assumption that mind involves no mixture with anything else at all, since otherwise it would have to be mixed with everything, just like all the rest.[32]

By giving mind this special position within the framework of his theory of physical mixture, Anaxagoras now finds himself led to go beyond the strictly matter-of-fact decision that mind is unmixed with other things. He ventures to interpret this fact in a way which we can describe only as metaphysical, even if he himself is unaware of such a distinction. Fortunately we still have his own words on this point:[33]

'Everything else has a share of everything; Mind, however, is infinite[34] and self-ruling, and is mixed with nothing, but is alone, itself by itself. For if it were not by itself, but were mixed with something else, it would have a share in *all* things if it were mixed with *any*. For in everything there is a portion of everything, as I have said above; and if any other things were mixed with it, they would prevent it from controlling anything as it now does when it is alone by itself. For it is the thinnest of all things and the purest; and it has every kind of knowledge about everything, and the utmost strength. And Mind controls all things that have soul, both greater and smaller. And it was Mind, too, that controlled the whole whirling movement and made it possible for it to whirl at all. At first this whirling arose from a small beginning, but it is now whirling farther and will whirl farther still. And Mind knew all the things that were then being mixed and separated off and parted from one another. And Mind arranged all such things as were to be and were (that is, the things which now are not), and such as are at present; and it arranged this whirling, too, which the stars and the sun and the moon and the air and the ether—as they separate off—perform. But it was this whirling itself that caused their separating-out. And the thick separates itself from the thin, the warm from the cold, the light from the dark, and the dry from the moist. And many parts of many things exist. But no thing is altogether separated off or distinguished from anything else except Mind. And all Mind is alike, both the greater and the smaller. But nothing else is like anything else; on the contrary, each individual thing is and was most manifestly those things of which it contains the most.'

It has recently been pointed out that the verbal form of Anaxagoras' statements about *Nous* betrays a peculiar resemblance to the style of the hymn, of which it is evidently a conscious imitation.[35] We have already shown that Anaximander probably used a similar form in his own writings when he spoke of the *apeiron* as the Divine—that which guides all things and holds all things together.[36] Indeed, Anaxagoras is here following an established stylistic tradition which can be shown to have been followed by almost all the pre-Socratic philosophers with more or less individual variation.[37] This fact is particularly important in the case of Anaxagoras; for in none of the surviving fragments is there any direct evidence that he ever referred to Mind as the Divine. That this must, however, have been his doctrine appears now to be a certainty both from the hymn-like form in which the predicates of *Nous* are expressed, and even from the content of these statements. The epithets 'infinite', 'self-ruling', 'unmixed', and 'itself by itself' thoroughly justify the elevated style in which the philosopher speaks of this highest principle.[38] Anaxagoras holds that the Mind is particularly well qualified for the role of ruling the world because of the very property that distinguishes it from other things—its purity and freedom from admixture. Earlier thinkers ascribed Mind to the divine principle quite independently of these physical considerations. This was done by Xenophanes, for instance, whose God 'makes all things tremble by the power of his thought alone'.[39] The fact that the express ascription of consciousness to the highest principle did not begin with the physiological thinkers[40] but with the theologian of Colophon, is enough to prove its original independence of any physical motives. Parmenides knew nothing of it, and Empedocles was obviously following directly in Xenophanes' footsteps when he described the god *Sphairos* as 'a holy and unutterable Mind, darting through the whole cosmos with its swift thoughts'.[41] All this made a deep impression on Anaxagoras, but failed to satisfy him as a philosopher of nature. One would like to know whether he was influenced by Heraclitus and if so to what extent. Heraclitus had already set up the postulate that the Wise (σοφόν) is separate from everything else; and he attached so much importance to this doctrine that he said explicitly: 'None of all those whose teachings I have heard goes so far as to recognize this.'[42] It was therefore a critical point for him; unfortunately we do not understand exactly what this 'separateness' means, and we must be careful not to interpret it too hastily in terms of later ideas. Anaxagoras' new conception of 'being by itself' is, as he finally makes clear, to be thought of as contrasted with his conception of the mixture of all things with everything, and serves him as a vehicle for the idea of something sovereign, dominating, independent.[43] In this way Mind becomes for the first time a physical principle in the proper sense, on which the whole construction of the world is based, although earlier thinkers may perhaps have entertained a similar idea more or less consciously. Mind, he feels, would forfeit its power of dominion if it were mixed with everything.[44] Hence arises the further consideration that a genuine cosmogony requires a second cause that is not subjected to mixture—something to provide the initial impetus for the vortical motion to which the separating-out of things from the original mixture gives rise. In the main this conception is a purely physical one. It has been compared with the divine causality which some modern astronomers felt they needed for setting the original mechanism of their cosmology in motion.[45] But Anaxagoras' theory includes a second motif besides that of physical kinetics: his *Nous* is that all-guiding knowledge which ever since the beginning has comprehended each and every individual process of mixture, separating-out and particularization in the world's development, in the past no less than in the present and future. *Nous* has anticipated the motions and revolutions of the stars and meteorological bodies like air and ether in their present form, and has ordered everything from the first according to a definite plan (διεκόσμησε).[46]

The idea of this preconceived world-plan is quite worthy of the rational physics of the fifth century; it is peculiarly fitting in a period that ascribes decided significance to τέχνη in all realms of being and even finds it present in nature itself.[47] The mechanism of the creative vortical motion is the ingenious device by which Anaxagoras, like other of his contemporaries, tried to explain the formation of the world. The fact that he made the divine Mind guide the vortex in a specific direction gave his physics its new teleological aspect. This is what caught Plato's attention and gave Aristotle occasion for the celebrated remark that among the earlier thinkers Anaxagoras, with his theory of the world-creative Mind, seemed like a sober man among the drunk, even if he made no detailed use of this teleological type of observation in his physics, but employed *Nous* only in his cosmogony and in certain instances where he was at a loss for a mechanical explanation and had to fall back on it, if only as a *deus ex machina*.[48] Probably Anaxagoras would not have considered this a very serious objection. Certainly he must have felt that he had assured the rationality of his world-plan when he envisaged a mechanical process as automatic as possible, whether pre-established as a whole in all its phases within the divine Mind or merely anticipated by it.

The conception of the Mind as unmixed, which is so important in Anaxagoras' doctrine of the divine world-principle, also enables him to ascertain the place of mankind and even philosophy itself in the system of the world as a whole. All Mind is like unto itself, declares Anaxagoras, whether larger or smaller.[49]

We must notice that he recognizes certain distinctions between minds, just as he has spoken earlier of differences between things that have soul or life and those that do not; but these differences by no means imply that it is absolutely impossible to find any qualitative resemblances between the infinite divine Mind and the finite human mind. Our mind is the Divine in us, which enables us to approach the divine Mind and its plan for the world with genuine understanding. It is true that this idea is not expressed explicitly in the fragments, but we must assume that Anaxagoras thought at least this highly of the Mind. How else could he have come to think of it as the very essence of the Divine?[50] There is a mystical element in this rationalism that reminds us slightly of Empedocles' conviction of the soul's divine origin; but Anaxagoras has no experience of the sins and pollutions of the soul-demon, or of its purification and return to the godhead along endless paths of woe. To Anaxagoras the Divine is pure reason—the activity of the Mind as task-master. Man has direct access to the Divine by the similar powers that he bears within himself. Anaxagoras' philosophy is physics through and through; it obviously contains no anthropology in the theological sense and completely lacks any centre of gravity of that sort. Nevertheless, the axis of this physics has God and man as its two poles—or, more exactly, the divine principle of nature and the human knowledge that comprehends it; and this structure is what gives Anaxagoras his place in the line of those same impressive thinkers who served as his models. But we must not forget that when we think of him as an oracle for the great Pericles and a precursor of the Platonic and Aristotelian philosophy of the Mind, such an historical perspective brings him too close to our eyes and unduly magnifies his stature.

With these teleological conceptions one of the most consistent and historically influential motifs makes its way into the study of the Divine from the philosophical side. The concept of *telos*, to be sure, belongs primarily to Socraticism;[51] but that which Socraticism seeks in everything—the good, the intelligible, and the perfect—is already virtually present in Anaxagoras' principle of *diakosmesis* and the idea of order which it involves. It simply is not employed here as a consistent principle of explanation for particular phenomena.[52] And yet this stage was actually reached in fifth-century physics, for our tradition reveals a number of strictly teleological explanations of natural phenomena that apparently go back to a source from this period. The research of the last decades has shown with increasing certainty that the author of this system was Diogenes of Apollonia. Although he was rather second-rate as a natural philosopher, he gave us no small insight into the way in which the development of the Ionian natural science was affected by the interweaving influences of the times—influences peculiarly mingled in Diogenes himself.

Diogenes evidently lived for a long time in Athens, where the comic poets capitalized on his theories.[53] Like Anaxagoras, he was primarily a student of nature with an eye for specific facts. But these leanings were accompanied by a powerful drive for speculating about the world in general, not omitting theology.[54] In his doctrine of the first principle he turned away from Empedocles and Anaxagoras and back to Anaximenes of Miletus. While all the profounder minds of his time assumed a multiplicity of principles, he returned to the theory of a single primal substance, of which all other things are merely modifications. According to his view, even if it may appear that there are certain simple stuffs in nature, like water, fire, air, and so on, it would be impossible for these to combine with one another or to affect one another if they were not fundamentally one and the same.[55] Diogenes finds the real basic principle in the air,[56] which takes on the most various forms. In order to produce these modifications, nature requires a certain measure which it must keep. Summer and winter, night and day, rain, wind, and sunshine all depend on this measure. 'And as for the rest, one will find, if one is willing to reflect upon it, that it has all been arranged as well as possible.'[57] The purposeful arrangement which Diogenes, like Anaxagoras, finds in the world, compels him to assume that the distribution of forces and effects is a work of the thinking Mind.[58] He sees evidence for believing that air is the primal stuff, for he considers that it is not only the vital element which all things breathe, but also something which soul and mental power depend on so intimately that they vanish as soon as the breath leaves the body.

'And it seems to me that that which has the power of knowing [νόησις] is the thing that men call air, and that it steers all things and controls all things. For I feel that this is God, and that it extends everywhere and disposes all things and is contained in all things. And there is nothing that does not have a share in it.'[59]

There are a large number of ways in which things may participate in the divine primal stuff, as in soul and in power of mind. 'And this itself is an eternal and undying body; other things, however, are such that some of them come to be while others pass away.'[60] In another fragment Diogenes describes the primal stuff as 'great, and mighty, and eternal, and undying, and of great knowledge'.[61]

This elaborate theology from his treatise *On Nature*, which was still being read at the time of Simplicius,[62] must not mislead us into supposing that the whole work sounded like this. We possess a very long and splendid fragment purely medical in content—a discussion of the veins[63]—which shows us how much detailed research and description were mingled with theological interpretation in Diogenes' writings. All these matters are closely connected. Diogenes' theology is a theory of universal animization. It is based on the assumption that different stages of animization have occurred in a certain order, and that the divine Mind, which is also the prime elemental body, consciously produces this order out of itself.[64] Obviously the reasons for Diogenes' deliberate reversion from the pluralism of the later philosophers of nature like Empedocles and Anaxagoras to the doctrine of a single original being were primarily theological. On the one hand, this assumption seemed more satisfying than Empedocles' theory of the six contending divinities, Love and Strife and the gods of the four elements, even when they take the form of the one unified *Sphairos*, which prevails for only a certain length of time.[65] On the other hand, Diogenes succeeded in avoiding the difficulty of how the Mind could exert any influence upon the world of intermingling stuffs if it were as distinct from them as Anaxagoras maintained. In Diogenes' primal principle matter and Mind are united, and we obviously must think of the Mind as working from within outward.[66] Anaxagoras himself had not distinguished Mind sharply from 'the other things': despite its freedom from any admixture, it remained for him 'the thing [χρῆμα] that is purest and thinnest'.[67] He was therefore not yet aware of a real

opposition between matter and Mind. Though he needed the
Mind primarily as a cause of motion, he still conceived of it
as something material, endowed with the power of thought.
Hence it was easy for Diogenes to obliterate the distinction
between Mind and matter once again, without abandoning
Mind as a teleological principle of order.

Apparently Diogenes was the first to try to demonstrate the
sway of a purposeful divine thought in nature by interpreting
particular phenomena from this point of view—the method that
was to play so important a role in the Stoic theology later on.
Presumably it was by way of Xenophon that Diogenes' ideas
reached the Stoa; for in more than one passage of the *Memorabilia* Xenophon attributes to Socrates certain theological
speculations which evidently come from this source.[68] It may
be true that Socrates and his companions had actually discussed
some piece of writing like that of Diogenes. At any rate, Plato
makes Socrates report in the *Phaedo* that he has examined the
work of Anaxagoras with great eagerness to find out what he
has to say about Mind as the cause of natural processes, and
has found him disappointing.[69] We may assume that in all
probability Socrates was interested in Diogenes, too, for the same
reasons, and paid even more attention to him. Xenophon himself does not mention Diogenes by name. He makes Socrates
converse with a young friend notorious for his indifference to
the cult of the gods, and try to refute his deistic attitude—for
while the young man believes in the gods' existence, he refuses
to admit that they feel any concern for mankind.[70] Socrates
accordingly maintains that the nature of man himself, both
bodily and mental, reveals the providing care of a higher wisdom.[71] The arguments that Socrates brings forward are undoubtedly not his own. We might easily have assumed that
they were, in view of his partiality for teleological explanations
of nature (so well attested by Plato), if we did not find the same
and similar explanations in the zoological works of Aristotle.
Aristotle certainly did not take them from Xenophon's *Memorabilia*, but must have resorted to someone among the philosophers
of nature who would count as particularly authoritative in such
observations.[72] We also find many similar traces in Attic
comedy and in the tragedies of Euripides.[73]

All this contemporary evidence suggests that at the time of

Socrates, Euripides, and Aristophanes there was a certain student of nature teaching in Athens who sought to prove the dominion of an intelligent principle in nature by calling attention to the planned purposefulness with which the human organism is put together. The more particular details supporting this suggestion cannot be introduced here.[74] Certainly the way in which Xenophon applies his arguments for the divine πρόνοια to the practical religious problem of the individual's attitude towards the State religion must be ascribed to Xenophon himself, as has long been recognized.[75] On the other hand, his discussions of the purposeful adaptation of the human organism are strictly naturalistic in character; they breathe the spirit of a genuinely theoretical explanation of nature in terms of the principle of its technical perfection. They are therefore theology in another sense altogether. This method of explanation reminds us strikingly of the iatro-mathematical school of the modern Enlightenment with its efforts to understand the corporeal side of man's nature as a system of purposeful mechanical arrangements comparable to true machinery: the heart as a pump, the lungs as bellows, the arms as levers, and so forth. In the same spirit Xenophon's Socrates-Diogenes explains the eyelashes as sieves (ἠθμός), the eyebrows as a cornice (γεῖσον) placed on the forehead as on the roof of a temple, the eyelids as doors (βλεφάροις θυρῶσαι), the intestines as a system of conduits (ὀχετοί).[76] Other sources add further features to the imagery of this theory: the ears as troughs, the eye as a wheel corresponding to the sun, the nose as a wall.[77] This technological interpretation of nature is entirely systematic, as is plain to see. It did not originally have the meaning that it now has in Xenophon, namely, of proving that these are all ways in which the gods provide for men's needs; it was obviously intended to show that the productions of nature cannot be the work of blind chance, but presuppose the purposeful intelligence of some creative principle. As Xenophon has both these objectives in mind, it is hard to tell which parts of the discussion really belong to Diogenes, and we must accordingly exercise a certain critical restraint. But we can go at least one step farther without danger.

Naturally Diogenes could not base his arguments for a purposeful divine creator on analysis of man's nature alone. He

also had to try to demonstrate the presence of this same purposefulness in the course of nature as a whole and in the evident
disposition of heavenly bodies according to some plan.[78] In
fact we find this view clearly expressed (cf. p. 165) in a
fragment that has come down to us under Diogenes' name.[79]
But even in Xenophon, who has occasion to speak of this
problem in several passages of the *Memorabilia*, it seems to be
closely connected with the proof of the purposefulness with
which human nature is arranged.[80] The earlier thinkers had
raised the problem of the form (μορφή) of the Divine, on the
frank assumption that while the existence of the Divine was a
fact and needed no demonstration, its nature and form could
not help being entirely different from the representations of the
folk-religion.[81] The line of thought struck out by Diogenes,
however, begins with the 'works' (ἔργα) of the Divine. To
determine the form of the gods is hard, Socrates explains in the
fourth book of the *Memorabilia*; but their works lead us to
a knowledge of their power, by which the All is imperceptibly
ruled and preserved.[82] In this way the whole point of the
theological discussion is fundamentally shifted: the problem
of the form of the Divine lapses into the background as insoluble, and the existence of the Divine as such becomes the
real matter to be proved. The Divine can be known only
indirectly, for it remains hidden behind its works, just as the
soul guides the man without ever becoming visible to our sight.[83]
The relation between soul and body corresponds exactly to
that between God and the world; this analogy follows inevitably
from Diogenes' identification of his principle—the air—with
soul and Mind and the animization of the All.[84] That Xenophon's analogy between the invisible deity and the soul itself
actually comes from Diogenes is rendered even more probable
by the recurrence of the conception in that portion of the first
book of the *Memorabilia* to which we have already referred—
the section where we find the characteristic comparisons of the
human organism with various technical implements.[85]

The comparison of God and soul in this passage is connected
with a kind of argument which makes particularly clear how
much the inner point of departure of Diogenes' theology has
come to differ from that of the earlier thinkers. They had approached nature with the exuberant consciousness that 'all

things are full of gods'.[86] In the new period nature has lost its
divine character; the eye of man no longer finds traces of the
demonic at every step, and philosophy is faced with a difficult
problem. Is not Man, with his reason, isolated and alone in the
universe? Is there any Mind or soul in the world apart from
him? Such a conception would lay far too heavy a burden upon
his shoulders; it would also indicate appalling arrogance on the
part of little Man himself, at least for a people who shared the
Greek feelings about the cosmos.

'Do you believe', Xenophon's Socrates asks the young Aristodemus, 'that you have any wisdom within you? . . . And do you still
suppose that there is no spark of wisdom anywhere else in the world?
And do you believe all this, even though you know that you have
in your body only one tiny bit of earth out of the mass that exist,
and only a little of all the moisture that there is, and that your body
is composed entirely of small portions of every other kind of thing
that is present in large quantities [in nature]? And do you still
think that mind alone is nowhere else to be found, and that you have
somehow gathered it up as if you had come upon it by some happy
accident? And are you convinced that all these immense and utterly
countless things [the heavenly bodies] hold their courses with such
admirable order by the power of mere unreason?'[87]

When his interlocutor objects that he cannot see the causes
of these things and therefore is sceptical about them, Socrates
again brings in the analogy of the human soul, which is likewise
invisible.[88] If this point of contact with the argument of the
fourth book is itself good ground for tracing both these arguments and Xenophon's statements about the Mind in the universe to the same source, then Plato's *Philebus* is corroborative
evidence; for there this same peculiar line of proof appears in
much the same words with an appeal to the authority of certain
older philosophers of nature who extolled the *Nous* as lord and
ruler of the universe.[89] This reminds us of Anaxagoras' *Nous*,
but it also includes Diogenes'. We have seen how Diogenes,
in his great theological fragment, following the example of
Anaxagoras, lauds his first principle in hymn-like language as
a thinking Mind by which all things are ordered.[90] It is through
him rather than through Anaxagoras that this argument
reached Xenophon and Plato. This is quite clear from the

testimony of Theophrastus, who tells us, in the course of expounding Diogenes' theory of perception, that according to the views of this philosopher 'the inner air within is what does our perceiving, inasmuch as it is a tiny portion of the divinity'.⁹¹

Thus Anaxagoras and Diogenes added a new teleological form of argument to the earlier stages of natural theology. By this time the 'primal ground' presupposed in the Milesian physics has come to be conceived less dogmatically and tends more and more to become a mere abstract matter or stuff. As this process continues, it becomes increasingly paradoxical that this blind mass of matter should yet prove to be of service in so many works of nature artfully arranged and purposefully fashioned forth. All the greater, therefore, is the need for an additional, second force as a conscious creator of the world-order analogous to the human mind, regardless of whether it is to be distinguished sharply from the rest of the corporeal world as 'the purest and thinnest body', as in Anaxagoras, or thought of as immanent in the material basic principle itself and identified with it, as in Diogenes. In both cases it is by our experience of the world-order as a constructive and purposeful organization that we are able to grasp the nature of that divine intelligence which stands behind this world-order or is effective within it; and this new experience of the cosmos would be unthinkable if it were not for that peculiarly developed feeling for all kinds of mechanical and technical purposefulness which we find in the new era—a feeling that springs from the heightened technical knowledge and skills of the period. The rational purposefulness which underlies both man's activities and even his very existence has here attained its highest peak of development, particularly in works of art; and in this process it calls man's attention to the rationality of nature as well, and thereby shows him how he can, purely by sober interpretation of the reason that there prevails, and quite apart from any mythical apotheosis of natural forces, approach the secret of that power by which all nature is led: ὄψις τῶν ἀδήλων τὰ φαινόμενα (Anaxagoras).

CHAPTER X

THEORIES OF THE NATURE AND ORIGIN OF RELIGION

W E shall conclude our historical review of the older Greek philosophers' ideas of God by considering the age of the Sophists; for when we come to Socrates and Plato, we meet a new and very different phase of development, so significant historically and so rich in traditional material that it deserves an altogether separate treatment. In dealing with the Sophistic movement we shall think of it in a sense wide enough to include certain related phenomena and doctrines, as far as they may belong to the same period.

Up to this time the speculations of the pre-Socratics about the Divine displayed a decided singleness of character in their intellectual form, despite their diversity of aspects and the multiplicity of their points of departure. Their immediate goal was the knowledge of nature or of Being. The problem of the origin of all things was so comprehensive and went so far beyond all traditional beliefs and opinions that any answer to it had to involve some new insight into the true nature of those higher powers which the myths revered as 'the gods'. In the all-creative primal ground of becoming, no matter how much this idea was further particularized, philosophical thought had always discovered the very essence of everything that could be called divine. All the individual features and forms of the gods with which the mythological consciousness had occupied itself became dissolved in it, and a new conception of deity began to take shape. This process paralleled the advancing insight into the nature of reality and made new headway at every stage it traversed. Thus we arrive again at the selfsame source of assurance of the Divine by which the Greek faith in the gods had been nurtured from the first: to the Greek spirit, *Weltanschauung* had again become *Gottanschauung*—simply and directly, but on another plane. Even the word 'God' itself, which is used by a number of these thinkers, now takes on the same new ring it had acquired in the Milesian philosophy of nature from the very beginning in the formulation 'the Divine':[1] all the perfections (ἀρεταί) ever attributed to any divine persons of the cult-religion by the epithet 'God' are now collected and transferred to that primal ground which philosophical thought regards as involving the essence of supreme power over all existence, and therefore alone worthy to possess this predicate (for the Greeks always thought of the word 'God' as predicative). If we ask upon what this new evaluation is based, we find that the real motive for so radical a change in the form of the godhead lies in the idea of the All (ὅλον, πᾶν). The philosophers are continually speaking of the Divine as all-encompassing, all-governing, and so forth, on the assumption that its claim to the name of God is thereby directly established.[2] In the face of such thinking as this, nothing finite and limited has any right to the title of divinity. Accordingly, we find an unremitting intellectual struggle to grasp the nature of this All-divine. The course of its development leads all the way from the simple Boundless of the earliest hylozoists,[3] out of which all existing things are produced, to the Mind that plays so great a part in the teleological views of nature in Anaxagoras and Diogenes.[4]

Hence the philosophical struggle which we have been examining has its place as an integrating factor in the development of Greek religion; yet we have usually set it apart as philosophy, as if it were something else altogether. The common element lies, as we have already indicated, in the fact that whenever the Greeks experienced the Divine, they always had their eyes on reality, and all their experiences were oriented in that direction. But at the earliest stage of the philosophy of nature they approached reality with entirely new intellectual powers and grasped it in entirely new forms. Accordingly, the achievements of this philosophy strike us at first as no more than the emergence of a radically destructive and fundamentally anti-religious force such as we often attribute to reason and to science. If one thinks of religion not as a form developing with a life of its own, but simply as a bare fact of history given once and for all, as is very plausible in the light of the Christian conception of a single and final revelation by God, this view is perhaps correct. But Greek religion is much richer and less restricted in its development. It does not consist in any revealed teachings reconcilable with rational thinking only to a limited degree; it springs rather from a lavish profusion of mythical views of the world, the characteristics of which are constantly changed and revised with each new shift of perspective. The religious sense of the Greeks is not of such a sort that their conception of Zeus, for instance, would be dogmatically hardened and debarred from reinterpretation. Accordingly, the conception of Zeus which we find in art and in poetry draws new life from philosophy,[5] while that which philosophy calls 'the Divine' is, as Heraclitus puts it, 'both willing and unwilling to be called by the name of Zeus'.[6] In fact, it is impossible not to find in the Divine of which these thinkers speak many features that remind us of Zeus, even though we cannot treat it as identical with the old god of the skies. Indeed, the development of the philosophical idea of God from the *apeiron* to the *Nous* is undeniably accompanied by an increasing resemblance to Zeus. At first the whole spiritual element of the old conception of the gods seemed to have evaporated in the bare idea of the All; but as this idea developed into that of the Divine, the spirit was reinstated, and we again come round to something more like the mythological conception of the gods on a higher stage of the spiral cycle.[7] From this point of view, moreover, the fact that the philosophical theory of God is the work of individual thinking rather than a heritage of collective lore from the immemorial past, is no argument against the religious quality of this intellectual faith. Indeed, the religious problem is so closely tied up with the problem of cosmogony, which sets the cognitive faculties in motion and puts them to work on the problem of the divine nature, that this religious quality follows inevitably. As is plain from the hymn-like form of the statements these thinkers make about the Divine, knowledge and reverence for the gods are one and the same for them.[8] To this extent it is quite right to designate the philosophy of the pre-Socratic period as a *modus deum cognoscendi et colendi*—that is, as religion, even if the gap between this and the popular beliefs about the gods is never again entirely closed.[9]

In its final phase the rise of philosophical religion leads to a consciousness of the problem of religion itself—the problem of accounting for the universal dispersion of the idea of God and of discovering its sources. Any type of thinking that derives all existence from nature and its characteristic law and order must come to the point of regarding even the belief in God as a product of human nature in interaction with the world that surrounds it, and therefore as something natural in itself. It is only gradually and at a later period that the philosophical consciousness begins to look upon man's nature as part of the nature of the universe.[10] Here the philosophers follow in the footsteps of the medical men, who are the first to draw the logical conclusions from the new conception of a single and unified nature governed throughout by universal laws, and to inquire into the laws of man's corporeal nature.[11] A second approach to the problem begins with the purely philosophical question of man's position in the cosmos, already raised by Heraclitus;[12] here the intellectual nature is involved quite as much as the corporeal. But the real fathers of rational anthropology are the fifth-century Sophists. In this respect they resemble the philosophers of the modern Enlightenment, who perform a similar function and have many close points of contact with them. Both in practice and in theory the Sophists base their activity as teachers upon the idea of the *physis* of man. According to their doctrine, all education is a product of *physis*, *mathesis*, and *askesis*.[13] Over and above their interest in the natural disposition of the individual man, this insight inevitably leads them to consider the general laws of human nature—all the more so since the training in political virtue which they strive to inculcate presupposes a well-fixed concept of State and society and of the general natural conditions underlying them. But these conditions are nothing other than the laws of human nature, from which these forms of social life have arisen. The Sophist Protagoras of Abdera worked out his views of the nature of man's common life in the State in a special work with the title *On the Order of Things at the Beginning*. There he attempted to envisage the beginnings of the human race and to determine by a genetic approach the causes that had led to the development of the earliest civilization.[14] Such attempts at analysis from the standpoint of sociology and the philosophy of culture cannot help bringing up the problem of the origins of religion as one of the most potent factors in man's social life. But this is not the only point at which the Sophists touch upon the religious problem; they also encounter it in connexion with the problem of knowledge and certainty, which likewise was treated by Protagoras. Moreover, they are really the first psychologists to consider the phenomenon of religion from this point of view. These various aspects cannot be kept altogether separate; for they are merely different forms of a single attitude of approach—an attitude which no longer demands an objective philosophical knowledge of the divine essence such as the older philosophers of nature had proclaimed, but which regards the traditional religious conceptions of the Divine as among the constituents of human nature as such, and seeks to approach them rather from the standpoint of the subject by analysing man himself.

In the myth of the rise of the human race and human civilization that Plato ascribes to Protagoras in his dialogue of that name, the worship of God is presupposed as an essential element of human culture. Here we read that 'as man had a share of the Divine, he was first of all the only living creature to believe in gods, because of his kinship with the godhead; and so he set himself to building altars and images of the gods'.[15] Of course, the mythical form in which Protagoras clothes his views of the origin of culture prevents us from weighing every word of this sentence with too much precision, particularly when it comes to his metaphysical deduction of the religious impulse from man's relatedness to God. But in depicting the rise of human culture, Protagoras must surely have seen the full import of the fact that man alone has any acquaintance with religion and divine worship. Plato's myth makes very clear the context into which Protagoras attempted to fit it. Protagoras here looks upon religion primarily as an anthropological fact to be understood in the light of its meaning and function in human civilization and social structure. We shall see later that behind this positive attitude there also lurks the problem of the objective certainty and truth of the belief in God, a different aspect altogether, which receives Protagoras' attention in his work *On the Gods*.[16]

In the speech of Socrates in Xenophon's *Memorabilia* which we have analysed in our last chapter,[17] we already possess a similar or at least comparable discussion of religion as a product and expression of the characteristic nature of man as distinct from the animals. It has recently been shown that Xenophon was not content to draw some of his ideas from Diogenes' teleological theory of nature, but probably fused it with a Sophistic tractate which attempted to prove the gods' solicitude for men in a more anthropomorphic sense, by adducing man's own religious endowments as a sign of it.[18] The art of divination is here mentioned as a particularly impressive example.[19] As is well known, this argument gave rise to a whole literature in Hellenistic philosophy; we need only recall Cicero's tract *De Divinatione*, which follows a pattern quite familiar in Hellenistic philosophical literature. In Xenophon we are still very near the beginnings of the argument based on divination; and therefore our more extreme critics have felt that both this passage and all the rest of this theological chapter should be bracketed as a later Stoic interpolation. But Aeschylus' Prometheus had already boasted of inventing the arts out of his love for men in their helpless subjection to natural forces; and among these arts he included mathematics, astronomy, grammar, and divination.[20] We have here a direct precedent for Xenophon's argument. The difference is merely that he or his model formulated everything in somewhat broader terms, replacing the one god Prometheus, the traditional helper of suffering humanity, by the gods in general.[21] In Xenophon Socrates considers the question whether divination may not sometimes be deceptive, and replies that the collective experience of untold generations is a more reliable criterion than individual intelligence. Socrates points out that states and nations, the longest-lived and wisest of all human institutions, are also the strongest religious forces in the world, just as older men, who by reason of their years may be supposed to have superior insight, are more god-fearing than younger ones.[22] The problem of the truth and certainty of religion is here thrust into the background in favour of a new kind of attitude that makes practical experience rather than critical intelligence the real yardstick. This situation reminds us of that which we meet in the third book of Cicero's *De natura deorum*, where Cotta, the Roman Pontifex Maximus, while not denying the competence of philosophical understanding in religious matters, sets up against it the *auctoritas* of the religious tradition and religious experience.[23] The concept of *auctoritas*, however, which is later to be of such decisive importance for the attitude of the Church in questions of faith, is entirely missing in Greek thought. In its place we find Xenophon referring to the wisdom vested in the religious institutions of States and peoples by virtue of their immemorial age.[24] This defence of the popular religion is obviously a far cry from mere credulousness. Any man capable of this statement must already have undergone the experience of radical philosophical doubt; and even if he returns to positive religion, he still speaks of it from an intellectual distance that is readily perceptible. It is not so much the details of religion that he defends as the whole. This is a new attitude towards religion, and it is based upon something very like a philosophy. It might be best characterized as a kind of pragmatism; for it utilizes the conception of verification by fruitfulness rather than by objective truth, and traces religion back to the subjective spiritual constitution of mankind.[25] Xenophon says that the idea of the gods as powers which bring blessings or destruction is one which is 'implanted' or 'inborn' in men; and from the fact that man possesses this psychological structure he infers the reality of a provident divine creative force as its producer.[26] This conclusion is not so remarkable if one has already accepted the premise that the experience of untold generations demonstrates the wisdom and bounty with which the religious side of man's mind has been equipped.

In Xenophon that which is only briefly suggested in Protagoras' myth is now fully developed. The problem is to discover from what inborn natural disposition of mankind religion has taken its rise. Awareness of this question is a significant stride forward from the earlier naturalistic attempts to determine the nature of the Divine. As an historical product of human nature, religion itself now appears to be something necessary and subject to natural law. This discovery provides a new argument for the purposefulness of man's mental organization, in addition to the older proofs based on his physiological structure.[27] While the older theology of the natural philosophers replaced the traditional ideas of the gods with its own conception of the Divine, the new anthropological and psychological approach proceeds to rehabilitate the popular religion, which has hitherto seemed irreconcilable with philosophical truth. Instead of rational criticism and speculative revision of the idea of God, we now find a more understanding attitude which shows how a whole world of given intellectual forms reflects the wisdom underlying man's natural endowments, and is to that extent divine. When Xenophon's youthful interlocutor asks Socrates how such unimaginable power and wisdom may fittingly be honoured, he receives the thoroughly consistent reply that the best way is to follow the established usages of the State religion, just as the Delphic oracle recommended when plied with similar questions. The Delphic oracle is here introduced in order that even this practical problem may be solved in conformity with wisdom old and tried.[28]

The Sophists' attempt to reveal the teleological basis of religion by reconstructing the earliest stages of human society inevitably leads to the question of how the idea of the existence of divine beings can ever have entered the mind of man. The first man to raise this question thinks of it more in universal than in historical terms. The problem is that of the permanent psychological causes of the idea of God. Two theories have come down to us, each of them arising in the time of the Sophists. One of them comes from Prodicus of Ceos, and will steadily find adherents later on, particularly among the Stoics. As far as I know, the earliest traces of its influence upon his contemporaries are to be found in the *Bacchae* of Euripides, where it appears in speeches arguing for and against the divinity of Dionysus.[29] Prodicus teaches that those things in nature which are wholesome and nutritive for mankind have been looked upon as gods by the earliest of men and honoured accordingly. This rather general formulation, which comes from an Epicurean source utilized by Cicero in his *De natura deorum* as well as by Philodemus in his tract *On Piety*,[30] is amplified with further details in a parallel account by Sextus Empiricus. Sextus tells us that according to Prodicus, sun, moon, rivers, springs, and indeed all things wholesome and useful for men were regarded as gods by the people of ancient times, just as the Nile was worshipped by the Egyptians. Accordingly bread has been looked upon (νομισθῆναι) as Demeter, wine as Dionysus, water as Poseidon, fire as Hephaestus, and so on with everything else that is useful to man.[31] In another passage Sextus includes meadows and lakes in this same group, and thus treats the origin of the belief in nymphs and similar deities of nature.[32] The mention of agriculture in connexion with Demeter encourages us to suspect that Prodicus tried to derive the mystery-religion with its initiatory rites from this root, and there is confirmation for this belief in Themistius. The mystery-religion must have seemed a particularly good point of departure for conjecturing about the religious ideas of primitive times, for it was supposed to go back to extreme antiquity. This it presumably does, though it presupposes a fairly advanced civilization in which agriculture and settled living are already well established.[33] All these instances of deification of natural forces and things useful and healthful in human lives must have impressed Prodicus by their very numbers and compelled him to give his observations a highly general form. To trace the idea of God back to those things in nature which serve men's purposes was all the easier for him because the teleological motif had more effective demonstrative force in the philosophical thought of his time than any other. There was nothing farther removed from the rationalism of the Sophists than genuine historical thinking. They never realized how little plausibility there was in naïvely seizing upon the abstract teleological type of argument current in the scientific efforts of their own times and reading it back into the primitive stages of human thought.

Nevertheless, we have already seen that in the religious philosophy of the Hellenistic age Prodicus' teachings were taken very seriously ;[34] and, in fact, they do contain a kernel of truth, as we shall presently show. The theories of Democritus took their place beside those of Prodicus,[35] and deserve mention here because of their similar method of approach to the problem. Democritus may also seem to merit our consideration as a philosopher of nature like his predecessors; but the great exponent of atomism did not work out any original theology, such as we find in Anaxagoras or Diogenes, which would oblige us to give special attention to this phase of his philosophy of nature. His description of nature in terms of the interplay of countless atoms in empty space ruled by the power of chance left no room for teleology and the deification of any moving forces or single primal ground. Nevertheless, Democritus saw a serious epistemological problem in the very existence of religious ideas in the mind of man. He was convinced that the immediate source of these ideas was to be sought in the apparitions of the gods that men behold in their dreams. He did not explain these as hallucinations, but attributed them to real objects actually perceived. Democritus called these objects 'images' ($\epsilon\check{\iota}\delta\omega\lambda\alpha$), and thought of them as fine membranes freeing themselves from the surfaces of actual things and stimulating human sense-organs.[36] We need not here discuss the physiological aspects of this hypothesis. Democritus thought of these images as having either good or baneful effects, and believed in their significance as portents; but he explained all this as a purely natural process. And it was to this process, as Sextus reports, that he ascribed the rise of the belief in gods among the earliest peoples.[37] Thus he did not deny the gods altogether, but relegated them to a twilight realm of materialized psychical phenomena, where even though divested of their own peculiar power and significance, they could still bring about good fortune or bad. He described these images as great and far exceeding human stature and hard to destroy, though not absolutely indestructible.[38] Thus Democritus recognized eternity and imperishability as properties really belonging to the gods, or at least as claims approaching reality, though he robbed them of their proper significance. He even went so far as to retain prayer as the most fundamental way of expressing one's faith in the reality of the Divine. But prayer, too, had come to mean something rather different, for the philosopher could bring himself to admit only one kind as reasonable—the wish 'to encounter propitious images'.[39] He had no faith in the idea of life after death as taught in the mysteries, for he held that everything that nature brings forth is subject to decay or, more strictly speaking, to dissolution. 'Some men who know nothing of the dissolution of mortal nature, but are well aware of the badness of their own ways of life, wear themselves out all their lifetime with troubles and anxieties, while they invent lying myths about the time which comes after death.' These words have come down to us as a fragment from Democritus' ethical work *On Tranquillity*.[40] Here the philosopher departs from his theory of images, declaring that certain types of religious conceptions are merely the unreal offspring of a bad conscience—obvious fictions, unwittingly compensatory, a source of lifelong self-inflicted torment for the human mind. Retribution, in truth, does not come in the hereafter but in man's own inner life, which constitutes his actual Hell.[41] This idea does not spring from the cynicism of a pure student of nature utterly cold to the ethical side of the problem. It comes rather from the interplay which results when psychological and physiological thinking are mingled with a refined ethical cultivation such as the treatise *On Tranquillity* reveals on every page. Democritus will not have men's conduct based on false authorities, even if they are derived from the laws of the State; he has faith in the paramount efficacy of some such moral force as human self-respect,[42] and this faith accounts for the peculiarly impassioned tone with which he criticizes the belief in the hereafter.

The juxtaposition of the fiction-theory and the theory of images in Democritus' work shows that he attacked the problem of religion from two different sides, and prepares us for a third theory which is in principle like that of Prodicus. Here we are again indebted to Sextus. According to Democritus, he remarks,[43] it is through the wonders ($\pi\alpha\rho\alpha\delta\delta\xi\omega\nu$) of nature that men have arrived at the idea of God; when the first men watched the cosmic meteorological processes like thunder and lightning, stellar conjunctions, and eclipses of sun and moon, they were filled with fear and believed that these things were caused by the gods. Similarly, in the papyrus fragments of Philodemus' treatise *On Piety*, we find still other meteorological processes like summer, winter, spring, and autumn named in connexion with Democritus as things that have come 'from above'; and we learn that it is this knowledge that has led men to honour the causes by which these processes are produced.[44] If we array these new examples along with thunder, lightning, eclipses, and other dire phenomena, we can refer them all to a single psychological motive on the border-line between awe and fear. It now becomes evident that our author's derivation of religion from apparitions in dreams and his theory of the origin of belief in an after-life, heterogeneous though they may appear, both harmonize very nicely with the same general psychological attitude. We then see at once that his attempt to explain the first intimations of the beyond as arising in the bad consciences of wrongdoers fits very well with the fear-theory. In this instance, to be sure, we are dealing with a truly inward anxiety, not the kind of fear which outward sense-impressions, such as thunder and lightning, produce. But obviously the hypothesis of images must be connected with the fear-motive; for what Democritus emphasizes in the images that appear to us in dreams is nothing other than their magnitude and supernatural stature ($\mu\epsilon\gamma\dot{\alpha}\lambda\alpha\ \tau\epsilon\ \kappa\alpha\dot{\iota}\ \dot{\upsilon}\pi\epsilon\rho\phi\upsilon\hat{\eta}$)—in short, their terrifying appearance.[45] This derivation of religion from the sense of fear or awe really touches one of its strongest roots. Perhaps we may also venture a similar approach to Prodicus' theory that man has apotheosized those bounteous powers of nature which he finds to his advantage; for if we divest this theory of the rationalistic teleological form in which it is clothed and substitute a more psychological explanation, it would mean that man has come to revere the Divine because of his feeling of gratitude for the things in this world that seem to him good. This approach is not only an admirable supplement to Democritus' fear-theory; it is also a necessary one.

Apparently Democritus, like his townsman Protagoras in Plato's myth,[46] did more than treat the origin of religion as an abstract psychological problem. He even gave it a place in his concrete sociological theory of how culture arose—the subject of his principal work, the *Mikros Diakosmos*. At least, this seems to be the best place to put the beautiful fragment which Clement of Alexandria has preserved for us: 'Some of the wise men lifted their hands towards that place which we Hellenes call the abode of Air, and said that Zeus holds converse with himself about all things, and that it is he who knows all things, and gives and takes away, and he is king of all.'[47] Obviously this refers to that memorable moment in the dark primeval age when the idea of deity first dawned upon men's minds. Democritus is quite in accord with the spirit of his own enlightened era when he thinks of religious ideas as originating not by the flickering-up of a vague feeling among the many, but rather by the act of a few heroic souls who step before the multitude with solemn gestures, raise their hands in prayer to heaven, and speak these words, which seem like a manifest confirmation of Democritus' fear-theory, and show that in this fear the germ of reverence is latent. These men are venerable, men of wisdom, what the Greek calls λόγιοι—the name Herodotus gives to the sages of the ancient Asiatic peoples. Here we are reminded of the form and concept of the philosopher as such, and tend thoughtlessly to read it back into the pre-Socratic period as Plato and Aristotle might have done, though the word 'philosopher' did not as yet have this significance, if it even existed at all. Indeed, Democritus here has in mind the type of philosopher or λόγιος on whom the intellectual development of Ionian culture has put its stamp; he has merely projected the type into primitive times. Not only does his language express with truly plastic force the curious relationship—partly one of close kinship, partly one of contrast and opposition—between the philosophical thinker and the multitude; in his choice of words and even in the tone of the fragment, Democritus has preserved the style of the pre-Socratics. Thus these wise men appear as a belated illustration for our view of the older Hellenic thinkers. Democritus shows us how the philosopher, overcome with awe and amazement at the sight of nature's sublimities, becomes a herald for the godhead in the form in which he sees it. These old-time sages are not thought of as the inventors of the popular polytheism; they speak rather of a single god whom they call Zeus, whose mind embraces all things in its knowledge, and who guides all things and is king of all. This series of hymn-like predications rings with the language and manner of the accounts of the natural philosophers, from Anaximander to Anaxagoras and Diogenes, of that divine nature which their search for the primal ground of Being has revealed.[48] Thus, at the end of the long line of testimonials to the new knowledge of the Divine, this knowledge is reflected back into the earliest age of the human race, and an attempt is made to explain all religion from the personally experienced prototype of just such reverent seeking and research. While Democritus himself may have been less inclined than his predecessors to make definite statements about deity as such, nevertheless his concern with the origin of the idea of God shows how lively a part he plays in the tradition of the pre-Socratic θεολογήσαντες, and how directly he was aware that his own study of the natural world was one branch on the tree of man's primordial striving to know the divine nature of reality.

It is understandable that Democritus, the man of research who spent his life in constant intimacy with the natural world and was aware of his predecessors' numerous attempts to fathom the nature of the Divine through their studies of the cosmos, should have sought to explain the origin of religion very largely by the impressions which natural phenomena make upon the human mind. The Sophist Prodicus likewise arrived at an explanation of this sort, though by another route. But besides the cosmic religion towards which the mind of Hellas displayed a profound susceptibility even in the late ancient period, the Sophists found themselves forced to consider another source of religious assurance, of which Democritus was already conscious when he explained the belief in the hereafter. This is the world of morals. As we have already remarked, the Sophists were the first to make a careful theoretical study of the nature of State and society in connexion with their claim of training men in political ἀρετή. That they studied the problem of the validity and origin of the accepted moral standards and the laws of the State is plainly illustrated by a fragment from a lost work *On Truth* by Antiphon the Athenian, which was recovered several decades ago. The author considers that the distinguishing of a twofold justice—the natural and the conventional—is a discovery of the first importance.[49] This distinction, which is known to be much older, and has already been applied by Parmenides and Empedocles to certain cosmical and ontological matters, becomes of the greatest practical significance when it is used by Sophists like Antiphon, Hippias, and the 'Callicles' of Plato's *Gorgias* to demonstrate that the prevailing laws and accepted social *mores* are a product of mere convention and arbitrary human decisions.[50] Antiphon defines justice as conformity with the laws of the State in which one lives.[51] By such a definition he makes room for his conviction of the relativity of the laws of the State, which he opposes to the conception of natural justice. According to his theory, the laws are shackles with which the lawgiver binds the individual, and are quite inimical to nature.[52] The man who acts naturally has only one standard for his actions—namely, that which he finds agreeable or disagreeable, productive of pleasure or of pain.[53] Antiphon concludes, therefore, that man will obey the law only under compulsion, and will repudiate it as soon as that compulsion disappears. Moreover, he speaks of the presence of witnesses as a decisive factor in human conduct.[54] The fact that the average man will not act in the same way before witnesses as he will when none are present strikes Antiphon as an argument for his thesis—the distinction between natural and conventional morality and justice.

The presence or absence of witnesses plays an important role in the Sophistic and Platonic discussions of ethical problems, as I have shown in that section of my book *Paideia* where I discuss the problem of the moral authority of law and the disturbances it undergoes in the life of this period.[55] Plato's tale of the ring of Gyges in the *Republic* illustrates most strikingly the ethical importance of witnesses. He asks whether a man would act justly of his own free will if he possessed a magic ring which would make him invisible.[56] Democritus, as we have seen already, introduces the idea of self-respect into his ethical maxims because he, too, is no longer able to conceive of mere outward obedience to law as a sufficient basis for action.[57] When the validity of the State law was inwardly shaken by the criticisms of the Sophists and by their efforts to define it as the expression of the advantage of those temporarily at the head of the State,[58] the re-establishment of an inner norm independent of legislative changes became the greatest of all human problems. In earlier times this norm was furnished by religion, which gave the law its support. But can it continue to do so when the all-too-human origins of law are criticized, and not without some cause?[59] Can it endorse legislation based on selfish interests? Or rather must not religion, too, become involved in the collapse of legal authority?

This is the point of departure, for the remarkable criticism of religion that we find in the remaining long fragment of Critias' lost satyr-drama, the *Sisyphus*.[60] Many a convinced oligarch who found himself compelled to live under a democracy was sceptical of the pride which that democracy took in the laws as such;[61] and it is from the oligarchic circle that there emerge those devastating criticisms of the law—the very pillar of the democratic order—which we meet in Plato's Callicles.[62] No one else has succeeded in better expressing what this upper social stratum thought of the arbitrary character of those laws which the overwhelming majority of the people revered as truly god-given.[63] Presumably Critias, with his enlightened radicalism, was still dissatisfied with arguments of the kind put forward by Callicles in Plato's *Gorgias*. He therefore inserted in his *Sisyphus* a long account of the origin of religion, presumably putting it into the mouth of the crafty hero of his piece. In primeval times, he tells us (and here we note at once the influence of such prototypes as Democritus and Protagoras), men's life was confused and chaotic until the art of statecraft was developed and legislators arose to chain life down to a definite

fixed order. To compel law-observance among the contending
sons of nature, punishments were introduced for any trans-
gressions of which they might be convicted. But in order to
secure obedience even in the absence of witnesses, the wise
lawgivers hit upon the device of inventing an ideal witness who
sees all things and hears all things and instils in men the fear
of his punishment. In short, they invented God. Just as the
sages of Democritus step forward from the ranks of primitive
men and point to the phenomena of the heavens, so does
Critias' wise and cunning statesman mount the stage, presenting God to men: 'There exists', this person tells us (for he is
speaking in the style of the natural philosophers),

'A demon who abounds with deathless life,
Hearing and seeing with his mind, replete
With wisdom, holding everything together,
And moving godly nature in its course.
And he will hear all things that mortals speak,
And he can watch all things that they may do;
And if you plan some secret deviltry,
This never will escape the gods, for theirs
Is sapience immeasurably great.'
These were the words with which he introduced
The sweetest of all teachings; but the truth
He kept concealed with fraudulent discourse.
He said the gods resided in that place
Which men would dread the most, that place from which,
As he well knew, mortals have been beset
With fears or blest with that which brings relief
To their tormented lives—there, high above,
In that great circuit where the lightnings flash,
Where thunder's baleful tumult may be heard,
And heaven's starry countenance is seen
(That lovely work of Time's skilled joinery),
Where molten stones of stars descend ablaze,
And wet rain starts its journey to the earth.
Such were the consternating fears he sent
To men, and such the means by which the gods
Were settled in their proper dwelling-place
(A pretty trick, accomplished with a word);
And thus he quenched out lawlessness with laws.

We need hardly remark that this long *rhesis* is entirely made up of reminiscences from pre-Socratic theology. Not only do the sages of Democritus[64] find their analogue in Critias' clever lawgiver; even the depiction of divinity itself shows many features we have already met in Xenophanes and others. Our author also cashes in on the theories of Democritus and Prodicus as to the origin of religion, and fuses them in a common smelter.[65] He does not, however, follow these writers in making the idea of deity spring from fear and the sense of gratitude by a purely natural and automatic process; on the contrary, Critias' legislator looks at the heavens from which both the benefits and terrors of nature descend, and sees there the most effective place for lodging his ideal witness, the all-knowing God.[66] This subversive critique of the prevailing law is based on the notion that God is merely a device in the reigning political system to take the place of the policeman in cases where that eye of the law is not available, and the attempt to derive religion from a deliberate political fiction follows quite consistently. God is the 'as if' that serves to fill the gaps in the organization of the political system already dominant.[67] It is doubtful whether these theories were ever really proclaimed on the Athenian stage; the *Sisyphus* may rather have been a closet-drama, for we may take for granted that such works existed by the close of the fifth century. At any rate, this politico-moral theory of the origin of the idea of God breathes a far more radical spirit than the naturalistic explanations of Democritus and Prodicus which it presupposes.

Among the Sophists we find every shade of the philosophy of religion, from positive defence of religion as a natural endowment of mankind, essentially wise and serving to preserve the State, to the breakdown of the whole realm of ideas which it involves as mere subjective impressions or even as deceptive fictions. It is characteristic of the Sophists and their period that in approaching this problem they begin with the nature of the religious subject instead of following the older philosophers of nature and starting with the reality of the Divine. The Divine is now caught up in the general maelstrom of relativization and subjectivization of all normative standards. If the theories of Democritus and Prodicus were intended to make plausible the rise of the idea of God in man's consciousness, they still had nothing to say about the truth of this idea. Prodicus remarks that the beneficial things in nature have been looked upon as gods by the earliest of men. The Greek expression which he uses—νομισθῆναι—is connected with νόμος ;[68] behind this lurks the thought that these conceptions of divine beings are really based on νόμος alone and not on φύσις—an idea which the verb νομίζω occasionally expresses elsewhere.[69] Even when a Sophist regards religion with as positive a practical attitude as that of Protagoras in Plato's myth, there is always a conscious and fundamental theoretical doubt of its absolute truth. Protagoras' treatise On the Gods, which was publicly burned in Athens, began with the words: 'When it comes to the gods, I am unable to discover whether they are or are not, or even what they are like in form. For there are many things that stand in the way of this knowledge—the obscurity of the problem and the brevity of man's life.'[70] The words 'or even what they are like in form' are missing in some of the authors by whom this famous sentence is quoted, and they have been questioned by many critics.[71] It is clear, however, that the statement is a reference to the two chief problems that have occupied the pre-Socratic philosophers with regard to the gods—the problems of the existence and the form of the Divine. In the light of what we have seen already, it is self-evident that the latter reference is here indispensable.[72] Only so can we clearly see what Protagoras is opposing. He is backing away from the whole previous philosophical treatment of the problem of the Divine, by denying that there is anything certain about it. Such an opening note might seem to leave nothing more to be said, as has often been remarked. If, in spite of this, Protagoras could still devote an entire treatise to the problem of the belief in God, he must have been satisfied with a somewhat lesser degree of certainty as his work progressed. In that case, however, he could hardly do more than apply the standard of human opinion; and that would be most fitting for the man who had declared that 'Man is the measure of all things'.[73] In this way we can also understand the meaning of the 'I am unable to discover' in the first sentence of his treatise On the Gods, and we can see for what he is here preparing the way. With these words he restricts the scope of his sentence about the impossibility of knowing the gods, and makes it an expression of an individual opinion.[74] This must have seemed the only standpoint which would enable him to combine a fully precise approach to the question of objective certainty with his own personal recognition of the positive fact of religion and its undeniable significance for man as a social being.[75] This approach must also have been extremely congenial to the tendencies of the times; for in spite of all the rationalistic criticism and all the current uncertainty, there was a growing feeling that religion was indispensable, and public opinion was becoming sensitive as never before to real and alleged attacks upon the gods of the State. But this conservatism must have come entirely from the side of practical politics and morals. Hence we can understand to some extent why Critias should suggest that the gods are an invention of wily politicians, for here the contemporary situation has simply been reflected back into primeval times. Protagoras' attitude is one of 'to be sure, but . . . '. Certainly we cannot call this a real solution of the problem. The crisis of the philosophical idea of God has now arrived. Any attempt to solve it will have to start from the side where it has at last become most plainly evident and bodes the most serious consequences; and this is the problem of the goal of human life and action, the problem of the Good that Socrates and his followers will soon be compelled to attack. In speculative theology no less than in philosophy as a whole, this moment marks the beginning of a new epoch.[76]

NOTES

THE following are the works most frequently referred to in the Notes:

Diels, Hermann, *Die Fragmente der Vorsokratiker*, 5. Aufl., hrsg. v. Walther Kranz. Berlin: Weidmann, 1934-5. (All references to the fragments of the pre-Socratics are made from this edition.)

Diels, Hermann, *Doxographi Graeci*. Berlin: Reimer, 1879.

Jaeger, Werner, *Aristotle*. Oxford: Clarendon Press, 1934.

Jaeger, Werner, *Paideia: The Ideals of Greek Culture*. Vol. i, 2nd ed., N.Y.: Oxford University Press, 1945 (the 2nd ed. of this volume has not yet appeared in England); vol. ii, N.Y., 1943; Oxford: Blackwell, 1944; vol. iii, N.Y., 1944; Oxford: Blackwell, 1945.

CHAPTER I

THE THEOLOGY OF THE GREEK THINKERS

1. Cf. Aug. *Civ. Dei* vi, *praef.*

2. Although the demonstration of the total or partial agreement of the Greek and Roman philosophers with Christian doctrine begins in book vi of the *Civitas Dei* with the analysis of M. Terentius Varro's doctrine of the gods, it reaches its climax only in book viii, where St. Augustine states that Platonism even 'transcends' the Stoic philosophy of Varro in approaching the truth. As for the general idea see viii *praef.*, second half. On the subordination of the pre-Socratic thinkers as forerunners of Socrates and Plato see ibid., ch. ii, where St. Augustine briefly treats Thales, Anaximander, Anaximenes, Anaxagoras, Diogenes, and Archelaus. In this chapter he apparently follows an historical handbook. Similar doxographic surveys of the theology of the Greek philosophers from the Epicurean and Stoic points of view are to be found in Cic. *De nat. deor.* i and ii. That Augustine used this type of history of Greek philosophy is clear from his congruencies with Hippolytus' *Philosophoumena* (see R. Agahd in Fleckeisen's *Jahrbücher*, 1898, pp. 93 ff.). Cf. also his reference to the division of the pre-Socratic period into an Italic and an Ionian school, which we find in the same context in Diog. L. *praef.* 13. Diog. L. *praef.* 1 speaks also of the wisdom of other nations: the Persians, Babylonians and Assyrians, Indians, Celts, Phoenicians, Scythians, Egyptians, and Libyans. In the *Civ. Dei* viii, ch. ix, where St. Augustine refers for a second time to the division of the pre-Socratics into an Ionian and an Italian school, he adds the *sapientes aliarum gentium* as well, and enumerates exactly the same nations as does Diogenes, with the single exception of the Phoenicians. Indirectly, Diogenes and St. Augustine go back to the same source (Sotion's *Diadochai*), but St. Augustine followed directly a more recent work which had used the same tradition (a Latin translation of Porphyry's *History of Philosophy*? See Agahd, op. cit., p. 106, n. 2).

3. Aug. *Civ. Dei* vi, ch. v, reveals the systematic structure of Varro's theology in that work. See what he says in his characterization of Varro's work in the preceding chapters, ii–iv. The *Antiquitates rerum humanarum et divinarum*

is quoted and analysed by St. Augustine so extensively that modern philology
has been able to attempt a partial reconstruction of the work. See R. Agahd,
*De Varronis rerum divinarum libris i, xiv–xvi ab Augustino in libris De civitate
Dei iv, vi, vii exscriptis*, Leipzig, 1896.

4. See Aug. *Civ. Dei* iv, ch. xxvii; vi, ch. v. In the latter passage he writes:
'. . . tria genera theologiae dicit esse (*scil*. Varro), id est rationis quae de diis
explicatur, eorumque unum mythicon [appellari], alterum physicon, tertium
civile. . . .' Varro took this division from a philosophical source, as his own
words quoted by St. Augustine prove: 'Deinde ait: "Mythicon appellant, quo
maxime utuntur poetae; physicon, quo philosophi; civile, quo populi."'
Cf. K. Reinhardt, *Poseidonios* (Munich, 1921), p. 408, n. 1, on Varro's Stoic
source.

5. Aug. *Civ. Dei* viii, ch. iv (p. 250, 17, Dombart): 'Iste ipse Varro propterea se
prius de rebus humanis, de divinis autem postea scripsisse testatur, quod
prius extiterint civitates, deinde ab eis haec (i.e. res divinae) instituta sint.'
Varro's idea of the primacy of the State in matters of religion is expressed
even more dogmatically in his words quoted by Aug. loc. cit. 26: ' Sicut prior
est, inquit, pictor quam tabula picta, prior faber quam aedificium, ita priores
sunt civitates quam ea quae a civitatibus instituta sunt.' Varro is writing
about the Roman gods and Roman religion. So far as they are Roman, they
seem to him to belong to the Roman nation as clearly as any other institution
of the State. But St. Augustine remarks that Varro made an interesting
restriction with regard to his own belief in the primacy of the State in religious
matters. He says that if Varro were concerned not specifically with the
Roman gods but with the nature of the Divine at large ('si de omni natura
deorum scriberet'), he would have placed religion first. In other words, his
Stoic distinction of mythical, political, and natural theology is in unresolved
conflict with his political and patriotic aim to immortalize the national
religious system of Rome. From the viewpoint of absolute truth as maintained by philosophy, God comes first and human things second. But apparently the Roman gods are not identical for Varro with absolute truth in matters
of religion. The Pontifex Maximus Aurelius Cotta in the third book of Cic.
De nat. deor. (i.e. Cicero himself) thinks he has found a way out of this
dilemma by founding the Roman State religion on *auctoritas* alone, i.e. taking
it as a matter of will and civic duty, while he takes a position of philosophical
scepticism with regard to the ability of the human mind to know absolute
metaphysical truth. Varro's *Antiquitates* was dedicated to Caesar the pontifex
(cf. Aug. *Civ. Dei* vii, ch. xxxv; Lact. *Inst. div.* i. 6, 7) and therefore must have
been published in 47 B.C. Cicero wrote his work *De natura deorum* in 45. It
gives the answer to Varro's problem. The combination in it of voluntaristic
authoritarianism and metaphysical agnosticism is even more Roman than the
patriotic conflict in Varro's heart.

6. Aug. *Civ. Dei* vi, ch. x (p. 269, 11, Dombart²): 'Hanc libertatem Varro non
habuit; tantum modo poeticam theologian reprehendere ausus est, civilem
non ausus est, quam iste concidit.' The *iste* of this passage is Seneca, 'nam in
eo libro quem contra superstitiones condidit, multo copiosius atque vehe-
mentius reprehendit ipse civilem istam et urbanam theologian quam Varro
theatricam atque fabulosam' (p. 267, 9, Dombart). Thus Augustine contrasts
Seneca's truly philosophical consistency with Varro's compromise. Augustine's
attitude seems to follow Seneca's example. But of course it ought not to be
overlooked that in Augustine's time the Roman empire had officially
adopted the Christian faith as its State religion. Thus the front which Christian

polemic opposed to the pagan gods was not directed against the religion protected by the State but against those patriots of the old school who thought that Rome and her destiny were identical with her old gods; see Aug. *Civ. Dei* i, ch. xxxvi. On the similar attitude of Isocrates and the Athenian conservatives in the 4th century see my *Paideia*, iii, p. 117.

7. Aug. *Civ. Dei* vi, ch. iv (p. 250, 20, Dombart): 'Vera autem religio non a terrena aliqua civitate instituta est, sed plane caelestem ipsa instituit civitatem. Eam vero inspirat et docet verus Deus, dator vitae aeternae, veris cultoribus suis.' A similar universalistic attitude towards the particular gods of the states (ἔθνη) is taken by Ps. Plato's *Epinomis* 984a and by Aristotle; cf. my *Aristotle*, p. 141.

8. Aug. *Civ. Dei* vi, ch. vi (p. 255, 27, Dombart) says in addressing Varro: 'Quanto liberius subtiliusque ista divideres, dicens alios esse deos *naturales*, alios ab hominibus *institutos*.'

9. Philodemus Περὶ εὐσεβείας (p. 72, Gomperz): παρ' Ἀντισθένει δ' ἐν μὲν τῷ φυσικῷ λέγεται τὸ κατὰ νόμον εἶναι πολλοὺς θεοὺς κατὰ δὲ φύσιν ἕνα. Cf. Cic. *De nat. deor.* i. 13, 32, who says literally the same. (They follow a common source: Phaedrus the Epicurean's book Περὶ θεῶν. Cf. Diels's *Doxographi*, p. 127.)

10. A passage such as the one quoted above in n. 8 makes it highly probable that Augustine opposed his dichotomy of *dei naturales* and *dei ab hominibus instituti* to the trichotomy of Varro, not merely as an improvisation of his own but with full awareness of the existence of such a dichotomy in the philosophical tradition. Antisthenes' famous division (cf. n. 9) is quoted expressly by some of the Latin Christian Fathers before St. Augustine; see Minucius Felix, *Oct.* 19, 8, and Lact. *Inst. div.* i. 5, epit. 4. Other Christian authors refer to Antisthenes' theology of the one invisible and shapeless God without mentioning the dichotomy; cf. E. Zeller, *Philosophie der Griechen*, ῐῐ. Teil, 1. Abt., 5. Aufl., p. 329, n. 1. Since Minucius Felix in his *Octavius* and Lactantius in the first book of his *Institutiones divinae* likewise used Varro's *Antiquitates rerum divinarum* as a source (cf. R. Agahd, op. cit. in n. 2, pp. 40 ff.), it appears that all three took Antisthenes' dichotomy from Varro; for he probably mentioned it in the first book of his *Antiquitates* in connexion with the trichotomy which he preferred to it, because he wished to safeguard the independent validity of the gods of the Roman state. In order to reconcile both divisions, St. Augustine tried to subordinate Varro's three *genera theologiae* to Antisthenes' bifurcate scheme by reducing the *genus mythicon* to the *genus civile*; cf. *Civ. Dei* vi, ch. vii: 'revocatur igitur ad theologian civilem theologia fabulosa theatrica scaenica.' Dramatic poetry was recited at the festivals of the gods of the State. Augustine adds the words *theatrica scaenica* to *fabulosa* in order to connect mythical theology with the State.

11. Aug. *Civ. Dei* vi, ch. v, cites *genus physicon* and *genus mythicon* several times directly from the text of Varro. But he says (p. 252, 23, Dombart): 'secundum autem (genus) ut naturale dicatur, iam et consuetudo locutionis admittit.' One may conclude from these words that the latinized term *theologia naturalis* must have been introduced before Augustine's time by some other Latin philosopher. It was probably he who directed St. Augustine's attention to Varro's theology (Marius Victorinus?).

12. On the following see my *Humanism and Theology* (The Aquinas Lecture 1943, Marquette University Press, Milwaukee), pp. 46 ff.

13. Plat. *Rep.* ii. 379 a : οἱ τύποι περὶ θεολογίας τίνες ἂν εἶεν; Plato himself explains the new word θεολογία: οἷος τυγχάνει ὁ θεὸς ὢν ἀεὶ δήπου ἀποδοτέον. The coining of the word indicates the importance from Plato's point of view of the mental attitude which it tries to express. Theology is in a way the very aim and centre of his thought. In his last work, the *Laws*, we find a complete system of theology when in book x Plato sets forth the importance of the soul for a theological view of reality. In the *Timaeus* he approaches the problem of the Divine from the point of view of nature and cosmogony; the Divine there appears as the demiurge. On these two ways of approach as sources of Plato's theology, cf. the most recent monograph on the subject, *Plato's Theology*, by Friedrich Solmsen (Ithaca, 1942). But although the *Timaeus* and the *Laws* are the most explicit discussions of God and the gods in Plato's dialogues, there are other treatments of the problem in Plato's moral philosophy. I should like to deal with them more in detail in a sequel to this volume, discussing the theology of Plato and Aristotle. In the meantime I refer to my outline in *Paideia*, ii, p. 285. There I have tried to show that the main and most original approach to the problem of God which we find in Plato's philosophy is what may be called the paideutic approach—God as the measurement of measurements.

14. See Bonitz's *Index Aristotelicus*, p. 324ᵇ53 ff., s.v. θεολογεῖν, θεολογία, θεολογική, θεολόγος.

15. It is probable, if not certain, that the development of this group of words as we find it in Aristotle's works had started in the Platonic school, as did most of his terminology, since his interest in the theological problem derived from his Platonic phase.

16. Cf. Arist. *Metaph.* E 1, 1026ᵃ19 and the parallel passage K 7, 1064ᵇ3 in the doublet of books ΒΓΕ which we have in our text of the *Metaphysics* in K 1–8.

17. Arist. *Metaph.* B 4, 1000ᵃ9: οἱ . . . περὶ Ἡσίοδον καὶ πάντες ὅσοι θεολόγοι μόνον ἐφρόντισαν τοῦ πιθανοῦ τοῦ πρὸς αὑτούς (they are contrasted with scientific thought); Λ 6, 1071ᵇ27: οἱ θεολόγοι οἱ ἐκ νυκτὸς γεννῶντες (Pherecydes), as opposed to οἱ φυσικοί; N 4, 1091ᵃ34 speaks of οἱ θεολόγοι who did not place the most perfect stage at the beginning of the world and compares them with τῶν νῦν τινες (Speusippus); A 3, 983ᵇ28: τοὺς παμπαλαίους καὶ πολὺ πρὸ τῆς νῦν γενέσεως καὶ πρώτους θεολογήσαντας (Homer and Hesiod, cf. 30). They are contrasted with Thales and Ionian natural philosophy. *Meteorol.* ii. 1, 353ᵃ35: οἱ ἀρχαῖοι καὶ διατρίβοντες περὶ τὰς θεολογίας.

18. See my *Aristotle*, p. 128.

19. Arist. *Metaph.* Λ 8, 1074ᵇ1: παραδέδοται δὲ παρὰ τῶν ἀρχαίων καὶ παμπαλαίων ἐν μύθου σχήματι καταλελειμμένα τοῖς ὕστερον ὅτι θεοί τ' εἰσιν οὗτοι καὶ περιέχει τὸ θεῖον τὴν ὅλην φύσιν. τὰ δὲ λοιπὰ μυθικῶς ἤδη προσῆκται πρὸς τὴν πειθὼ τῶν πολλῶν καὶ πρὸς τὴν εἰς τοὺς νόμους καὶ τὸ συμφέρον χρῆσιν. ἀνθρωποειδεῖς τε γὰρ τούτους καὶ τῶν ἄλλων ζῴων ὁμοίους τινὲς λέγουσιν.... The same words, οἱ ἀρχαῖοι καὶ παμπάλαιοι, are used by Aristotle with regard to the mythical theologies of Homer, Hesiod, Pherecydes, and others, in the passages collected in n. 17.

20. Edward Caird, *The Evolution of Theology in the Greek Philosophers* (2 vv., Glasgow, 1904).

21. Paul Elmer More, *The Religion of Plato* (Princeton, 1921).

22. Cf. n. 13.

23. Of the earlier literature on this subject, the posthumous book by Otto Gilbert, *Griechische Religionsphilosophie* (Leipzig, 1911), ought to be mentioned. The title is somewhat misleading, since it suggests a book concerned

with the ideas of the Greek philosophers on the nature of religion as a general phenomenon. Actually it deals with physics and ethics and includes their development up to the Hellenistic period. It discusses at length the meteorological views of individual thinkers in the pre-Socratic period. Clifford Herschel Moore's *The Religious Thought of the Greeks* (Cambridge, 1925) is of wider scope than the present book, as the word 'religious' implies. The poets are in the foreground, and the philosophy of the pre-Socratics is excluded, with the exception of Pythagoras, who is treated along with Orphism and the Mysteries. Moore apparently considers the other pre-Socratics as mere physicists, in Burnet's sense, who deserve no place in his scheme. A different and more appreciative attitude towards the pre-Socratics is to be found in a more recent monograph by R. K. Hack, *God in Greek Philosophy to the Time of Socrates* (Princeton, 1931). Étienne Gilson, *God and Philosophy* (New Haven, 1941), does not deal with the pre-Socratic philosophers explicitly, though the author recognizes their importance for his subject.

24. In O. Gilbert's book (see n. 23) the physical views of the pre-Socratics are taken into account throughout, but they tend to overshadow the religious aspect rather than put it into a clearer light.

25. Theodor Gomperz, *Greek Thinkers* (v. i, London, 1906), and John Burnet, *Early Greek Philosophy* (4th ed., London, 1930), are the most characteristic representatives of this type. The unilateral emphasis on the physical side of pre-Socratic philosophy in their works is a product of 19th-century scientism and its horror of everything metaphysical. Eduard Zeller, who belonged to the older German school and who was in reality the founder of 19th-century history of philosophy, was originally inspired by Hegel's thought, which was largely based on a philosophical interpretation of the history of ideas. Consequently, in spite of his increasing interest in the scientific element of pre-Socratic speculation, Zeller was much more aware of its metaphysical implications than his modern successors, even though in his first volume on the pre-Socratics he did not escape Hegel's dialectic construction of intellectual progress.

26. U. v. Wilamowitz-Moellendorff, *Der Glaube der Hellenen*, ii, pp. 207–12 and 243–58.

27. See Arist. *Metaph*. A 3, 983ᵇ27. He is probably referring to Plat. *Theaet*. 181 b. For other Platonic passages see W. D. Ross, *Aristotle's Metaphysics*, i, p. 130.

28. οἱ πρῶτοι θεολογήσαντες (Homer and Hesiod) are contrasted with ἡ νῦν γένεσις, *Metaph*. A 3, 983ᵇ28. οἱ πρῶτοι φιλοσοφήσαντες (Thales, &c.), *Metaph*. A 2, 982ᵇ11 and A 3, 983ᵇ6, are also contrasted with the philosophy of Aristotle's own age. The present philosophy can obviously be compared with both the πρῶτοι θεολογήσαντες and the πρῶτοι φιλοσοφήσαντες: it is the continuation of both.

29. Arist. *Metaph*. B 4, 1000ᵃ4 and 18. The words μυθικῶς σοφίζεσθαι refer to what Aristotle had said before about the type of Hesiod's theological thought.

30. See n. 28.

31. *Iliad* xiv. 201 and 302, 246. See n. 19, the words ἐν μύθου σχήματι and μυθικῶς προσῆκται πρὸς τὴν πειθὼ τῶν πολλῶν.

32. The story of Oceanus and Tethys told in *Iliad* xiv. 201 ff. shows the same keen interest in the genealogical background of the Olympian gods which we find in Hesiod's *Theogony* and later epic poems of the theogonic type. Wilamowitz, *Die Ilias und Homer*, p. 317, says that the poet of *Iliad* xiv had lost the

naïve attitude towards the old myths. The spirit of Ionian 'science' is already at work in him, and he is susceptible to theological speculation. In a similar case, with regard to the catalogue of the Nereids in *Iliad* xviii. 39 ff., Zenodotus (schol. Ven. A) speaks of the 'Hesiodic character' of the lines (cf. Hes. *Theog.* 243 ff.). Another Alexandrian critic, Callistratus, states that in the Argolic manuscript of the *Iliad* these lines did not exist at all.

33. Hes. *Theog.* 27.

34. See *Paideia*, i², p. 75.

35. Hes. *Theog.* 33 calls it, briefly, μακάρων γένος αἰὲν ἐόντων; but see the more detailed announcement of the contents of the *Theogony* in 105 ff., if these lines really belong to Hesiod and are not due to later rhapsodic expansion of his poem.

36. The very phrase in which Hesiod summarizes his epic, μακάρων γένος αἰὲν ἐόντων (*Theog.* 33), seems to be self-contradictory from the point of view of modern logic. But αἰὲν ἐόντες means 'lasting' and therefore 'deathless', not 'eternal' in the strict philosophical sense.

37. Cf. the constant reiteration of words like τέκε, γείνατο, ἐξεγένοντο, in Hesiod's *Theogony*.

38. The genealogies of heroes and heroines in epic or prose form of which we hear or possess fragments in later ancient authors, seem to have derived from the genealogical treatment of the gods. Most of them were therefore attributed to Hesiod, so far as they were in epic form. The present form of the text of Hesiod's *Theogony*, which obviously was expanded by later additions of the rhapsodes who recited it, shows at the end of the poem a gradual transition into the genealogy of the heroes.

39. See *Paideia*, i², pp. 65 ff.

40. It is most of all this consistent theological approach to the actual problems of life and thought which guarantees the unity of authorship for both the *Theogony* and the *Works and Days*. Cf. *Paideia*, i², p. 67.

41. I do not doubt that the famous lines (*Works and Days*, 11 f.), οὐκ ἄρα μοῦνον ἔην Ἐρίδων γένος, ἀλλ' ἐπὶ γαῖαν εἰσὶ δύω, with which Hesiod begins his admonition to Perses are, as has often been stated, an express reference to his own *Theog.* 226, where he had mentioned only one Eris. It is characteristic of Hesiod's mind that he begins with just such a subtle theological matter. It is obviously profoundly important to him and settles the entire problem of labour and evil in human life.

42. Rebels are the sons of Iapetos and Klymene, *Theog.* 507 ff. See the theological conclusion drawn from the catalogue of the several punishments of Menoitios, Atlas, and Prometheus at the end of the story, ibid. 613. Also, the exile of Kronos and the Titans in the underworld is understood by Hesiod in moral and theological terms.

43. Hes. *Theog.* 116.

44. Arist. *Phys.* iv. 1, 208ᵇ31.

45. Hes. *Theog.* 700.

46. Ibid. 116: ἦ τοι μὲν πρώτιστα Χάος γένετ', αὐτὰρ ἔπειτα Γαῖ' εὐρύστερνος, πάντων ἕδος ἀσφαλὲς αἰεί. . . .

47. Cf. Arist. *Metaph.* A 3, 984ᵇ23; A 8, 989ᵃ10; B 4, 1000ᵃ9.

48. Hes. *Theog.* 120.

49. See Plato, *Symp.* 178 b, who briefly surveys the repercussions in early Greek thought and literature of Hesiod's idea that Eros was one of the oldest deities.

50. Hesiod's relationship to the older mythical tradition resembles that of the Christian theologians to the tradition of the Bible. Although he applies his reason to the interpretation or reconstruction of the myths, their objective authority remains unshaken as the starting-point of his thought. Aristotle and even Plato seem not to have understood this when they used a phrase like ἐν μύθου σχήματι as almost equivalent with what we should call subjective and arbitrary. Arist. *Metaph.* B 4, 1000ᵃ9, says that Hesiod and all the other θεολόγοι have thought only of how to satisfy themselves (μόνον ἐφρόντισαν τοῦ πιθανοῦ τοῦ πρὸς αὑτούς), apparently referring to the mythical form of their thought in general.

CHAPTER II

THE THEOLOGY OF THE MILESIAN NATURALISTS

1. The oriental origin of some of Hesiod's religious ideas is postulated by R. Reitzenstein in Reitzenstein–Schaeder, *Studien zum antiken Synkretismus. Aus Iran und Griechenland* (Leipzig, 1926), p. 55 f. See also Ed. Meyer, *Ursprung und Anfänge des Christentums* (Stuttgart, 1921), Bd. ii, p. 190.

2. In the juridical language of the Attic orators τὰ ὄντα often occurs in the sense of a man's property, as an equivalent of the noun οὐσία, in phrases like τῶν ὄντων ἐκβάλλειν or ἐκπίπτειν τῶν ὄντων. In the broader sense of all that 'exists' the word must have been used from the very beginning of Greek natural philosophy. It meant then, speaking from the Platonic point of view, that which our senses perceive in the world without. Plato therefore found it necessary to differentiate the being of the invisible world of *noumena* from the ὄντα in this pre-Socratic sense and called it τὸ ὄντως ὄν. We find τὸ ἐόν and τὰ ἐόντα in the earliest pre-Socratic philosopher of whom we possess coherent fragments, Parmenides of Elea, and this may lead to the misunderstanding that τὰ ὄντα was from the beginning a metaphysical term; for some of the interpreters have given the word in Parmenides a meaning similar to that which it has in Plato: a 'being' of purely intelligible character. But Heraclitus, Melissus, and Empedocles used τὰ ὄντα in the sense of all natural existence, and it is more than probable that in doing so they were only following the example of their Milesian predecessors. Parmenides obviously took the word from them and analysed its logical implications with a view to revolutionizing the naïve, sensual concept of existence as adopted by the Milesians. The term τὰ ὄντα in the so-called fragment of Anaximander, where it means all existing individual things, in all probability reflects the true language of this early thinker. He and the other Ionian philosophers of nature simply followed Homer and the usage of epic language. Homer and Hesiod speak of τὰ ἐόντα as that which exists at present and contrast it with τὰ ἐσσόμενα and τὰ πρὸ ἐόντα, things as they will be in the future and as they were in the past. This very opposition proves that the word originally pointed to the immediate and tangible presence of things. Homer's ἐόντα did not exist in the past and will not exist in the future. They did not yet exclude γένεσις and φθορά, as Parmenides taught they did. In this regard the oldest thinkers were quite Homeric.

3. Thucydides i. 21 calls the tradition of the ancient poets and logographers incapable of disproof and for the most part changed by time into the fabulous

(τὰ πολλὰ ὑπὸ χρόνου αὐτῶν ἐπὶ τὸ μυθῶδες ἐκνενικηκότα. The words are really untranslatable). Plat. *Rep.* 522 a uses μυθώδεις λόγοι as opposed to ἀληθινοί and speaks of μυθικός τις ὕμνος, *Phaedr.* 265 c. Thucydides, loc. cit., derives the exaggerating tendency of poetical tradition from its hymnodic character. Arist. *Metaph.* B 4, 1000ᵃ18, Λ 8, 1074ᵇ3, *De caelo* ii. 1, 284ᵃ23 uses μυθικός in the same negative sense. But even if this adjective belongs only to the Attic period of the Greek language and did not exist at the time of Thales and Anaximander, the critical attitude towards the myth which it reveals originated much earlier, as is proved by Xenophanes, who calls the stories about Titans and Giants 'fictions of the ancients' (πλάσματα τῶν προτέρων). Solon, a contemporary of the Milesian thinkers, coined the phrase quoted by Aristotle, πολλὰ ψεύδονται ἀοιδοί, and even before them Hesiod had acknowledged that much of what the Muses inspired the poet to sing was ψεύδεα.

4. Arist. *Metaph.* Γ 3, 1005ᵃ31 speaks of the earlier philosophers as οἱ φυσικοί and defines the object of their speculation as περὶ τῆς ὅλης φύσεως σκοπεῖν καὶ περὶ τοῦ ὄντος.

5. *Iliad* xiv. 246 Ὠκεανοῦ, ὅς περ γένεσις πάντεσσι τέτυκται. Instead of using the dative construction (γένεσις for all), we might call him πάντων γένεσις, as he is called θεῶν γένεσις in xiv. 201. Burnet, *Early Greek Philosophy*, 4th ed. (London, 1930), pp. 11 ff., goes too far in trying to prove that φύσις had nothing to do with the origin of things and meant from the beginning only the primary substance. In the development of philosophical language it certainly came more and more to signify the persistent and fundamental reality out of which (ἐξ οὗ) everything has grown, but the process of growth which includes the beginning is likewise implied in it. The termination -σις leaves no doubt about that, and the equation of φύσις and γένεσις stated explicitly by Plato in *Laws* 892 c confirms it. No one could seriously maintain that γένεσις meant primarily that out of which a thing was made (τὸ ἐξ οὗ) and only secondarily or not at all the act by which it became. The same is true with regard to φύσις, and, as a matter of fact, all the φυσικοί were interested in cosmogony. This interest in what πρώτιστα ἐγένετο is as old as mankind itself and occurs in Greek literature as early as the beginning of Hesiod's *Theogony*. The conviction of the first natural philosophers that that out of which everything had come to be had no beginning itself did not diminish in the least their interest in the problem of the beginning of the world. See the following instances of φύσις = origin, process of growth: Emp. B 8, 1, φύσις οὐδενὸς ἔστιν ἁπάντων θνητῶν, οὐδέ . . . τελευτή (where φύσις = γένεσις, τελευτή = φθορά); Arist. *Phys.* ii. 1, 193ᵇ12, ἡ φύσις ἡ λεγομένη ὡς γένεσις ὁδός ἐστιν εἰς φύσιν. In the latter sentence we have both meanings clearly distinguished: (1) φύσις = origin, growth, and (2) φύσις = nature of a thing.

6. See Arist. *Metaph.* A 3, 983ᵇ18 (Thales, A 12). From this source the other ancient testimonia are derived.

7. Plat. *Laws* 899 b; see Arist. *De anima* i. 5, 411ᵃ7 (Thales A 22).

8. Plat. *Laws* 967 a. See also Aëtius i. 7, 11 (Diels's *Doxographi*, p. 301).

9. *Epinomis* 991 d. On the connexion of the stellar religion of Hellenistic philosophers with the astronomy of their time see my *Aristotle*, p. 138.

10. Arist. *De anima* i. 2, 405ᵃ19 (Thales A 22) mentions a (probably oral) tradition which credited Thales with the theory that the magnet had a soul because it attracted iron. Aristotle therefore places Thales in the class of those thinkers who thought the soul to be first and foremost a principle of motion—a somewhat too bold generalization. From the famous sentence that 'everything is

full of gods', Aristotle, in another passage of the *De anima* (i. 5, 411ᵃ7, Thales A 22), explicitly derives the view that Thales thought the whole universe animated. Thus Aristotle seems to try to combine that apophthegm with the tradition of Thales' theory of the magnet in order to prove his interpretation that Thales thought the whole world to be animated, even its inorganic part. Modern historians of philosophy have mostly accepted Aristotle's theory as dogma and built their reconstruction of Thales' philosophy on this basis. Even the later ancient authors who followed the lost *Φυσικῶν δόξαι* of Aristotle's pupil Theophrastus speak in rather dogmatic terms of the soul of the world which Thales assumed and interpret it as the spirit of the world (*νοῦς τοῦ κόσμου*, Aëtius; *mentem*, Cicero; see Thales A 23) in the manner of contemporary Stoicism. This 'spirit' they predicate as God. But obviously all this is mere conjecture, and we know nothing about Thales' concept of God. We have only the one sentence which Aristotle took as his point of departure: 'everything is full of gods'. Plato quotes it without mentioning Thales (see n. 7), whereas Aristotle ascribes it to him. In reality it matters very little whether Thales coined the epigram or not: the spirit of the early Greek philosophy of nature finds its genuine expression in these words. See J. Burnet, op. cit., p. 50.

11. Arist. *De part. anim.* i. 5, 645ᵃ17 (Heraclitus, A 9).

12. Burnet, op. cit., p. 50, n. 2, thinks the anecdote a mere variant of Thales' apophthegm. There did, indeed, exist a variant according to which Heraclitus and not Thales said that everything is full of gods (see Diog. L. ix. 7: [Heraclitus said] *πάντα ψυχῶν εἶναι καὶ δαιμόνων πλήρη*). But the story told by Aristotle refers rather to Thales' well-known phrase and wittily applies it to the present situation.

13. Aëtius, *Plac.* i. 3, 3 (Diels, *Doxographi*, p. 277, Anaximander A 14); Simpl. *De caelo* 615, 13 (Anaximander A 17).

14. Burnet, op. cit., pp. 54 ff. Cf. Rodolfo Mondolfo, *L'Infinito nel Pensiero dei Greci* (Florence, 1934). In his article 'L'Infinità divina nelle teogonie greche presocratiche' (*Studi e Materiali di Storia delle Religioni*, ix, 1933, pp. 72 ff.) the same author has tried to trace the idea of infinity in the post-Hesiodic theogonies which are an important witness for it. I do not discuss them at this point, but I have devoted a separate chapter to them because I am convinced that the picture of the historical development of the earliest natural philosophy has been increasingly confused in the last generation by the unwarranted assumption that all theogonic thought is pre-philosophical, even in the chronological sense. The wholesome deflation which our ideas of the Orphic religion of early Greece have lately undergone offers one more reason for caution in interpreting the beginning of purely rational thought in Ionia against a hypothetical background of Orphic speculation.

15. Simpl. *Phys.* 24, 13 (Anaximander A 9): *τῶν δὲ ἓν καὶ κινούμενον καὶ ἄπειρον λεγόντων Ἀναξίμανδρος μὲν Πραξιάδου Μιλήσιος Θαλοῦ γενόμενος διάδοχος καὶ μαθητὴς ἀρχήν τε καὶ στοιχεῖον εἴρηκε τῶν ὄντων τὸ ἄπειρον, πρῶτος τοῦτο τοὔνομα κομίσας τῆς ἀρχῆς.* Cf. Hipp. *Ref.* i. 6, 1–7 (Diels, *Doxographi*, p. 559, Anaximander A 11): *Θαλοῦ τοίνυν Ἀναξίμανδρος γίνεται ἀκροατής. Ἀναξίμανδρος Πραξιάδου Μιλήσιος·. . . οὗτος μὲν οὖν ἀρχὴν καὶ στοιχεῖον εἴρηκε τῶν ὄντων τὸ ἄπειρον, πρῶτος τοὔνομα καλέσας τῆς ἀρχῆς.* I have quoted the passage from Hippolytus along with that in Simplicius because it will be of some importance for the discussion of Simplicius' text.

16. Arist. *Phys.* iii. 4, 203ᵇ6 (Anaximander A 15): *ἅπαντα γὰρ ἢ ἀρχὴ ἢ ἐξ ἀρχῆς,*

τοῦ δὲ ἀπείρου οὐκ ἔστιν ἀρχή· εἴη γὰρ ἂν αὐτοῦ πέρας. ἔτι δὲ καὶ ἀγένητον καὶ
ἄφθαρτον ὡς ἀρχή τις οὖσα· τό τε γὰρ γενόμενον ἀνάγκη τέλος λαβεῖν, καὶ τελευτὴ
πάσης ἐστὶ φθορᾶς. διὸ καθάπερ λέγομεν, οὐ ταύτης ἀρχή, ἀλλ' αὕτη τῶν ἄλλων
εἶναι δοκεῖ καὶ περιέχειν ἅπαντα καὶ πάντα κυβερνᾶν, ὥς φασιν ὅσοι μὴ ποιοῦσι παρὰ
τὸ ἄπειρον ἄλλας αἰτίας οἷον νοῦν ἢ φιλίαν. καὶ τοῦτ' εἶναι τὸ θεῖον· ἀθάνατον γὰρ
καὶ ἀνώλεθρον, ὥς φησιν ὁ Ἀναξίμανδρος καὶ οἱ πλεῖστοι τῶν φυσιολόγων.

17. It is evident even from Aristotle's own words that the part of the passage
quoted above, n. 16 (*Phys.* iii. 4, 203^{b}6), cannot be a mere reflection by Aristotle
himself but must contain the very argument of the philosophers who assume
the *apeiron.* ' For at 203^{b}15, after referring to Anaximander, Aristotle goes on :
τοῦ δ' εἶναί τι ἄπειρον ἡ πίστις ἐκ πέντε μάλιστ' ἂν συμβαίνοι σκοποῦσιν; then he
enumerates these five reasons. Obviously they are not of purely Aristotelian
origin either, but at the same time they summarize Aristotle's own point of
view and thereby are different from the preceding argument, which Aristotle
expressly ascribes to 'Anaximander and most of the natural philosophers'.
See Harold Cherniss, *Aristotle's Criticism of Presocratic Philosophy*, p. 20.

18. In *Metaph.* A 4, 985^{a}18 and 29, after those thinkers who assumed only one
(material) principle, Aristotle names Anaxagoras and Empedocles as the
representatives of a second cause (ὅθεν ἡ κίνησις), because Anaxagoras introduced the νοῦς and Empedocles φιλία and νεῖκος. He here refers (985^{a}12)
explicitly to his *Physics.*

19. Arist. *Phys.* iii. 4, 203^{b}13 lists the predicates ἀθάνατον καὶ ἀνώλεθρον—these
words are spaced in Diels's *Vorsokratiker* as belonging to the quotation from
Anaximander—and preceding them, ἀγένητον καὶ ἄφθαρτον and περιέχειν ἅπαντα
καὶ πάντα κυβερνᾶν.

20. See the quotation in n. 16 (*Phys.* iii. 4, 203^{b}6, ἅπαντα γὰρ . . . πέρας).

21. See n. 15.

22. Simpl. *Phys.* 23, 31; cf. 25, 6; 27, 11 and 154, 14–23. See the list of all the
passages in which Theophrastus' Φυσικῶν δόξαι is explicitly quoted by Simplicius in his commentary on Aristotle's *Physics*, vol. ii, p. 1447 (ed. Diels).
Cf. the collection of the fragments by Diels in *Doxographi Graeci*, pp. 475 ff.,
for his reconstruction of Theophrastus' lost work.

23. See the two passages in n. 15.

24. Simpl. *Phys.* 7, 13: καὶ στοιχεῖα πρῶτος αὐτὸς [Plato] ὠνόμασε τὰς τοιαύτας
ἀρχάς, ὡς ὁ Εὔδημος ἱστορεῖ. This fragment, which is not listed in Spengel's
collection of the fragments of Eudemus (cf. Diels's edition of Simpl. *Phys.*,
p. 1445), seems to belong not to Eudemus' *Physics*, the work most quoted by
Simplicius, but to the Γεωμετρικὴ ἱστορία, which is quoted only on pp. 60, 22
and 31 (cf. 55, 23). Simplicius does not refer to Eudemus' *Physics* with
ἱστορεῖ. From Simpl. 7, 13–17 we infer that Eudemus first listed systematically inventions like that of the concept στοιχεῖον. In this passage it is also
stated that Plato was the first to distinguish elementary principles, which he
called elements, from *causa efficiens, causa finalis*, and *causa exemplaris*, the
ideas, whereas Aristotle later invented the concepts of matter and form. The
quotation from Eudemus is followed (p. 55, 23–7) by the statement that
Hippocrates of Chios invented the quadrature of the circle through *lunulae.*
Proclus, *In Eucl.* 352, 14, records that Eudemus in his *History of Geometry*
traced back a certain mathematical proposition to Thales. Apparently this
ἀνάγειν was characteristic of Peripatetic method in dealing with the history of
philosophy and science.

25. Burnet, op. cit., p. 57, n. 1. See the text of the passage from Simplicius above, n. 15.

26. A glimpse at Kranz's Index to Diels's *Vorsokratiker*, s.v. ἀρχή, especially the section ἀρχή = *Prinzip*, is very instructive. Most of the passages are so-called A-passages, i.e. taken from doxographic sources. Only a few seem to prove that ἀρχή occurs in this sense in B-passages also, i.e. direct fragments. But in the passage taken from Empedocles the term ἀρχή does not belong to the text of the fragment but rather to the words of the late author who quotes it. Diels wrongly spaces the word as if it were Empedoclean. The passages taken from Philolaus do not prove anything, since the book that exists under his name is as apocryphal as the rest of the 'Pythagorean' literature. It is a late product and belongs after Aristotle.

27. See Burnet, op. cit., p. 54, n. 2. I repeat here the text of Theophrastus in both forms. Simpl. *Phys.* 24, 13: Ἀναξίμανδρος . . . ἀρχήν τε καὶ στοιχεῖον εἴρηκε τῶν ὄντων τὸ ἄπειρον, πρῶτος τοῦτο τοὔνομα κομίσας τῆς ἀρχῆς. Hipp. *Ref.* i. 6, 1–7: οὗτος μὲν οὖν [Anaximander] ἀρχὴν καὶ στοιχεῖον εἴρηκε τῶν ὄντων τὸ ἄπειρον, πρῶτος τοὔνομα καλέσας τῆς ἀρχῆς. Burnet construes Simplicius' words as meaning: 'Anaximander said that the *apeiron* is the *arché* and element of all things, being the first to use this name (*scil. apeiron*) for the *arché*.' But should we not expect in this case πρῶτος τοῦτο τοὔνομα καλέσας τὴν ἀρχήν? The κομίσας of Simplicius seems to make it clear that it must mean: 'he was the first to *introduce* this name of *arché*,' referring thereby to the preceding words ἀρχὴν καὶ στοιχεῖον εἴρηκε τῶν ὄντων τὸ ἄπειρον. One might object and ask why he makes this statement of priority only with regard to ἀρχή and not to στοιχεῖον. But Simplicius had already made a similar statement about στοιχεῖον, *Phys.* 7, 13 (see n. 24), saying that that concept was introduced by Plato; so the reader does not expect it to be repeated here, where we are interested only in what Anaximander said. The word emphasized is ἀρχή; the words καὶ στοιχεῖον were added by Theophrastus only in order to make clear that in this context the principle is to be understood as the material cause. Hippolytus omits τοῦτο, though it may belong to the true text of Theophrastus. By doing so and by replacing κομίσας by καλέσας, Hippolytus wanted to exclude any interpretation other than this: 'Anaximander was the first to use the term *arché*.' In this he was quite correct; see n. 28.

28. Simpl. *Phys.* 150, 23, πρῶτος αὐτὸς [*scil.* Anaximander] ἀρχὴν ὀνομάσας τὸ ὑποκείμενον. τὸ ὑποκείμενον here is the Peripatetic word for the *apeiron*, which Aristotle elsewhere also calls ὕλη in his own terminology. The words unmistakably mean: 'he gave it the name ἀρχή', and so they were correctly understood by Usener and Diels. They are almost literally the same as those in Simpl. 7, 13 about Plato: στοιχεῖα πρῶτος αὐτὸς ὠνόμασε τὰς τοιαύτας ἀρχάς. Thus we cannot translate them as Burnet does: 'Anaximander named the substratum as the material cause.' The sense of ὀνομάζειν is in both passages simply 'give the name of'.

29. See n. 24.

30. See n. 16.

31. Melissus B 4: ἀρχήν τε καὶ τέλος ἔχον οὐδὲν οὔτε ἀίδιον οὔτε ἄπειρόν ἐστιν.

32. Melissus B 2.

33. See n. 16.

34. Anaximander A 9.

35. Diog. L. i. 36 (Thales A 1).

36. Anaximander A 15. See n. 16.

37. Arist. *Phys.* iii. 7, 207^{b}35–208^{a}4.

38. Ibid. 4, 203^{b}11 ; see n. 15.

39. Besides the passage ibid. 4, 203^{b}11 (Anaximander A 15), καὶ περιέχειν ἅπαντα καὶ πάντα κυβερνᾶν, the word περιέχειν is apparently quoted from Anaximander by Theophrastus, Hipp. *Ref.* i. 6, 1 (Anaximander A 11), ταύτην δ' ἀΐδιον εἶναι [scil. τὴν ἀρχήν] καὶ ἀγήρω ἦν καὶ πάντας περιέχειν τοὺς κόσμους. The words ἀΐδιος καὶ ἀγήρως have the genuine colour of the original, and so has the word περιέχειν. This word occurs again in the only preserved fragment of Anaximenes (Aët. i. 3, 4, Anaximenes B 2). It is applied to the highest principle, the air which rules the world. It may very well be authentic in the report on Empedocles (Aët. ii. 11, 2), where it is used of the οὐρανός and the σφαῖρος, and in similar passages about Heraclitus and others (see Kranz's Index to Diels's *Vorsokratiker*, s.v. περιέχειν). It occurs twice in Anaxagoras, frg. B 2 (Simpl. *Phys.* 155, 30) and B 14 (Simpl. 157, 5), and in a manner which reminds one of Anaximander: τὸ περιέχον and τὰ ἀποκεκριμένα are opposed to each other, and the περιέχον is called ἄπειρον τὸ πλῆθος. There the νοῦς is active both in the περιέχον and its secretions. Ps.Philolaus uses the word with regard to the world-soul, which in his view takes the role of the ruling principle. This is of course an imitation of the genuine pre-Socratic philosophy, and the same holds for frg. B 18 of Critias, who speaks of the πόλος as τὸ περιέχον ἅπαν in language that closely resembles that of some earlier thinkers. κυβερνᾶν is used with regard to the activity of the highest principle in the fragments of Heraclitus, Parmenides, Diogenes (see Kranz's Index, s.v.), and in our passage on Anaximander, where it seems to occur in this sense for the first time. It is also to be found in imitations of pre-Socratic philosophical language in Ps.Philolaus and 'Hippocrates'; in both these authors it refers to the divine principle of the cosmos.

40. Plat. *Phil.* 28 c says that all the σοφοί agree (συμφωνοῦσιν) that νοῦς is the king of heaven and earth. This is of course somewhat generalized, since not all thinkers believed that νοῦς was the highest principle. It seems to fit philosophers like Anaxagoras and Diogenes best. But the solemn words βασιλεύς, τὰ σύμπαντα διακυβερνᾶν (28 d), and πάντα διακοσμεῖν (28 e) are common in pre-Socratic language, regardless of the special nature of the highest principle.

41. See K. Deichgraeber, 'Hymnische Elemente in der philosophischen Prosa der Vorsokratiker' in *Philologus*, lxxxviii, 1933, p. 347.

42. Aristotle is himself fully aware of the special character of that language and its importance for the understanding of philosophical meaning. In *Phys.* iii. 6, 207^{a}18 f., he speaks of the solemnity (σεμνότης) which the representatives of the *apeiron* assume in their predications about it: ἐντεῦθεν λαμβάνουσι τὴν σεμνότητα κατὰ τοῦ ἀπείρου. He refers especially to the predication of the *apeiron* as τὸ πάντα περιέχον. He says that they transfer that category from the ὅλον, to which it actually belongs, to the *apeiron*, because in their speculation it takes the place of the ὅλον. According to this interpretation, they understand by *apeiron* something outside which nothing exists (οὗ μηδέν ἐστιν ἔξω) and for this reason give it the place of what later philosophy called 'the whole'.

43. Plat. *Phil.* 28 d says that early thinkers taught that the highest principle τὰ ξύμπαντα . . . διακυβερνᾷ (cf. 28 e, πάντα διακοσμεῖν). He characterizes

ξύμπαντα as a stereotyped element of their solemn theological language and interprets it as meaning τόδε τὸ καλούμενον ὅλον. He thus agrees with Aristotle, who says that they took the *apeiron* for the ὅλον (= τὸ πάντα περιέχον). See n. 42.

44. (A) The word τὸ θεῖον. There is no doubt that the word τὸ θεῖον occurred in the philosophical language of pre-Socratic thinkers, even though our fragmentary tradition has preserved but little evidence. In the two quotations from Empedocles (B 133) and Heraclitus (B 86) the word τὸ θεῖον or τὰ θεῖα occurs, but Diels seems to think that it does not belong to the text quoted. However, something like it must have been said in the text, and Kranz in the Index refers to the passages, s.v. θεῖον. Since no direct testimonia are available, the imitation by contemporary authors must serve as a substitute for us. Critias, in the long Sisyphus fragment preserved by Sextus Empiricus ix. 54 (Critias B 25), visualizes his wise man (σοφὸς γνώμην ἀνήρ, v. 12), who invents religion, as a sort of pre-Socratic philosopher. He says of him that he introduced the idea of the Divine (τὸ θεῖον εἰσηγήσατο, v. 16) and equipped it with the predicates of immortal life, the power of seeing and hearing with its mind, and of moving divine nature (φύσιν θείαν φορῶν). All these features are obviously taken from the language of pre-Socratic theology. He says explicitly that these are the statements (λόγοι) which the wise man made about the Divine (v. 24). The rest of his description of the Divinity makes the origin of his picture from the cosmological philosophers and their λόγοι even more evident. It reminds us of Democritus' famous words about the wise men of old (λόγιοι ἄνθρωποι) who raised their hands towards the upper air and said: 'Zeus speaks everything and knows everything and gives and takes away, and he is King of all' (Democr. B 30). Cf. Critias l.c. vv. 27 ff. The bold identification of τὸ θεῖον with ἡ φύσις, which is characteristic of pre-Socratic thought, is to be found also in the medical literature of the Hippocratic age. The author of the book *On the Divine Disease* rejects the old but superstitious idea of the divine character of epilepsy by pointing out that the cause of this disease is as natural as that of any other, and that everything in the nature of our diseases is divine and everything is human. They all start from the same influences: cold, sunshine, changing winds, and weather. These physical factors are the forces which are the cause of all things (Hippocrates, ed. Littré, vi. 394). In this sense it is true μάλιστα τὸ θεῖον ἐν ἀνθρώποισιν αἴτιον εἶναι (*De natura muliebri*, Littré, vii. 312). From passages like this it becomes clear that in using the concept of the Divine, pre-Socratic natural philosophy made a statement about the primary cause, since traditional religious thought traced everything that happened back to the gods (αἰτιᾶσθαι τὸ θεῖον).

(B) καὶ τοῦτ' εἶναι τὸ θεῖον. With these words Anaximander (A 15) proceeds to identify his *apeiron* with τὸ θεῖον. His *modus procedendi* is quite natural. He cannot begin with the concept of God or the Divine, but starts with experience and the rational conclusions based on it. Having arrived in this way at the conception of a first cause, the predicates of which are equal to those which earlier religious belief used to attribute to the gods, he takes the last step, which is the identification of the highest principle with the Divine. This method was followed by ancient philosophers of later centuries. It is only natural that our main evidence should come from later times, since our direct fragments of the works of the pre-Socratics are scarce. But Aristotle's report on Anaximander and the other philosophers who stated the existence of the *apeiron* as the first cause must be authentic in this respect also. The most obvious argument for this is the grammatical form of his sentence, the *oratio obliqua*: καὶ τοῦτ' εἶναι τὸ θεῖον, which gives the derivation of the divine character of the *apeiron* from its very predicates (περιέχειν ἅπαντα καὶ πάντα κυβερνᾶν) as an explicit statement of those thinkers and, so to speak, as their supreme thought.   It follows the *verbum dicendi* ὥς φασιν ὅσοι μὴ ποιοῦσι παρὰ τὸ ἄπειρον ἄλλας αἰτίας οἷον νοῦν ἢ φιλίαν. By this restriction Anaxagoras and Empedocles are eliminated, and only the pure *apeiron*-theorists like Anaximander and Diogenes and Melissus are left. Theirs is also the reason which is added after καὶ τοῦτ' εἶναι τὸ θεῖον: ἀθάνατον γὰρ καὶ ἀνώλεθρον, ὥς φησιν ὁ Ἀναξίμανδρος καὶ οἱ πλεῖστοι τῶν φυσιολόγων. It is very important in the development of the philosophical theology of the earliest Ionian thinkers that we have this statement, which gives us not only the word τὸ θεῖον but also the method by which they arrived at final certainty about what we might think a transcendental problem. What happens in Anaximander's argument (and that of his successors in this line) is that the predicate God, or rather the Divine, is transferred from the traditional deities to the first principle of Being (at which they arrived by rational investigation), on the ground that the predicates usually attributed to the gods of Homer and Hesiod are inherent in that principle to a higher degree or can be assigned to it with greater certainty. This new approach to the question of the Divine was apparently imitated by later philosophers. Since we prefer direct evidence from the fragments to any doxographic testimonium, here are the words of Diogenes of Apollonia (Diog. B 5), quoted by Simplicius, who says that he still had the original work of this thinker and made excerpts from it for his commentary on Aristotle's *Physics* (p. 25, 7, ed. Diels): καί μοι δοκεῖ τὸ τὴν νόησιν ἔχον εἶναι ὁ ἀὴρ καλούμενος ὑπὸ τῶν ἀνθρώπων, καὶ

> ὑπὸ τούτου πάντας καὶ κυβερνᾶσθαι
> καὶ πάντων κρατεῖν.
>
> αὐτὸ γάρ μοι τοῦτο θεὸς δοκεῖ εἶναι
> καὶ ἐπὶ πᾶν ἀφῖχθαι
> καὶ πάντα διατιθέναι
> καὶ ἐν παντὶ ἐνεῖναι·
>
> καὶ ἔστιν οὐδὲ ἕν ὅ τι μὴ μετέχει τούτου.

Diogenes first states as the first cause 'what men call the air' (implying that it is something higher than that of which we think in pronouncing the simple word 'air'); he identifies with the air the thinking principle (τὸ τὴν νόησιν ἔχον) which his teacher Anaxagoras had introduced and called νοῦς. Then Diogenes attributes to this highest cause a series of predicates which resemble those of Anaximander's statement about the *apeiron* both in their stylistic form and in their philosophical intention : they are hymnodic in form ; the first two predications vary the concept of ruling, which is expressed in more than one way (κυβερνᾶσθαι, κρατεῖν, the omnipotence being expressed by the anaphora πάντας-πάντων); then this very principle (αὐτὸ τοῦτο) at which Diogenes has arrived by rational speculation is equated with God, ὁ θεός; the equation is characterized as a subjective act of judgement (δοκεῖ εἶναι), which is added to the rational analysis of nature as a final step. This identification is safeguarded by three (or four) other predications which are aimed at establishing the identity of the air with God by showing the way in which this highest cause rules the world (ἐπὶ πᾶν ἀφῖχθαι, πάντα διατιθέναι, ἐν παντὶ ἐνεῖναι). The last line, after the threefold πάντα, repeats this thought by saying that there is *nothing* which does not participate in it (τούτου, effectively placed at the end, in chiastic form, re-emphasizes the αὐτὸ τοῦτο of the beginning and the ὑπὸ τούτου of the preceding sentence). This example proves Anaximander's influence on the language and method of thought of his successors in the most perfect way ; they illustrate each other. Diogenes has amplified Anaximander's form, if the words of the latter, as reported by Aristotle, are not too poor a reflection of the original.

Now we turn to the later philosophers and trace the same phenomenon in the tradition of post-Socratic philosophy. By that time the language of the philosophers had lost much of the original power of expression which it had possessed during the pre-Socratic period, when even a second-rate mind like Diogenes' aspired to a high level of diction (cf. his statement on style, frg. B 1). The form of argumentation became more stereotyped in the philosophers of later times, but at this stage it still reflected the influence of their predecessors upon them in form and content. Aristotle, in his lost dialogue Περὶ φιλοσοφίας (frg. 23, Rose, Cic. De nat. deor. ii. 15), wanted to prove that the stars have a soul and reason, and he ended his argument with the words 'ex quo efficitur in deorum numero astra esse ducenda'. The same is proved by pointing to the voluntary movement of the stars, frg. 24. A number of similar identifications of θεός with mens = νοῦς, mundus = κόσμος, πρῶτον κινοῦν, caeli ardor = αἰθήρ, caelum = οὐρανός, are quoted by Cicero and Philodemus from Aristotle's Περὶ φιλοσοφίας, book iii (frg. 26, Rose). Aristotle seems to have followed earlier philosophical theologians in all the passages concerning the existence of God which occur in his dialogues. An example which comes especially close to Anaximander's form of expression and argument is preserved by Simplicius in his commentary on Aristotle's De caelo (289, 2, Heiberg): λέγει δὲ περὶ τούτου ἐν τοῖς περὶ φιλοσοφίας· καθόλου γὰρ ἐν οἷς ἐστί τι βέλτιον, ἐν τούτοις ἐστί τι καὶ ἄριστον. ἐπεὶ οὖν ἐστιν ἐν τοῖς οὖσιν ἄλλο ἄλλου βέλτιον, ἔστιν ἄρα τι καὶ ἄριστον, ὅπερ εἴη ἂν τὸ θεῖον (Arist. frg. 16, Rose). Here Aristotle first concluded from the hierarchy of perfection in nature that there must exist a 'most perfect being', and this he identifies with τὸ θεῖον. The teleological argument is his own, but the form in which he puts it is inherited from earlier philosophers, who approached God from their specific principle (Anaximander from the apeiron, Anaximenes and Diogenes from the air, &c.). Sextus Empiricus, Adv. dogm. iii. 20, has preserved Aristotle's explanation of the origin of religion from dream-vision and from the regular movements of celestial bodies. Both arguments begin with the observation of natural phenomena and end with the conclusion εἶναί τι θεῖον or εἶναί τινα θεόν (frg. 10, Rose).

The same form of theological argument was used by the Hellenistic philosophers. The Stoics (frg. ii. 1016, Arnim) are represented by Sextus, Adv. phys. i. 114, as trying to prove that the cosmos has an intelligent nature which is moved by itself in a certain orderly way: νοερὰν ἔχειν φύσιν . . . ἥτις εὐθέως ἐστὶ θεός. The conclusion that the intelligent nature which moves itself in orderly fashion is God seems, from their point of view, to follow εὐθέως. This word also throws light on the pre-Socratics who argued in the same or a similar way. See the same identification made by some of the Stoics in Sextus, Adv. phys. i. 118, where the nature of the cosmos is called κρατίστη, because it is the cause of order (διακόσμησις) in the entire universe. From this it is concluded that it is intelligent (λογική τέ ἐστι καὶ νοερά) and eternal (ἀίδιος), and then the author whom Sextus is quoting adds: ἡ δὲ τοιαύτη φύσις ἡ αὐτή ἐστι θεῷ, 'a nature like this, however, is identical with God'. See also Sextus, op. cit. i. 100, where we find οὗτος δέ ἐστι θεός at the end of a demonstration that the universe is the product of the supreme intelligence of a demiurge. Cleanthes (frg., i, 529, Arnim) argues, quite in the Aristotelian manner (Sextus, op. cit. i. 88 ff.), that there must be a most perfect living being which is higher than man's virtue and wisdom and is not susceptible to failure; then he adds: τοῦτο δὲ οὐ διοίσει θεοῦ (cf. Sextus, op. cit. i. 91). See Sextus, op. cit. i. 76: ἔστι τις ἄρα καθ' ἑαυτὴν αὐτοκίνητος δύναμις, ἥτις ἂν εἴη θεία καὶ ἀίδιος, and at the end of the same paragraph: ἀΐδιος τοίνυν ἐστὶν ἡ κινοῦσα τὴν ὕλην δύναμις . . . ὥστε θεὸς ἂν εἴη αὕτη.

This evidence could be augmented easily by tracing the method of Greek philosophers with regard to the problem of God, but it may be sufficient to follow it through the main periods of Greek thought and show that there is a remarkable continuity of approach, even though the conception of nature itself varies. The physical argument is pre-Socratic in origin, although it is taken over and modified by later philosophers. This explains the similarity of all the arguments which rest on this basis, so far as their logical structure is concerned. The structure of the famous argument *ex consensu omnium gentium* is of an entirely different kind. It takes as its starting-point human nature and psychology, thereby characterizing itself as derived from another philosophical attitude, that of the Sophists. (See pp. 176 ff.)

45. Thales is said by Diog. L. i. 36 and Clem. Alex. *Strom.* v. 14 (ii. 389, 17 ff. St.) to have been asked the question τί τὸ θεῖον; But this late anecdote cannot be used as early evidence for the existence of the word τὸ θεῖον. I have suggested (p. 29) that the apophthegm was coined from what Anaximander had said in his book about the same problem.

46. Herodotus' frequent use of the noun τὸ θεῖον seems to presuppose that in the meantime it had become rather popular. It has no strictly philosophical meaning in the language of Herodotus. On the other hand, it is obvious that it deliberately leaves unsolved the question whether the single gods of the popular religion are realities or whether the historian believes in a more general and impersonal idea of the Divine. Aesch. *Suppl.* 100 speaks of τὸ δαιμόνιον in this sense in a passage which contains rather Xenophanic ideas about the way in which the Divine acts in human life. On this difficult passage see *infra*, p. 212. It has already been said on p. 203 that the Hippocratic medical literature of the fifth century knows the word θεῖον in the philosophical sense as referring to divine nature as a whole. All these are traces of the influence of the early natural philosophers on the thought and language of the classical period.

47. See Erland Ehnmark, *The Idea of God in Homer* (Uppsala, 1935). The author rightly criticizes the view expressed by some scholars that immortality is the only distinctive predicate which can be ascribed with certainty to the Homeric gods.

48. See p. 67. Not only the poets of the post-Hesiodic theogonies but also the earliest philosophers are explicitly credited by our tradition with having criticized the concept of divinity underlying all theogonic speculation: that the gods were born sometime, although their lives are not limited by death. Cf. the criticism by Xenophanes in Arist. *Rhet.* ii. 23, 1399[b]6: οἶον Ξενοφάνης ἔλεγεν ὅτι ὁμοίως ἀσεβοῦσιν οἱ γενέσθαι φάσκοντες τοὺς θεοὺς τοῖς ἀποθανεῖν λέγουσιν (Xenoph. A 12).

49. See Anaximander A 17.

50. This is also the opinion of John Burnet, op. cit., p 59, against Zeller, who interprets the existence of innumerable worlds only as successive existence.

51. Cic. *De nat. deor.* i. 10, 25 (see n. 49).

52. Emped. B 21, 12, and B 23, 8. Both passages call the gods δολιχαίωνες. The word seems to be used by Empedocles in the stereotyped manner of an epic epithet. Sophocles, *Ant.* 987, calls the Moirai and the Nymphs (*O.T.* 1099) μακραίωνες. Cornutus, *De nat. deor.* 17, transfers the predicate μακραίων to the stars, which are 'visible gods' in the theology of philosophers since the time

of Plato's *Timaeus*. They have not an eternal but only a long life (αἰών), like Anaximander's worlds, and from the viewpoint of later philosophers their deity is vulnerable by the same argument which Cicero's Epicurean source launches against Anaximander's *nativi dei*: 'sed nos deum nisi sempiternum intellegere qui possumus?' The deity in the strict sense of Anaximander's *apeiron*, which is really without beginning and end, is here used as criterion for the deity of his own minor gods. Nothing could prove more clearly that from Anaximander's own point of view there was no contradiction in his two different ranks of cosmic deities. Under the rule of the one eternal God, the *apeiron*, he established the innumerable company of long-lived gods, the κόσμοι, who were its offspring.

53. See Simpl. *Phys.* 24, 13 f. (Anaximander A 9). The information given by the Neoplatonic commentator on Aristotle is taken from Theophrastus' work on the history of natural philosophy (frg. 2, Diels, *Doxographi*, p. 476).

54. Friedrich Nietzsche, *Philosophie im tragischen Zeitalter der Griechen*, i (Leipzig, Kroener Verlag), p. 429. Erwin Rohde, *Psyche*, 7.–8. Aufl. (Tübingen, 1921), ii, p. 119, n. 1.

55. Erwin Rohde, loc. cit. (see n. 54).

56. Arist. frg. 60, Rose: εὐθὺς φύσει συνέσταμεν καθάπερ φασὶν οἱ τὰς τελετὰς λέγοντες, ὥσπερ ἂν ἐπὶ τιμωρίᾳ πάντες; . . . ζῆν ἡμᾶς ἐπὶ κολάσει μεγάλων τινῶν ἁμαρτημάτων. The penalty which we are paying by living our present life is obviously the punishment for a crime which we committed in or by a former life.

57. Anaximander A 9. See Burnet, op. cit., p. 54.

58. See my interpretation of the famous passage in *Paideia*, i², p. 159 f. with notes. Cf. Heraclitus B 62. R. Mondolfo, *Problemi del pensiero antico* (Bologna, 1936), p. 23 f., has given an elaborate *epikrisis* of the various interpretations of the fragment of Anaximander, including my own in *Paideia*, I² (see Mondolfo, op. cit., p. 27 f.). To him I refer the reader for a complete critical survey of the situation with regard to this difficult problem.

59. From our Greek text-books, it is true, we learn that τάξις means 'order', and so Diels understands this passage. But in Greek we say the judge τάττει δίκην or τάττει ζημίαν or τιμωρίαν; for instance, τάττει θάνατον; that fits the situation best, since it is with the penalty (τίσις) which things have to pay for their ἀδικία that the fragment of Anaximander is concerned. τάξις must therefore have the meaning 'ordinance' here and cannot mean 'order'. In this old juridical sense the noun is used by Plat. *Laws*, 925 b; τάξις is, more generally speaking, every rationing or assessment. See the passages referred to in *Paideia*, i², p. 455, n. 50.

60. On Time as judge, see Solon, frg. 24, 3 Diehl, ἐν δίκῃ χρόνου; cf. also frg. 3, 16; 1, 16; 1, 28; 1, 31, for *diké* and *timé*, with my remarks in *Berl. Sitzb.* 1926, p. 79. On the permanent character of Solon's *diké*, see my interpretation, loc. cit. and *Paideia*, i², p. 144.

61. See the contemporary poet Mimnermus, frg. 2, Diehl, and Semonides of Amorgus, frg. 3 and 29, Diehl.

62. Anaximenes B 2. Karl Reinhardt, *Parmenides* (Bonn, 1916), p. 175, expresses doubt with regard to the authenticity of this fragment. He seems to think that it is rather a formulation by Aëtius, our doxographic source, or of the authority he followed (Theophrastus), of what he supposed to be Anaximenes' view on the relationship of air and world. No one can refute such doubts

once they are voiced, and it cannot be denied of course that the φησίν with which Aëtius 'quotes' the sentence proves nothing. It was the habit of later Greek writers to introduce the author of an opinion differing from their own in this naïve personal way (with φησίν), in order to make the reader realize more clearly that the speaker is referring to another man's view before attacking it. This is exactly the situation in Aët. i. 3, 4 with regard to the thesis of Anaximenes. Nevertheless, the sentence seems to express the view of the old philosopher as we should expect it. It states not only the dominant position of Anaximenes' principle, air, in his picture of the universe, but also the reason why it must be air. For air, and only air, seemed to explain the fact that this principle was at once the element from which everything had originated and the cause of life in the world, whereas Thales' water or Anaximander's *apeiron* offered no explanation for it. So the words have their value for us, whether they are literally authentic or not. The fact that the dialect is not Ionian but Attic does not prove much, since a prose paraphrase might easily have changed the original colouring of the language.

63. That the word ψυχή = 'soul' in the fragment of Anaximenes offers no reason for doubt. One may say that the poetry of the sixth century does not use the word in this sense. But poetry follows the language of Homer, in which ψυχή means 'life' or the 'ghost' which is the shadow of the dead in Hades (see *supra*, pp. 77 ff.). The compulsion of established norms of style in the literary genus prevented the poets from using the word in the sense in which it was obviously accepted by the time of the next great natural philosopher of Ionia, Heraclitus, whose generation overlaps that of Anaximenes. Heraclitus B 45 speaks of ψυχῆς πείρατα, the limits of the soul, and he says that the ψυχή has profound λόγος (cf. B 115). This proves that it is really the soul, although it is at the same time something material, as is shown by B 36, where he says that ψυχαί turn into water, and water into ψυχή; see also B 12: ψυχαί are evaporated from moisture. The dryer they are the better; cf. B 117 and 118. In an ethical sense the word occurs in B 85, although the distinction of θυμός and ψυχή in that passage is not quite clear. It cannot be doubted that if it was possible for Heraclitus to use ψυχή in the double sense of air and of soul a few decades later, it was possible for Anaximenes too. Possibly Heraclitus even took over this strange twofold meaning of the word from his immediate predecessor, whose philosophical intention it fitted better than that of any other of the physicists. He meant it to indicate the two aspects of his principle, air and soul. From the fact that it had these two aspects in man, he inferred by analogy that it must also have them in the universe, which is entirely ruled by *pneuma* and air. On Diogenes of Apollonia and the revival of Anaximenes' doctrine in the second half of the fifth century, see *supra*, p. 165.

64. Anaximenes A 10, A 11.

CHAPTER III

XENOPHANES' DOCTRINE OF GOD

1. Cf. Diog. L. *prooem.* 13. Diogenes represents a widespread tradition, for the same division appears in other ancient authors. See *supra*, p. 191. On Xenophanes and the Italic school, see loc. cit. 15.

2. Diog. L. ix. 18 (Xenoph. A 1): γέγραφε δὲ ἐν ἔπεσι καὶ ἐλεγείας καὶ ἰάμβους καθ' Ἡσιόδου καὶ Ὁμήρου, ἐπικόπτων αὐτῶν τὰ περὶ θεῶν εἰρημένα. ἀλλὰ καὶ αὐτὸς ἐρραψῴδει τὰ ἑαυτοῦ.

3. Diog. L. ix. 18 (Xenoph. B 8).

4. Ath. xii. 526 A (Xenoph. B 3).

5. Ath. *Epit.* ii. 54 E (Xenoph. B 22).

6. Diog. L. ix. 22 (Xenoph. A 18) describes Hesiod, Xenophanes, Empedocles, and Parmenides as philosophers who wrote in poetic form (διὰ ποιημάτων φιλοσοφεῖ). But that does not mean that they all used the same poetic form, the didactic epic. Apuleius, *Florida,* c. 20 (Xenoph. A 21), expressly contrasts Empedocles' didactic epics with the poetical form of Xenophanes, the satires or *silloi*: 'canit enim Empedocles carmina, Plato dialogos . . . Xenocrates satiras.' Casaubon's emendation *Xenophanes* for *Xenocrates* is evidently correct. Diels preferred Rohde's conjecture *Crates* only because both believed in the existence of an epic poem Περὶ φύσεως by Xenophanes, but philologically this emendation has very little probability. The philosopher who was famous for writing in the form of σίλλοι (*satirae*) was Xenophanes, and the translation of the word σίλλοι by *satirae* is perfectly proper.

7. Diog. L. ix. 18 (cf. n. 2) distinguishes among Xenophanes' works poems in hexameters (ἐν ἔπεσι), elegiac poems, and iambics. The latter belonged to the σίλλοι, but this group also contained poems in dactylic and elegiac metres. Diogenes' learned source did not mention an epic by Xenophanes on nature, the existence of which most modern scholars have assumed (see nn. 10, 11). As greater epic poems of Xenophanes he mentions only the Κολοφῶνος κτίσις and τὸν εἰς Ἐλέαν τῆς Ἰταλίας ἀποικισμόν (ix. 20) in 2,000 lines. This information goes back to an Alexandrian source. Sotion's *Diadoché* is quoted in the same paragraph. But Sotion's ultimate source must be some pinacographic work of Callimachus' school, in which the exact number of the lines was indicated, as is done in many other passages derived from the same learned tradition. Mimnermus of Colophon, who wrote before Xenophanes, had also dealt with the κτίσις of his city in a smaller elegiac poem, of which a fragment is preserved (see Mimn. frg. 12, Diehl).

8. Strabo xiv. 643 (Xenoph. A 20): Ξενοφάνης ὁ φυσικὸς ὁ τοὺς Σίλλους ποιήσας διὰ ποιημάτων. Note that Strabo, who is using for his work the learned grammatical literature of the Hellenistic period, here mentions the *silloi* of Xenophanes in close connexion with his title ὁ φυσικός. The words διὰ ποιημάτων recall Diog. L. ix. 18, who says that Parmenides, like Hesiod, Xenophanes, and Empedocles, διὰ ποιημάτων φιλοσοφεῖ. Obviously the words διὰ ποιημάτων mean only 'in poetical form' and do not prove that they all used exactly the same poetical form, that of the didactic epic. Xenophanes, according to Strabo's source, wrote satires in poetical form. He was famous for them. Proclus, who disapproves of Xenophanes' satires 'against all other philosophers and poets' (*In Hes. op.* 284, Xenoph. A 22), obviously considers them the characteristic form of his philosophical utterances. Schol. ABT to *Iliad* ii. 212 (Xenoph. A 23) assert that Homer and not Xenophanes was the inventor of the σίλλος and quote the Thersites scene of the *Iliad* to prove it. But there σίλλος does not mean the literary form used by Xenophanes, but simply 'slander'.

9. See the pure hexameters in B 11, B 12, B 15, B 16, and the alternation of hexameter and iambic trimeter in B 14. The fragments of Timon's sillographic poems were collected by H. Diels, *Poetarum philosophorum fragmenta* (Berlin, 1901), p. 184 f. See Timon's praise of Xenophanes, Diog. L. ix. 18.

10. Diels lists fragments B 23–41 under the title Περὶ φύσεως. See also K. Reinhardt, *Parmenides* (Bonn, 1916), p. 94 f. Recently K. Deichgraeber has

defended the existence of a lost poem of Xenophanes, Περὶ φύσεως, in the form of a didactic epic (*Rhein. Mus.* 87, 1938, pp. 1–31).

11. See J. Burnet, *Early Greek Philosophy*, 4th ed., p. 115. On the whole, Burnet's arguments will hold, even though we should not depend too much on the fact that Simplicius (*In Arist. De caelo*, 522) was no longer able to find this book by Xenophanes. By his time many of the books of the pre-Socratic thinkers were lost. The two quotations Ξενοφάνης ἐν τῷ περὶ φύσεως by the grammarians Crates of Mallus and Pollux (Xenoph. B 30, B 39) suggest the existence of a poem concerned with cosmological problems, but a glimpse at the fragments of Empedocles' epic *On Nature* shows that the few lines of Xenophanes which Diels would attribute to the Περὶ φύσεως are of a different calibre and do not really prove the existence of a didactic epic by him. They fit quite well into the form of the σίλλοι in which he attacked the views of philosophers (i.e. natural philosophers) as well as poets, according to Proclus (see n. 8). The title Περὶ φύσεως was of course added by later Hellenistic grammarians when they tried to classify the old poems. But how liberal they were in labelling their contents as ethics, politics, physics, &c., in accordance with the terminology of their own time, may be illustrated by the example of Plutarch, *Solon* 3. According to him, the main emphasis in Solon's thought lay on ethics and politics. In his physics, he remarks, Solon is still very simple and archaic (ἐν δὲ τοῖς φυσικοῖς ἁπλοῦς ἐστι λίαν καὶ ἀρχαῖος). For this Plutarch quotes two distichs from two of Solon's political elegies (frg. 10, 1–2, and frg. 11, Diehl), which he combines as though they belonged to one and the same poem. He obviously takes them from a doxographic source which compared Solon's physics with that of his contemporary Thales, and came to the conclusion that Thales' thought on nature was much more advanced. Solon speaks in one of the distichs of lightning and thunder. Fortunately, we can still read at least one of these in its original context. There the causal sequence of lightning and thunder is compared to the rise of tyranny from the accumulation of power in the hands of one man. The other distich must belong to a similar, i.e. political, context. But if we did not know this, we might assign them on the authority of Plutarch to a lost poem by Solon on physical problems. Similarly, Pherecydes of Syrus is said by Diog. L. i. 116 to have been 'the first to write on nature and the gods' (πρῶτον περὶ φύσεως καὶ θεῶν γράψαι), but we must not take this to mean that he was a real physicist. He was no more of a physicist than was Hesiod, of whom Hippolytus, *Phil.* c. 26 (Diels, *Doxographi*, p. 574, 14) says: Ἡσίοδος δὲ ὁ ποιητὴς καὶ αὐτὸς περὶ φύσεως . . . λέγει ἀκηκοέναι παρὰ Μουσῶν. Burnet's hypothesis of a lost *sillos* by Xenophanes which was concerned wholly with such questions seems sufficiently to explain its inscription Περὶ φύσεως and Xenophanes' classification as φυσικός by later doxographers. The same thing happened to Heraclitus (see *supra*, p. 110), though with much more justification. Far more reliable witnesses credited Xenophanes with a theological mind but denied his being a real physicist (see n. 12).

12. Arist. *Metaph.* A 5, 986^b 18 calls Xenophanes the first monist (ὁ πρῶτος ἑνίσας) but denies the existence in Xenophanes' thought of any logical specification of the nature of this 'One', such as that given by Parmenides or Melissus. Xenophanes spoke of the One, Aristotle says, looking at the whole *ouranos* (i.e. the visible universe). He calls him 'rather primitive'. Theophrastus in his *Phys. opin.*, quoted by Simplicius, *In Arist. Phys.* 22, 22 f. (Xenoph. A 31), mentions that Xenophanes believed in one principle alone, but (like Aristotle) Theophrastus does not think that his view should be classified as pertaining

to natural history at all. See the similar statement by Galen, *In Hippocr. De nat. hom.* xv. 25 K. (Xenoph. A 36). Sabinus, a commentator on Hippocrates, had ascribed to Xenophanes the theory that the earth was the element from which everything originated and thereby put him on the same level with Thales or Anaximenes. But Galen correctly points out that Theophrastus did not list this view at all in his *Phys. opin.* The δόξα goes back to Xenoph. B 27, ἐκ γαίης γὰρ πάντα καὶ εἰς γῆν πάντα τελευτᾷ, which has indeed nothing to do with natural philosophy.

13. T. Gomperz, *Greek Thinkers* (London, 1906), p. 155. See the passage in Diog. L. ix. 18 (Xenoph. A 1) quoted in n. 2, in which Xenophanes is said to have recited his own poems (καὶ αὐτὸς ἐρραψῴδει τὰ ἑαυτοῦ).

14. See Xenoph. B 1.

15. This is the somewhat bold picture of Xenophanes which Gomperz, loc. cit., tried to make plausible. But the grammatical foundation of it is weak. The words ἀλλὰ καὶ αὐτὸς ἐρραψῴδει τὰ ἑαυτοῦ (see n. 2) are not opposed to the works of Homer, but only to the preceding γέγραφε δὲ ἐν ἔπεσι καὶ ἐλεγείας καὶ ἰάμβους, 'he wrote hexametric poems, elegies, and iambics, but he also recited them in public himself'. The word ἐρραψῴδει lent itself quite naturally to that unusual kind of performance, but it does not imply that in order to be able to recite his own poems he had to be a Homeric rhapsode. Cf. Plutarch, *Vit. Solon.* 8 on Solon's elegy Αὐτὸς κῆρυξ ἦλθον, which he recited himself in the market-place.

16. Plat. *Ion* 536 d calls the rhapsode Ion Ὁμήρου δεινὸς ἐπαινέτης; see also 542 b. Ion is represented as a specialist who knows his Homer thoroughly (but nothing else) and who teaches Homer as the source of all wisdom.

17. Plat. *Rep.* 606 e. Herodian, Περὶ διχρ. p. 296, 6 (Cr. *An. Ox.* iii, Xenoph. B 10).

18. Clem. Alex. *Strom.* v. 109 (Xenoph. B 23).

19. Sextus, *Adv. math.* vii. 49. 110. Plut. *De aud. poet.* 2, p. 17 E (Xenoph. B 34).

20. Later Greek doxographers, and especially the sceptic school, used to interpret these words in the sense of dogmatic agnosticism. (See Sextus, *Adv. math.* vii. 48, who lists Xenophanes as the first of οἱ ἀνελόντες τὸ κριτήριον.) But obviously the awareness of the uncertainty of his ideas did not prevent Xenophanes from pronouncing them. We find a similar thought expressed by the Hippocratic author of *On Ancient Medicine* in the proem of his book (c. 1); but there it is said to be the advantage of medical science that it rests on verifiable experience, whereas natural philosophy is rejected because its views can never be confirmed by facts.

21. Cicero divides the inquiry *De nat. deor.* ii. 1 into the following topics: (1) *esse deos*, (2) *quales sint*, (3) *mundum ab his administrari*, (4) *consulere eos rebus humanis*. The question *quales sint* implies the problem of the true form or shape of the gods; see *De nat. deor.* ii, c. 17.

22. See Cic. *De nat. deor.* ii, c. 17 ff.

23. I follow in this the direct fragments, especially B 23, where it is said that God's δέμας does not resemble that of mortal men. According to the pseudo-Aristotelian treatise *De Xenophane Melisso Gorgia* (977ᵇ1 = Xenoph. A 28 (7)), Xenophanes taught that his God was spherical in shape; but this is obviously due to a later interpretation of frg. B 23 under the influence of Parmenides, who calls his Being (Parm. B 8, 43) εὐκύκλου σφαίρης ἐναλίγκιον ὄγκῳ. This is not the only example of such a Parmenidean interpretation of

Xenophanes in that treatise. On the difficult problem of the authenticity of the picture which the *De Xenophane Melisso Gorgia* gives of Xenophanes' doctrine, see p. 51.

24. See Xenoph. B 23, 1.

25. See *supra*, p. 33.

26. Xenoph. B 24.

27. Ibid. B 1, 13–14, exhorts men to praise 'the god' in hymns at the ideal symposium which he describes in this poem, and he defines this by adding 'with pious myths and pure words'. What he means by this is shown in lines 21–4. There he turns against the Homeric and Hesiodic myths of the fights of Titans, Giants, and Centaurs and the conception of the gods implied in them. No doubt his new and purified idea of God had some practical influence on the form of his worship, and it is this that he calls for in the last line of his elegy: θεῶν ⟨δὲ⟩ προμηθείην αἰὲν ἔχειν ἀγαθόν. This προμηθείη θεῶν is the right way of honouring them. As honouring the gods was the essence of Greek religion, this application of his ideas is of great interest for the historian of religion.

28. Xenoph. B 26.

29. See, for instance, Hom. *Iliad* ii. 17, 786; iii. 129; v. 353; viii. 42, 392, 399; xxiv. 340 ff.; *Od.* i. 96 ff., etc.

30. Xenoph. B 25.

31. Arist. *Metaph.* Λ 7, 1072ᵇ 3.

32. Aesch. *Suppl.* 96–103 (Murray). With Wilamowitz and Murray I accept Wellauer's emendation, which restores to the corrupt passage τὰν ἄποινον δαιμονίων of the codex Mediceus the decisive concept ἄπονον, which is necessary for both metrical and logical reasons. πᾶν . . . δαιμονίων I do not understand with Wilamowitz as meaning ὧν δαίμονες δρῶσι, but rather as 'every divine power'. Not the action of God, but God Himself is ἄπονος. The objection that τὰ δαιμόνια could not yet have this meaning in Aeschylus' time does not convince me. In the following line, φρόνημα is the object of ἐξέπραξεν, not subject, as Wilamowitz understands it. Not the thought, but God, is enthroned on high. The problem whether the words ἥμενον ἄνω have to be changed for metrical reasons can be dismissed here.

33. Arist. *Metaph.* A 5, 986ᵇ18 ff. (Xenoph. A 30).

34. Hom. *Iliad* viii. 18–27. The author of the *De Xenophane Melisso Gorgia* (977ᵃ 23, Xenoph. A 28) makes Xenophanes argue that 'if God is the strongest of all things, he must be one, for if there were two or more he could no longer be the strongest and best of all; for each of the many, being God, would be equally the strongest'. But no such argument occurs in the preserved fragments; rather, it is in open contradiction to fragment B 23, which says that one God is the greatest of gods and men. This implies a relationship of the highest God to the other gods like that in the passage from Homer quoted in the text. The exalted Homeric conception of the power of Zeus may well have determined the thought of Xenophanes, just as it impressed Aristotle (see n. 35).

35. Arist. *De mot. an.* 4, 700ᵃ1.

36. Hom. *Iliad* i. 528–30.

37. Xenoph. B 25. κραδαίνει does not refer to the circular motion of the *ouranos* but to the shaking of the firmament. It is a sign of the power of God which

recalls the description of Zeus in Homer (*Iliad* i. 530), μέγαν δ' ἐλέλιξεν "Ολυμπον. But the universe (πάντα) now takes the place of Olympus.

38. Xenoph. B 11, B 12.

39. Ibid. B 14.

40. We find the same criticism of the theogonic idea that the gods were born and therefore not eternal in Epicharmus B 1. See ch. iv, p. 55.

41. Clem. Alex. *Strom.* v. 110 (Xenoph. B 15).

42. Clem. Alex. op. cit. vii. 22 (Xenoph. B 16).

43. Goethe, *Gott, Gemüt und Welt*, vv. 23-4 (Sämtliche Werke, Jubiläumsausgabe, Bd. iv, p. 4).

44. See Aug. *Civ. Dei* viii, especially c. 11.

45. The new philosophical God is related to nature and to the universe, not to the *polis*, as were the old gods of the Greeks.

46. Xenoph. B 2, 11-22. In this poem he praises his own σοφίη as the foundation of εὐνομίη in the *polis* and contrasts it with the *areté* of the victors in the Olympic games. They are overpraised by human society, for they are unable to contribute anything to the common good. Here Xenophanes refers his new philosophical religion to a new rational concept of the best social order. See *Paideia*, i², p. 173.

47. See Friedrich Solmsen, *Plato's Theology* (Ithaca, N.Y., 1942), pp. 163 and 168 f.

48. Xenoph. B 26, 2: οὐδὲ μετέρχεσθαί μιν ἐπιπρέπει ἄλλοτε ἄλλῃ.

49. Max Pohlenz, *Göttinger Gel. Nachr.*, 1933, pp. 53 ff., has given a survey of the development of this concept. But the θεοπρεπές, discussed in the text hereafter, is omitted from his survey.

50. On the concept of τὸ πρέπον in Greek rhetorical and poetical theory, see J. Stroux, *De Theophrasti virtutibus dicendi* (Leipzig, 1912), pp. 28, 31, 35, 78. On its influence on Greek medicine, see W. Jaeger, *Diokles von Karystos* (Berlin, 1938), pp. 47-50. The word ἁρμόττον is used as synonymous with πρέπον.

51. See line 1345 in Euripides' *Heracles*, δεῖται γὰρ ὁ θεός, εἴπερ ἔστ' ὀρθῶς θεός, οὐδενός—if God is 'truly God', i.e. if his nature corresponds to the correct idea of God. This idea implies that he cannot be in need of anything. What is behind this concept of a θεός who is ὀρθῶς θεός is the claim of Xenophanes that our idea of God ought to be in harmony with what befits God. Euripides' rationalism made him fond of Xenophanes. This is shown by such obvious imitations as his criticism of the uselessness of athletic strength in the first edition of his *Autolycus* (see Ath. x. 413 c, Xenoph. C 2). The whole passage in the *Heracles* also seems to be borrowed from Xenophanes, as Diels observed; it attacks the idea of the gods committing adultery or dominating over one another, an idea which we found in Xenoph. B 11, B 12, A 32. Even though we do not find the idea that God is not in need of anything in the preserved fragments of Xenophanes, it obviously had its origin in his thought.

52. Plat. *Rep.* 378 c ff. criticizes the way in which the poets represent the gods, and he sets up τύποι θεολογίας for the education of the guards in his ideal State. The poets have to follow these rules if they want to be admitted to his republic. Plato's words recall those of Xenophanes when he refers to enmities and fights among gods, gigantomachies, and theomachies; cf. Xenoph. B 1, 21-4, B 11, and B 12.

53. The words of the Stoic Lucilius Balbus, Cic. *De nat. deor.* ii. 28, 70, refer literally to the same passage of Xenophanes which is quoted in Plat. *Rep.* (see n. 52). Cicero's Stoic source (Posidonius?) undoubtedly had both Xenophanes and Plato in mind when writing these words.

54. See *supra*, p. 2.

55. Aug. *Civ. Dei* vi. 5 (vol. i, p. 253, Dombart).

56. The concepts of θεοπρεπές and ἱεροπρεπές deserve a separate historical investigation.

57. See, for instance, the so-called Heraclitus, *Quaestiones Homericae* (ed. Soc. Philol. Bonnensis Sodales), c. 1, who says of Homer: πάντα γὰρ ἠσέβησεν εἰ μηδὲν ἠλληγόρησεν.

58. Anonymus, *De sublimitate* c. ix. 7, remarks that certain passages in Homer represent the gods in a perfectly impious manner if one does not interpret them allegorically (see also Dion. Hal. *Dem.* c. 8, p. 144, 1–7, Us.–Rad.). In § 9 he compares other passages of the *Iliad*, in which he finds a more adequate description of divine majesty, with the words of the 'lawgiver of the Jews' Moses in the cosmogony of Genesis. The source from which the author quotes Genesis is not the Septuagint but his predecessor in the discussion of the sublime, the rhetorician Caecilius of Caleacte, whom Suidas calls 'a Jew, so far as his religion is concerned', i.e. a proselyte. See also the Jewish authors Josephus, *Ant. Jud.* i. 3, 15 (p. 7, 4 f. Niese ed. maior) and Philo, *De aet. mundi* 5, p. 6, Cumont.

59. See n. 33.

60. What Aristotle says (see n. 33) of the somewhat vague character of Xenophanes' intuition of the principle of 'the One', which he conceived merely by looking up at the οὐρανός, must have favoured such an historical construction of the relationship between Xenophanes and Parmenides. First came the almost visual intuition and after it the clear logical concept. Hegel distinguished similarly in his philosophy of religion between the *Stufe der Vorstellung* and the *Stufe des Begriffs*.

61. Karl Reinhardt, *Parmenides* (Bonn, 1916).

62. See n. 33.

63. Pseud. Arist. *De Xenophane Melisso Gorgia* 977ᵇ2 ff.

64. Aristotle states (*Metaph.* A 5, 986ᵇ18 ff.) that Xenophanes said of his God neither that he was limited nor that he was unlimited, and he condemns Xenophanes' thought as rather primitive. This statement was incorporated into the doxographic literature, as is clear from Simpl. *Phys.* 22, 22 ff., who quotes Theophrastus' *Phys. opin.* (see Xenoph. A 31): καὶ οὔτε πεπερασμένον οὔτε ἄπειρον [scil. τὸ ὄν] . . . Ξενοφάνην τὸν Κολοφώνιον . . . ὑποτίθεσθαί φησιν ὁ Θεόφραστος, which means that, according to Theophrastus, Xenophanes taught neither that his principle was limited nor that it was unlimited. Theophrastus, in other words, has simply repeated what his master Aristotle says in his *Metaphysics*, as he has done so often in his doxographic work. But Simplicius shows how easily Theophrastus' words could be misunderstood in the sense in which they were taken by the author of the *De Xenophane Melisso Gorgia*; for after quoting Theophrastus, Simplicius shifts to another source (from § 3 on), and this source is obviously the author of the *De Xenophane Melisso Gorgia*, as is clear from the order of the predicates of God which he enumerates in the following paragraphs (3–7). One of the predicates which Xenophanes ascribed to his God is, according to this author, that God is neither limited

nor unlimited. Simplicius reproduces this immediately after quoting what he found in Theophrastus; obviously he did not notice that the two reports do not agree, but understood Theophrastus in the sense of the author of the *De Xenophane Melisso Gorgia*, i.e. he misunderstood him completely. What Theophrastus really meant to say is what Aristotle said in the *Metaphysics*, and nothing more.

65. This *diadoché* is to be found first in Plato's *Sophist* 242 c–d, where the Elean stranger says that the various schools of thought had taught either three, or two, or one kind of Being. The Eleatic tribe, he says, starting with Xenophanes 'and even earlier' (he obviously means Homer or the Milesian school), assumed the unity of all things. This is of course a playful and half-ironical way of speaking. The next step is taken in Arist. *Metaph.* A 5, 986ᵇ18 ff. There we find Plato's combination laid down as historical fact. Parmenides became a pupil of Xenophanes, 'as they say', because Xenophanes was the first to stress the unity of Being (ὁ πρῶτος ἑνίσας). But even Aristotle admits that the two thinkers did not have the same thing in mind, and the factual basis for establishing a teacher–pupil relationship between them is very slight indeed. But once it was stated in book i of Aristotle's *Metaphysics*, which was the bible of Theophrastus and the later ancient doxographers, the *diadoché* was accepted by all text-books on the history of philosophy as an established fact.

66. See nn. 11 and 12.

CHAPTER IV

THE SO-CALLED ORPHIC THEOGONIES

1. See Epicharm. B 1:

—ἀλλ' ἀεί τοι θεοὶ παρῆσαν χὐπέλιπον οὐ πώποκα,
  τάδε δ' ἀεὶ πάρεσθ' ὁμοῖα διά τε τῶν αὐτῶν ἀεί.
—ἀλλὰ λέγεται μὰν Χάος πρᾶτον γενέσθαι τῶν θεῶν.
—πῶς δέ κα ; μὴ ἔχον γ' ἀπό τινος μηδ' ἐς ὅ τι πρᾶτον μόλοι.
—οὐκ ἄρ' ἔμολε πρᾶτον οὐθέν ;—οὐδὲ μὰ Δία δεύτερον
  τῶνδέ γ' ὧν ἀμὲς νῦν ὧδε λέγομες, ἀλλ' ἀεὶ τάδ' ἦς.

Diels, Reinhardt, and other scholars believe in the authenticity of this fragment. From the viewpoint of language and style this seems not unlikely, and the content seems quite possible for Xenophanes' time. Epicharmus may have been influenced by the criticism of his famous contemporary.

2. See ch. iii, n. 19.

3. Diog. L. viii. 83 (Alcmaeon B 1): Ἀλκμαίων Κροτωνιάτης τάδε ἔλεξε Πειρίθου υἱὸς Βροτίνῳ καὶ Λέοντι καὶ Βαθύλλῳ περὶ τῶν ἀφανέων [περὶ τῶν θνητῶν] σαφήνειαν μὲν θεοὶ ἔχοντι, ὡς δὲ ἀνθρώποις τεκμαίρεσθαι καὶ τὰ ἑξῆς. Zeller and others thought the words περὶ τῶν θνητῶν a gloss which had crept into the text, whereas Diels defends them by saying that Alcmaeon's book dealt both with ἀφανέα and θνητά. But the antithesis of ἀφανέα and θνητά is strangely illogical, and the words περὶ τῶν θνητῶν disrupt the structure of the sentence. One should not defend this syntactical harshness by saying that it is due to the archaic style.

4. *On Ancient Medicine*, c. 1.

5. See p. 43, where we have shown that even Xenophanes, though he attacks the

anthropomorphic gods of the tradition, does not imply that God is without form. But His real form remains undefined.

6. Arist. *Metaph.* A 3, 983^{b}29 contrasts the παμπάλαιοι καὶ θεολογήσαντες πρῶτοι with the πρῶτοι φιλοσοφήσαντες (^{b}7), who represent a later stage of intellectual development; in the same way he contrasts (B 4, 1000^{a}9) οἱ θεολόγοι with οἱ δι' ἀποδείξεως λέγοντες (^{a}19).

7. See the fifth edition of Diels's *Vorsokratiker*, vol. i, edited by Walter Kranz.

8. See the vase-painting of the seventh century, and compare Archilochus as the leading representative of naturalistic expression in contemporary literature.

9. See Herod. v. 67 on the τραγικοὶ χοροί in honour of Adrastus, which were given to Dionysus by Cleisthenes; the testimonia on Arion's dithyrambs performed at Corinth are collected and discussed by A. W. Pickard-Cambridge, *Dithyramb, Tragedy and Comedy* (Oxford, 1927). Cf. chapters ii, iii, and App. A of this work on the oldest tragedy and comedy.

10. Plat. *Rep.* 364 b–e. This religious propaganda-literature did not bear the name of Orpheus exclusively but also went under the name of Musaeus, Selene, and others.

11. On abstinence from meat (ἄψυχος βορά) as an Orphic commandment, see Eur. *Hipp.* 952 ff., Aristoph. *Frogs* 1032 ff., Plat. *Laws* 782 c.

12. See n. 10.

13. See V. Macchioro, *Eraclito: Nuovi studi sull' Orfismo* (Bari, 1922), and the same author's *From Orpheus to Paul, A History of Orphism* (London, 1930).

14. Most of these oldest testimonia on Orphic rites and religious practices were collected by Otto Kern, *Orphicorum Fragmenta* (Berlin, 1922), pp. 80 ff., under the somewhat misleading title *fragmenta veteriora*. These passages mostly contain only references to Orphic things. Some of them are to be found under the title 'Testimonia' in the first part of the book, in which older and more recent materials have not been sufficiently separated.

15. The remains of Orphic poetry were collected by Chr. Aug. Lobeck, *Aglaophamus* (Regimontii, 1829), 2 vols. See M. Hauck, 'De hymnorum Orphicorum aetate' (*Breslauer philol. Abhandlungen*, 1911). Cf. O. Kern, *Berl. phil. Woch.*, 1912, p. 1438, and the same author's *Die Herkunft des orph. Hymnenbuchs* (*Genethliakon für C. Robert*, Halle, 1910).

16. See the collection of the fragments made by Kern, op. cit., pp. 130 ff. and 140 ff.

17. Lobeck, op. cit., p. 611, Kern, *De Orphei Epimenidis Pherecydis Theogoniis quaestiones criticae* (Berlin diss., 1888). But cf. now the same author's *Orphicorum Fragmenta*, p. 141. There he expresses doubt whether the *Rhapsodies* or Ἱεροὶ λόγοι were composed much before the Neoplatonic age, even though he maintains the existence in them of certain traces of the influence of much older poems. See also G. Rathmann's dissertation, inspired by Kern, *Quaestiones Pythagoreae Orphicae Empedocleae* (Halle, 1933).

18. U. v. Wilamowitz-Moellendorff, *Der Glaube der Hellenen*, ii (Berlin, 1932), 199. Since I wrote these chapters, Ivan Linforth's book, *The Arts of Orpheus* (Berkeley, 1941) has been published; this follows in Wilamowitz's footsteps. It underscores the critical doubts of that scholar as to the historicity of the picture of Orphism which modern historians of religion have reconstructed. W. K. C. Guthrie, *Orpheus and Greek Religion* (London, 1935), has followed a middle road between the extremes, but is on the whole much more positive than Wilamowitz and Linforth.

19. See O. Kern, 'Empedokles und die Orphiker', *Arch. f. Gesch. d. Philos.* i (1888), 498.

20. I have shown *supra*, p. 34, that this 'Orphic' interpretation of the fragment of Anaximander goes back to a period when the correct text of the fragment had not yet been discovered by H. Diels in the Simplicius manuscripts. Nevertheless, the old interpretation is maintained by some, although its textual basis has been destroyed. A leading representative of the mystical interpretation of the pre-Socratics was K. Joël, *Der Ursprung der Naturphilosophie aus dem Geiste der Mystik* (Jena, 1906); see the same author's *Geschichte der antiken Philosophie* (Tübingen, 1921), pp. 149 ff.: 'Der mystische Geist und seine Klärung zum Logos.'

21. See Kern *O.F.* 27, Arist. frg. 7, Rose (where the reference to the *De anima* should be i. 5, 410^{b}28 and not 1410^{b}28). Kern questions the Aristotelian origin of the view that Onomacritus was the author of the poem. He writes φασίν instead of φησίν in frg. 7 R. of Περὶ φιλοσοφίας, which is taken from Philoponus' commentary on the *De anima*; Guthrie, op. cit., pp. 58 ff., leaves this question undecided. According to Cic. *De nat. deor.* i. 38, 108, Aristotle had stated in the Περὶ φιλοσοφίας that 'a poet Orpheus never existed'. Philoponus (who confirms the fact that according to Aristotle the 'Orphic poems' were not written by Orpheus) takes this to mean that only the δόγματα stemmed from Orpheus, not the poems, which were written by Onomacritus. In my *Aristotle*, p. 129 (cf. 136), I have followed Philoponus, according to whom Aristotle denied the authorship of Orpheus but not his historicity. But Guthrie's treatment of the fragment, loc. cit., has made this doubtful. I conclude that the Orphic poem mentioned by Aristotle had theogonic content from the fact that he quoted it for the view of its author that the soul originated from the (*pneuma* in the) universe and came into the body carried by the winds. Aristotle refers to the so-called Orphic ἔπη again in *De gen. an.* ii. 1, 734^a 16, for a similar detail regarding the origin of the human body. Both opinions on the origin of soul and body were evidently part of a cosmogony in the 'Orphic poem'; and the cosmogony was no doubt put against a theogonic background and not treated in a purely abstract and scientific manner, even though it may already have been influenced by the contemporary theories of natural philosophers. This epic seems to be different from the redaction of the *Oracles of Musaeus* (Χρησμοὶ Μουσαίου) ascribed to Onomacritus by Herod. vii. 6 (see n. 23).

22. Herod. vii. 6.

23. See H. Diels, 'Über Epimenides von Kreta' in *Ber. Berl. Ak.*, 1891, pp. 387 ff. The *Oracles of Musaeus* must have been interpolated (if they contained any older tradition at all) by Onomacritus, who inserted 'prophetic' references to events of the time when the Persian war was imminent; see Herod., loc. cit.

24. This, if anything, is made clear by O. Kern's collection of testimonia in *O.F.*, pp. 1 ff.

25. For this picture of the Orphic Church see O. Kern, *Religion der Griechen*, ii (Berlin, 1935), 148. The idea, however, that the theogonic epics contained the dogma of the Orphic religion is not restricted to Kern alone but goes back to Erwin Rohde's *Psyche* and is widely held.

26. See O. Kern, op. cit., p. 147.

27. See my 1943 Aquinas Lecture, *Humanism and Theology* (Marquette University Press, 1943), especially pp. 36 ff., 58 ff., 82 ff. There I have traced the origin of the concept of theology in Greek philosophy and outlined its reception by the early Christian Church. See also the first chapter of the present book.

28. *Gregorii Nysseni Opera* ii, ed. W. Jaeger (Berlin, 1921), 271, 19 (*Contra Eunom.*, lib. iii, tom. ix. 59): τὸ δὲ ἐν δόγμασι δεῖν μόνοις οἴεσθαι τὴν εὐσέβειαν εἶναι, τίνος οὕτως ἴδιον ὡς τῶν Ἑλλήνων ἐστίν; This statement is the product of the profound experience and learning of a fourth-century leader of the Christian Church who belonged to the Cappadocian school of theology, a group which has contributed more than any other to the definite establishment and formulation of the dogma of the Church. But they knew the limits of all dogmatic faith and the dangers of that specifically Greek intellectualism which was then dominating discussion among educated Christians and at the councils of the ecclesiastical hierarchy. Well-trained in the tradition of Greek philosophy, Gregory of Nyssa and his group were aware of the Hellenic origin of this intellectualism and of the insistence on dogmatic clarity and precision in religious matters. See also op. cit., p. 270, 21, where Gregory stresses the importance of 'the community of the mystic symbols and customs on which the strength of the Christian religion rests'. From the point of view of the present inquiry it does not matter whether or not we like this dogmatization of religious substance; what we have to admit is the fact that it is a specifically Greek attitude of mind.

29. The words δόγμα and σύστημα were used in this sense for the first time towards the end of the classical period of Greek culture. They are particularly characteristic of the Hellenistic age.

30. On this deep respect for written tradition in Greek poetry at large and on the correction of predecessors made by the poets, see my *Paideia* ii, pp. 219–20.

31. Arist. *Metaph.* Λ 6, 1071^{b}26 (Kern, *O.F.* 24).

32. Damasc. *De princ.* 124 [i. 319, 8 Ruelle], Kern, *O. F.* 28 (Eudem., frg. 117, Spengel).

33. Aristoph. *Birds*, 690 ff. (Kern, *O.F.* 1).

34. Hes. *Theog.* 123–5.

35. Aesch. *Eum.* 321, Murray.

36. Light and darkness are one of the ten pairs of opposites which Aristotle (*Metaph.* A 5, 986^{a}22 ff.) enumerates in the συστοιχία of principles adopted by some of the Pythagoreans.

37. Arist. *Metaph.* N 4, 1091^{b}4 (Kern, *O.F.* 24). Cf. *Metaph.* Λ 6, 1071^{b}26.

38. Plato does not say expressly that the hexameter which he quotes as Orphic in *Phileb.* 66 c, ἕκτῃ δ' ἐν γενεῇ, φησὶν Ὀρφεύς, καταπαύσατε κόσμον ἀοιδῆς, is taken from a theogonic poem. Abstractly speaking, this line may refer to a sequence of generations either of gods or of mortals, as Lobeck, *Aglaophamus*, ii, pp. 788 ff., pointed out. But Lobeck rightly refused to interpret it, as K. O. Müller did, as a successive incorporation of the soul in six different kinds of animals or bodies. If we rule out this interpretation, which would fit Pythagorean doctrine rather than Orphic tradition, it seems most probable to think of six generations of gods; this view is recommended by the fact that Plato quotes (*Cratyl.* 402 b–c) another couple of lines from an Orphic theogony, in which Oceanus and Tethys appear as the first (?) generation in the succession of gods. Note that the manner in which Plato quotes this tradition is exactly the same in both cases: φησὶν Ὀρφεύς—λέγει δέ που καὶ Ὀρφεύς. A theogony is also quoted by Plat. *Tim.* 40 d, where he is concerned with the origin of the gods. According to this passage Oceanus and Tethys were not the first couple, but they were preceded by Uranus and Gē. From Oceanus and Tethys, on the other hand, stemmed Phorcys, Kronos, and Rhea; from Kronos and Rhea, Zeus and Hera and their brothers and sisters; and from them in turn

others were derived. The children of Zeus and Hera are the fifth generation in this series. If we assume that Uranus and Gē were only the first *couple*, but must have originated from Chaos or some other primordial deity (see n. 51), we have indeed the six generations which we need; for it is hard to go beyond the sixth, the children of Zeus and Hera, who are the last ones listed by Plato. It may be well to remember that there were six generations of gods also in the Neoplatonic version of Orphic theogony. This is important for the interpretation of the six γενεαί in the Orphic poem quoted by Plato, because it confirms that the number six was firmly established in theogonic tradition. See Orph. B 12, with Diels's footnotes (*Vorsokratiker* i).

39. Aristoph. *Birds*, 690 ff. (Kern, *O.F.* 1).

40. See *supra*, p. 34.

41. See in Aristoph., op. cit. 696, the words περιτελλομέναις ὥραις, which are a poetic paraphrase of χρόνος.

42. See *supra*, pp. 15 ff.

43. Aristoph., op. cit. 695 ff.

44. See Damasc. *De princ.* 124 [i. 320, 17 Ruelle]; Epimen. B 5 Diels (Eudem., frg. 117, Spengel).

45. See Damasc., loc. cit.; Orph. B 12 Diels (Eudem., frg. 117). Cf. Diels's footnote *ad loc.*

46. See H. Diels in *Festschrift für Theodor Gomperz* (Vienna, 1902): 'Ein orphischer Demeterhymnus', p. 1 and especially pp. 13 ff.

47. The words Ἰρικεπαῖγε σῶισομ με are to be found in a mystery papyrus of the third century B.C., discovered in the Egyptian village of Gurob and first published by J. G. Smily, *Greek Papyri from Gurob* (Dublin, 1921), n. 1. (See Kern, *O.F.* 31, lin. 22.)

48. The fragments of Epimenides' *Theogony* or Χρησμοί are collected in Diels's *Vorsokratiker*, i. See the excerpt from Eudemus, *supra*, n. 44.

49. Epimen. B 5.

50. See J. Burnet, *Early Greek Philosophy* (4th ed.), pp. 109, 186, etc.

51. According to Eudemus, the *Theogony* of Orpheus made Night the beginning (Orph. B 12); Aristoph. *Birds* 693 also begins his parody of an Orphic *Theogony* from Chaos and Night. See *supra*, p. 64.

52. Hom. *Iliad* xiv. 201.

53. This is how we may interpret the words of Eudemus *ap.* Damasc. 124 (Epimen. B 5): ἐξ ὧν [*scil.* Ἀέρος καὶ Νυκτός] δύο Τιτᾶνας .... Eudemus does not say who these 'two Titans' are, but if we look up the catalogue of the children of Uranus who are called Titans in Hes. *Theog.* 129 ff. (see vv. 207 ff. and 630), it seems possible that Oceanus and Tethys are to be understood by the δύο Τιτᾶνας of Epimenides, for they are the only ones who form a traditional couple that could and did play a part as ἀρχή in the oldest theogony, i.e. in Homer (see n. 52). Philodemus, *De piet.* 47 a 2, p. 19 (Gomperz), compares the Homeric variant, Oceanus and Tethys, with Epimenides' first couple, Air and Night; and Epimenides may have felt obliged by this famous tradition to incorporate the Homeric version somehow into his new genealogy by making Oceanus and Tethys, 'the Titans', the children of Air and Night, thus giving them the second instead of the first place. His reason for any such correction must have been that he wanted to make the genealogical myth agree with the

physical facts as he understood them. For another version of Epimenides' genealogy of the gods, see n. 55.

54. 'Epimenides' B 5 found this version of the world-egg in another source, different from Hesiod and Homer, probably an epic poem of the 'Orpheus' type.

55. Epimen. B 7. It is true, the words *'Ωκε]ανοῦ καὶ Γ[ῆς γεννήμα]τ' εἶναι*, which are taken from Philodemus' *De piet.* 46 b 7, p. 18 (Gomperz), are based on conjecture, but the reconstruction of the passage is rather probable. At first sight it seems hard to understand how Gē could be called a Titan by 'Epimenides', since she is the mother of the Titans in the theogonic tradition of Hesiod. But there is a possibility of reconciling Philodemus' version with that of Eudemus (see n. 53) if we assume that the highly speculative theogony of 'Epimenides' gave the word 'Titans' a new allegoric sense, and that he presented as the first couple Air–Night (= dark empty space), and as the second couple Oceanus–Gē (= the elements water and earth). We find a similar correction of the traditional theogonic myth in Pherecydes (see p. 67). He made Gē (Chthoniē) the wife of Zeus (Zās), although she was his grandmother in the *Theogony* of Hesiod; like 'Epimenides', Pherecydes justified this innovation by an allegoric interpretation, for both Zās and Chthoniē represented the highest physical principles in his system.

56. See Xenophanes' view that everything originated from earth and water, B 29.

57. See the *Theogony* of Hieronymus (*ap.* Damasc. 123, Kern, *O. F.* 54), who also made water and earth (*ὕδωρ καὶ γῆν*) the first principles of his cosmogony. Of course, he could not have called them by these names; *ὕδωρ* and *γῆ* are the interpretation of Damascius, and in the mythical language of the *Theogony* of Hieronymus the names were Oceanus and Gē. He seems to have taken this couple from 'Epimenides'' *Theogony*. See n. 55.

58. Pherecyd. B 1.

59. Acusil. A 4.

60. See Xenoph. B 14, Epicharm. B 1.

61. Prob. *ad* Virg. *Buc.* 6, 31, App. Serv. ed. Hagen, p. 343, 18 (Pherecyd. A 9). The same explanation is given by Hermias, *Irr.* 12 (ibid.).

62. The form *Κρόνος* is preserved by both Probus and Hermias; see n. 61. According to the literal quotation in Diog. L. i. 119, Pherecydes called him *Χρόνος*.

63. See *supra*, p. 34.

64. On the origin and function of etymology in early Greek theological thought, see Max Warburg, 'Zwei Fragen zum Kratylos' (*Neue Philologische Untersuchungen*, hrsg. v. W. Jaeger, Bd. v, 1929, p. 65 f.). Etymology is one of the most important and most frequent methods of early Greek theology.

65. Arist. *Metaph.* N 4, 1091^b 8 (Pherecyd. A 7). This 'mixed' character of Pherecydes' speculation seems to be what Diogenes Laertius is hinting at when he says (i. 116) that Pherecydes was the first to write *περὶ φύσεως καὶ θεῶν*. His theogony involved as one of its elements *τὸ φυσιολογεῖν*; it was physics under the guise of theology.

66. Arist. *Metaph.* B 4, 1000^{a}18 (cf. ^{b}9).

67. This observation was of special importance for Aristotle, since he made the 'most perfect being' the principle of the universe. He criticizes the Pythagoreans and Speusippus the Platonist because they put the imperfect at the beginning. See *Metaph.* Λ 7, 1072^{b}31.

68. See the long fragment discovered in a papyrus, Pherecyd. B 2.

69. Damasc. *De princ.* 124 (Eudemus, frg. 117), Pherecyd. A 8. Porph. *De antr. Nymph.* 31 (Pherecyd. B 6) says that Pherecydes distinguished in his cosmology various μυχοί and that he used the words ἄντρα, βόθροι, πύλαι, and θύραι as synonyms of μυχοί. Hence the title Πεντέμυχος (see Damasc. loc. cit.). Suidas has the variant Ἑπτάμυχος, which he seems to take from Porphyry's *History of Philosophy* (Pherecyd. A 2). The variant shows that the title was added by later writers, probably the grammarians of Alexandria, who did not agree on the interpretation of Pherecydes' cosmological scheme. Damascius explains πεντέμυχος as πεντέκοσμος.

70. Damasc. loc. cit. (= Eudemus) says that Chronos made—out of his own (?) γόνος—fire, *pneuma*, water . . . and distributed them in five μυχοί, and from them he derived a numerous lineage of gods. In the lacuna of this text two other elements are missing. Kern conjectures αὐτοῦ instead of ἑαυτοῦ and understands the γόνος to be that of Zās. Cf. Pherecyd. B 7, where the word ἐκροή is ascribed to him. But the 'emanation' which this synonym for σπέρμα or γόνος seems to suggest must have indicated something physical and quite different from the later spiritualistic use of the term.

71. Orig. *Contra Cels.* vi. 42 (Pherecyd. B 5).

72. Orig. loc. cit. (Pherecyd. B 4).

73. Aesch. *Prom.* 351–72, Pindar, *Pyth.* i. 15–28.

74. See my note in *Paideia*, i[2], p. 454, n. 31.

75. There seems to me an urgent need to reinterpret Hesiod's *Theogony* and his entire thought from this point of view and to make a serious effort to distinguish Hesiod's own theological ideas, which are new, from the merely traditional elements of his speculation.

76. Nauck, *Tragic. graec. fragm.*, Aesch. frg. 70.

CHAPTER V

ORIGIN OF THE DOCTRINE OF THE SOUL'S DIVINITY

1. Erwin Rohde, *Psyche — Seelenkult und Unsterblichkeitsglaube der Griechen*, 7.–8. Aufl. (Tübingen, 1921).

2. Ibid., p. 2.

3. Ibid., p. 4. Even though Rohde insists that it is not correct to say that death is the end of everything in Homer, that which is left, the Homeric ψυχή, is not a soul in our sense of the word.

4. Hom. *Iliad* i. 3–5, xxiii. 105. Different is xxiii. 244.

5. Rohde, op. cit., pp. 4 ff.

6. Ibid., pp. 46–7.

7. Pindar, frg. 131 (Schroeder). See Rohde, op. cit., p. 6. The Greek words of Pindar which we have translated by 'image of life' are αἰῶνος εἴδωλον.

8. W. F. Otto, *Die Manen oder Von den Urformen des Totenglaubens* (Berlin, 1923), pp. 4 ff.

9. W. F. Otto, op. cit., p. 6, has observed this rightly. I remember that, even before Otto's book was published, I had frequent discussions on the problem

of the Homeric concept of soul with Ernst Bickel, then my colleague at the University of Kiel. We used to agree on the very same point which was later made by Professor Otto, the point of departure for his monograph cited in n. 8. Both Otto and Bickel seem to have represented in this the oral tradition of H. Usener's seminar.

10. W. F. Otto, op. cit., pp. 8–10.

11. See n. 7.

12. See, for instance, W. F. Otto, op. cit., p. 17. The best-known example of this meaning in Homer is found in *Iliad* xxii. 161, ἀλλὰ περὶ ψυχῆς θέον Ἕκτορος ἱπποδάμοιο. Tyrtaeus, frg. 7, 4 (Diehl) derives the compound φιλοψυχεῖν from this meaning 'life', just as he says ψυχέων φείδεσθαι. In later centuries ψυχή loses this meaning more and more; it retains it mostly in solemnly phrased passages which are influenced by epic tradition. On the other hand, the way in which Herodotus and Anaxagoras used the word ψυχή for 'life' proves that the Ionian dialect had kept this meaning alive from Homeric times.

13. See the Hades scene in *Odyssey* xi; there Odysseus is able to recognize the ψυχαί of all the dead whom he had known in life by their resemblance to the living men. This resemblance is strongly emphasized in *Iliad* xxiii. 65 ff., where the ψυχή of Patroclus appears to Achilles in a dream, πάντ' αὐτῷ μέγεθός τε καὶ ὄμματα κάλ' εἰκυῖα καὶ φωνήν. This 'soul' even wears the same clothes as Patroclus.

14. W. F. Otto, op. cit., p. 45.

15. See Otto's own polemic against Rohde's assumption of a sort of primitive syllogism by which the belief in the ψυχή and its existence was supposedly derived from experiences such as dream, death, ecstasy, &c.

16. Ernst Bickel, 'Homerischer Seelenglaube; geschichtliche Grundzüge menschlicher Seelenvorstellungen' (*Schriften der Königsberger Gelehrten Gesellschaft*, 1. Jahr, Heft 7, Berlin, 1925). Although I cannot follow Bickel's speculations on the *lebender Leichnam*, &c., I find valuable observations in his criticism of Otto's theory.

17. See especially Bickel, loc. cit., pp. 232 and 258. See also Joachim Boehme, *Die Seele und das Ich im homerischen Epos* (Leipzig–Berlin, 1929), p. 113.

18. Bickel, loc. cit., p. 259.

19. W. F. Otto has tried to prove that ψυχή in Homer invariably means 'life' if it does not signify the shade in Hades. But although ψυχή shows a strong tendency towards the meaning 'life' in the Homeric poems, there are passages in which its true meaning remains controversial. And in spite of the fact that the meaning 'life' prevails, there is no doubt that this represents an advanced phase of abstraction in the development of the word.

20. In *Iliad* ix. 409 it is said that the psyche ἀμείψεται ἕρκος ὀδόντων. Similarly in *Iliad* xvi. 856, ψυχὴ δ' ἐκ ῥεθέων πταμένη Ἄϊδόσδε βεβήκει.

21. Arist. *De anima* i. 5, 410b22 ff. (Orpheus B 11).

22. Homer shows no trace of this old belief.

23. In Greek lyric poetry the expression of the ego and of human emotion naturally prevails. Therefore the word θυμός, which in Homer, too, means 'soul' in the sense of consciousness, becomes even more important than before.

24. Aët. i. 3, 4 (Anaximenes B 2): οἷον ἡ ψυχὴ . . . ἡ ἡμετέρα ἀὴρ οὖσα συγκρατεῖ ἡμᾶς, καὶ ὅλον τὸν κόσμον πνεῦμα καὶ ἀὴρ περιέχει.

25. Diog. L. ix. 19 (Xenoph. A 1).

26. Arist. *Phys.* iv. 6, 213ᵇ22 (*Pythagor. Schule* B 30).

27. See n. 21. Cf. the parallel results of the previous chapter concerning the influence of natural philosophy on the theogonic epics of the sixth century.

28. See n. 24. Diogenes of Apollonia, who followed the doctrine of Anaximenes closely, certainly thought of his air-principle as animated and 'knowing much' (πολλὰ εἰδός, see frg. B 8). Similarly the author of the Hippocratic treatise *On the Sacred Disease* says (c. 19), τὴν δὲ φρόνησιν ὁ ἀὴρ παρέχεται.

29. See Bickel, op. cit., pp. 260 ff.

30. See *Iliad* xi. 334; *Od.* xxi. 154, 171.

31. On Anaximenes' concept of ψυχή see n. 24.

32. I have traced this development of the concept of *areté* throughout the history of the Greek mind in my *Paideia*; on the etymology and meaning of the word see vol. i², p. 5 and p. 418, n. 10.

33. For instance, *Iliad* xiii. 671, ὦκα δὲ θυμὸς ὤλετ' ἀπὸ μελέων (θυμός = ψυχή), *Od.* xi. 221, xv. 354.

34. On the historical development of the Greek concept of ψυχή see John Burnet, 'The Socratic Doctrine of the Soul', in *Proceedings of the British Academy,* 1915–16, pp. 235 ff.

35. See W. F. Otto, op. cit., p. 1, on the two basic conceptions of soul, the Homeric, which he identifies with the old popular belief, and the mystic.

36. This is the opinion of Otto Kern, *Religion der Griechen*, ii (Berlin, 1935), p. 147.

37. See *supra*, p. 82.

38. This antithesis of body and soul which occurs so frequently in later times did not yet exist in Homeric thought. When the ψυχή is opposed to the body in Homer, the corpse or body is generally called 'the man himself' (αὐτός); see n. 4, where an exception to this rule is noted.

39. See F. M. Cornford, 'The Invention of Space', in *Essays in Honour of Gilbert Murray* (London, 1936), p. 223. See also J. Burnet, *Early Greek Philosophy* (4th ed.), pp. 109, 186, 194, 229.

40. See *supra*, p. 79, and nn. 24 ff.

41. C. A. Lobeck, *Aglaophamus*, i, pp. 69 ff.

42. Pind. *Ol.* ii. 63 ff. and frg. 129–33 (Schroeder).

43. See Wilamowitz, *Pindar* (Berlin, 1922), pp. 248–52. Wilamowitz rightly observes that it was not necessary for Pindar to be initiated in order to be able to describe Orphic eschatology as he does. But Wilamowitz seems to underrate the impression which that faith must have made on the poet to enable him to write his verses.

44. Pind., frg. 129–30 (Schroeder).

45. Ibid., frg. 133 (Schroeder).

46. For abstinence from animal food as a characteristic of the Orphic βίος see passages referred to *supra* p. 216, n. 11.

47. See Pind. frg. 131 (Schroeder).

48. Arist. frg. 10 (Rose). On this fragment see my *Aristotle*, p. 161.

49. On an interesting prognostic application of this Orphic concept of the soul in Greek medicine (Περὶ διαίτης, book iv) see my *Paideia*, iii, p. 39.

50. Arist. frg. 15 (Rose). See my *Aristotle*, p. 160.

51. The Greek word which Aristotle (frg. 15) uses for that inner 'disposition' of the soul (and of which our term 'disposition' is the literal translation) is διατεθῆναι. διάθεσις, originally a medical term, was applied by Plato and Aristotle to the soul. Besides the rational demonstration of God's existence, Aristotle admits a second and more emotional source of certainty about the things divine (see my *Aristotle*, pp. 162 ff.). In *De caelo* ii. 1, 284ᵇ3 he calls this sentiment or *Ahnung* of the soul, in a metaphoric sense, a μαντεία περὶ τὸν θεόν.

52. See chapters vi–viii of this book. Even Democritus in his book Περὶ εὐθυμίης, which contained an outline of his ethical thought in the loose form of ὑποθῆκαι, seems to have spoken of the spirit (νοῦς) and the soul (ψυχή) as divine (θεῖα), though only in a metaphorical sense; see B 37 and B 112, if the 'Sayings of Democrates' are really his literary property. Cf. also frg. B 18.

53. On Socrates' care of the soul see my *Paideia*, ii, pp. 38 ff.

54. See Orpheus B 19.

CHAPTER VI

PARMENIDES' MYSTERY OF BEING

1. Karl Reinhardt, *Parmenides und die Geschichte der griechischen Philosophie* (Bonn, 1916), p. 256.

2. Reinhardt, loc. cit.

3. It has been proved *supra*, p. 53, that this conception of Parmenides' relationship to Xenophanes has led the author of the *De Xenophane Melisso Gorgia* to attribute some of the basic views of Parmenides to Xenophanes in order to make this alleged relationship appear more clearly.

4. See pp. 39 ff.

5. Parm. A 37.

6. Hes. *Theog.* 22 ff.

7. Ibid. 33: καί μ᾽ ἐκέλονθ᾽ ὑμνεῖν μακάρων γένος αἰὲν ἐόντων.

8. Parm. B 1.

9. Ibid. B 1, 29 ff.

10. Hes. *Theog.* 28.

11. On the development of the Greek concept of truth and its synonyms see Wilhelm Luther's monograph *Wahrheit und Lüge im ältesten Griechentum* (Borna-Leipzig, 1935). Luther rightly sees Hesiod as marking the beginning of a new epoch, pp. 121 ff.

12. Parm. B 1, 29–30.

13. Ibid. B 1, 1 ff.

14. Sext. Emp. vii. 111 ff.

15. Hermann Diels, in the introduction to his *Parmenides Lehrgedicht* (Berlin, 1897), has analysed the motive of revelation in the proem of Parmenides' poem and has linked it with the history of early Greek religion.

16. Diels, op. cit., has assumed Orphic influence, and others have followed him in this. On the Orphic question in general see *supra*, p. 58.

17. Parm. B 6, 6.

18. Aesch. *Prom.* 447. On traces of prophetic speech in the language of Heraclitus see p. 112.

19. Parm. B 7, 4 (formerly B 1, 35).

20. Parm. B 1, 2–3: ὁδὸν ... ἣ κατὰ πάντ' ἄστη φέρει εἰδότα φῶτα (πάντ' ἄστη N, πάντ' ἄτη L, πάντα τῆ Es). See the attempts of modern scholars to restore the text of this passage listed in Diels's *Vorsokratiker*, i⁵, ad loc.

21. See *Od.* i. 3, πολλῶν ἀνθρώπων ἴδεν ἄστεα καὶ νόον ἔγνω.

22. On the metaphor of the way in early Greek thought see Otfrid Becker, *Das Bild des Weges und verwandte Vorstellungen im frühgriechischen Denken* (*Einzelschriften zum Hermes*, Heft 4, Berlin, 1937). The author has traced the use and meaning of this metaphor throughout early Greek literature and devotes a special chapter to Parmenides (pp. 139 ff.).

23. In my *Paideia*, i², p. 460, n. 149, I have suggested the emendation of the corrupt word ἄστη (Parm. B 1, 3) into ἀσινῆ: the 'way' of truth leads the 'knowing man' (εἰδότα φῶτα) unscathed (*incolumem*) wherever he goes. Similarly, the religious language of Aesch. *Eum.* 315 says of the 'pure' man (καθαρός), i.e. of him who keeps his hands free from pollution, that 'he goes through life unscathed' (ἀσινὴς δ' αἰῶνα διοιχνεῖ). This strikes the note required by the context of Parmenides' proem. After I had advocated this restoration of the text I noticed that Meineke had anticipated it, which seems to prove its correctness. My suggestion was accepted by O. Becker (see n. 22), p. 140, n. 5.

24. Parmenides received his 'revelation' not by an act of personal grace but as the 'knowing man' (εἰδὼς φῶς). See B 1, 3.

25. Goethe's words on *heilig öffentlich Geheimnis* are an attempt at expressing the nature of true mystery.

26. See *Cebetis tabula*, cc. 12 and 21. The later ancient material on the two ways was collected by A. Brinkmann; see p. 620 of his article quoted in n. 27.

27. See A. Brinkmann, 'Ein Denkmal des Neupythagoreismus', *Rheinisches Museum N.F.* 66 (1911), pp. 616 ff.

28. Hes. *Works and Days*, 286 ff.

29. Pind. *Ol.* ii. 77. On the two ways which the souls of the good and the bad have to wander after death, see Plat. *Gorg.* 524 a and *Rep.* 614 c.

30. On the myth in Plato's *Republic* and his conception of *paideia* as preparation for the choice of the right βίος in the next life, see *Paideia*, ii. 370. Plato follows an 'Orphic' pattern, into which he introduces his idea of *paideia*. On *paideia* as the 'road' (ταύτη πορευτέον), see also *Epin.* 992 a. Cf. Plato's similar reinterpretation of the 'islands of the blessed' as the philosophical *paideia*; *Paideia*, ii. 300, 319.

31. Parm. B 6.

32. Ibid. B 6, 4 ff.

33. Ibid. B 1, 3, εἰδότα φῶτα.

Q

34. The phrase 'men of two heads' (Parm. B 6, 5) was first referred to Heraclitus by Jacob Bernays, *Ges. Abh.* i. 62, and scholars like Diels, Gomperz, Burnet, and others followed his interpretation. They thought that the characterization of these men fitted Heraclitus exactly : they assumed, according to Parmenides, that 'it is and it is not the same and not the same', and that 'all things travel in opposite directions' (παλίντροπός ἐστι κέλευθος); cf. Heracl. B 60, ὁδὸς ἄνω κάτω μία καὶ ὡυτή.

35. See K. Reinhardt, *Parmenides*, pp. 64 ff.

36. On the phrase ἡ φύσις τῶν ὄντων, which is frequent in the Greek physicists and must go back to the Milesian school, see *supra*, p. 19. But these natural philosophers simply took the word ὄντα from common usage. Thus Parmenides turns his polemic against philosophers and common usage alike. It is impossible to think of an individual thinker, such as Heraclitus, in the passage where Parmenides speaks of the 'deaf and blind people' οἷς τὸ πέλειν τε καὶ οὐκ εἶναι ταὐτὸν νενόμισται, for νενόμισται refers not to the opinion of one man or a few but to the perversity of the prevailing νόμος (= custom, tradition). Cf. Xenophanes B 2, 13, ἀλλ᾽ εἰκῇ μάλα τοῦτο νομίζεται, which refers also to the *communis opinio* of men. See also the parallel passage of Parmenides himself, B 8, 38–9 : τῷ πάντ᾽ ὄνομ(α) ἔσται ὅσσα βροτοὶ κατέθεντο πεποιθότες εἶναι ἀληθῆ : their views on this subject are 'mere words', and there is no truth in them.

37. Parm. B 8.

38. Ibid. B 7, 3–B 8, 1 (formerly B 1, 34–7).

39. Ibid. B 3, B 8, 34.

40. See now K. von Fritz in *Classical Philology*, xxxviii (1943), pp. 79 ff., on the meaning of νοῦς, νοεῖν, &c., in Homer, and ibid. xl (1945), p. 236, on the meaning of these words in Parmenides.

41. Parm. B 2, B 6.

42. Ibid. B 1, 29–30; B 8, 50 ff.

43. The author must ask the reader's indulgence for this consciously anachronistic use of a much later terminology.

44. See E. Hoffmann, *Die Sprache und die archaische Logik* (Tübingen, 1925), pp. 8–15.

45. This is convincingly pointed out by K. Reinhardt, *Parmenides*, pp. 80 ff.

46. The world of δόξα which Parmenides builds up (B 8, 50 ff.) is based on the convention of mortals (cf. νενόμισται, B 6, 8, and n. 36) that Being and Not-being are one and the same and yet not the same. It is the world seen with human eyes and is opposed to the world of Being as the goddess of Truth sees it. For it is really she who is speaking when Parmenides talks of 'mortals'.

47. Parm. B 8, 55 ff., and B 9.

48. On Eros see Parm. B 13; on mixture, B 9, B 12, B 16. I cannot agree with Reinhardt, op. cit., p. 74, that the concept of mixture, which was to play such an important part in later Greek philosophy, took its origin here and thus grew out of Parmenides' purely logical and metaphysical speculation. It must have been applied long before in medical and physical thought, from which Parmenides transferred it to his problem.

49. Parm. B 12, 3. See the interpretation of the rings by H. Diels, *Parmenides Lehrgedicht*, pp. 105, 107, which leaves some doubt, however, as to the meaning of στεινότεραι. Cf. Burnet, *Early Greek Philosophy*, p. 191.

50. Parm. B 10, B 11.

51. Ibid. B 16.

52. Ibid. B 1, 9–10.

53. Ibid. B 8, 56 ff., and B 9.

54. Burnet, op. cit., pp. 184 ff., thinks that Parmenides in the second part of his poem took Pythagorean views as his point of departure. Diels (see n. 49), p. 63, assumes that this part formed a kind of doxography in the later Peripatetic manner and that it listed the views of previous philosophers. Against both views see Reinhardt, op. cit., p. 28, n. 1.

55. See Kurt Riezler, *Parmenides* (Frankfurt, 1934), p. 50.

56. Parm. B 8, 13 ff.: τοῦ εἵνεκεν οὔτε γενέσθαι οὔτ' ὄλλυσθαι ἀνῆκε Δίκη χαλάσασα πέδῃσιν. Diels translated this passage: 'Drum hat die Gerechtigkeit Werden und Vergehen nicht aus ihren Banden freigegeben, sondern sie hält sie fest.' He took the infinitives γενέσθαι and ὄλλυσθαι as object of ἀνῆκε. But the object of Δίκη ἀνῆκε is τὸ ἐόν, which must be supplied from what precedes here as well as in ll. 22 and 26. (Kranz in the fifth edition of Diels's *Vorsokratiker* has adopted the correct interpretation.) I find ἀφῆκε construed in exactly the same way with the *accusativus cum infinitivo* by Gregory of Nyssa (Migne, *P.G.* xlv, 1273 D). He seems to transfer a thought of Parmenides to Christian theological speculation. See H. Fraenkel, *Parmenides-Studien* (*Gött. Gel. N.*, 1930, p. 159), who first rightly criticized Diels's interpretation of these lines.

57. Parm. B 8, 21.

58. This interpretation would make the first part of Parmenides' poem correspond with Aristotle's *Metaphysics*, the philosophy of Being as Being (ὂν ᾗ ὄν), and the second part with Aristotle's *Physics*, the theory of Being as moved (ὂν ᾗ κινητόν).

59. In other words, Parmenides' procedure is exactly contrary to what we should expect from the modern point of view.

60. These properties he calls 'sign-posts' (σήματα) on the road to truth, frg. B 8, 2.

61. J. Stenzel in *Handbuch der Philosophie: Die Metaphysik des Altertums* (Munich and Berlin, 1929), pp. 34, 36, 47.

62. Parm. B 8, 43–4.

63. Burnet, op. cit., p. 182, rightly points to the fact that Parmenides' concept of Being determined the three most influential theories of the material foundations of the universe which were set forth by later pre-Socratic thinkers: Empedocles' four elements, Anaxagoras' homoeomeries, and Democritus' atoms. But I cannot follow Burnet when he infers from this that therefore Parmenides' Being itself must have been 'matter', and that this was its real meaning. What happened to Parmenides' Being the moment one of his pupils interpreted it as material is shown by Melissus of Samos, who quite logically dropped one of its main characteristics, its finiteness, and made it like Anaximander's material ἀρχή, the *apeiron*, again.

64. Parm. B 1, 3.

65. Ibid. B 8, 4.

66. The road which leads to the knowledge of this Being is called 'far from the path of mortals', frg. B 1, 27. The man who goes this way and reaches its end, which is truth, is praised because of his blessed lot. The Christian concept,

which is always present in our minds, of a personal God must not obscure the fact that Parmenides' Being is in the sense of Greek religion 'divine', as is Plato's Idea of the Good. Cf. my *Paideia*, ii. 285 ff.

CHAPTER VII

HERACLITUS

1. See *supra*, p. 31.

2. The author of this view is Aristotle (*Metaph.* A 3, 984^{a}8), who, after naming Homer and Thales as representatives of the water-hypothesis and Anaximenes and Diogenes as representatives of the air-hypothesis, describes Hippasus and Heraclitus as preferring fire as the first material cause. There is complete unanimity about this among ancient doxographers from Theophrastus to Nemesius of Emesa, since they all depend in the last analysis on Aristotle.

3. Aët. i. 23, 7 (Diels, *Doxographi*, p. 320): Ἡράκλειτος ἠρεμίαν μὲν καὶ στάσιν ἐκ τῶν ὅλων ἀνῄρει.

4. This aspect of Heraclitus' philosophy was stressed by Plato; see *Crat.* 402 a. Arist. *Metaph.* A 6, 987^{a}34 ff. even regards the πάντα ῥεῖ as one of the fundamental motives of Plato's ontology. The words πάντα ῥεῖ are not to be found in our fragments of Heraclitus, and perhaps they go back not to him but to some of his later followers such as Cratylus or the Heracliteans mentioned by Plat. *Theaet.* 189 e, *Crat.* 440 c. They could refer to such statements as Heracl. B 12, B 49 a, B 91 as proof of this interpretation of Heraclitus' philosophy.

5. See K. Reinhardt, *Parmenides*, pp. 205 ff. Zeller and Burnet were still following the path of the ancient doxographers and accordingly interpreted Heraclitus primarily as a philosopher-of nature after the Milesian fashion. Reinhardt rightly remarks that what corresponds in Heraclitus to the ἄπειρον of Anaximander and to the ὄν of Parmenides is not fire but ἓν τὸ σοφόν. The 'one wise' is not a predicate of fire, but fire is the form of its physical manifestation and expression, as Reinhardt puts it. See also H. Cherniss, *Aristotle's Criticism of Presocratic Philosophy* (Baltimore, 1935).

6. See Bruno Snell, *Hermes*, lxi, p. 353; Wilamowitz, *Hermes*, lxii, p. 276.

7. See the analysis of the Hippocratic *Aphorisms* given by E. Littré, *Œuvres d'Hippocrate*, iv, pp. 435–43.

8. That Heraclitus was much read by some of the authors of our 'Hippocratic' collection need not be proved, since it is so well known. He was used most of all by the author of the Περὶ διαίτης.

9. The numbers in parentheses refer to the numbers of the fragments of Heraclitus in H. Diels's *Vorsokratiker*, i, 5th ed. They are inserted into the text only where fragments are quoted literally.

10. The last decades have produced a large literature on Heraclitus, the fruit of an ever-increasing philosophical interest in his thought. Of this I quote as the most thorough and complete reinterpretation of the fragments: Olof Gigon, *Untersuchungen zu Heraklit* (Leipzig, 1935). See my own treatment of Heraclitus in *Paideia*, i^2, pp. 178–84.

11. I construe ἀεί with ἐόντος (Diels) and not with ἀξύνετοι γίνονται (Burnet). See the full discussion of this sentence in Gigon, op. cit., pp. 1 ff. Cf. the Ionian

use of ἐών (= real, true) in Hipp. *De vet. med.*, c. 1. There medicine is called a τέχνη ἐοῦσα. With τοῦ λόγου ἐόντος ἀεί, cf. τοῦ λόγου ἐόντος ξυνοῦ (Heracl. B 2). For the content see B 34: ἀξύνετοι ἀκούσαντες κωφοῖσιν ἐοίκασι· φάτις αὐτοῖσιν μαρτυρεῖ παρεόντας ἀπεῖναι. Cf. also B 72. This style, though consciously rhetorical, takes its colours from old religious *Prophetenrede*.

12. Similar is B 50: οὐκ ἐμοῦ ἀλλὰ τοῦ λόγου ἀκούσαντας.

13. διαιρέων, not = διαιρούμενος, cf. Herod. vii. 16, where it is said of a γνώμη (οἷον ἐγὼ διαιρέω).

14. Heracl. B 89, 'the waking have one and the same cosmos'. Cf. also the contrast of waking and sleeping in B 21, B 26, B 73.

15. See Heracl. B 1, τοὺς δὲ ἄλλους ἀνθρώπους.

16. See νοεῖν, νόημα, Parm. B 7, 2; B 2, 2; B 3, B 6, 1 and 6; B 8, 8, 17, 36, &c. (but Parm. B 16, 3, φρονέει); Heraclitus uses φρόνιμος, φρονεῖν, φρόνησις in B 2, B 17, B 64, B 112 (?), B 113, B 116. On the practical meaning of φρόνησις see my *Aristotle*, pp. 81–4. Heraclitus says that τὸ φρονεῖν ἀρετὴ μεγίστη (B 112). (Kranz prefers the variant σωφρονεῖν.)

17. See Aesch. *Ag.* 176.

18. Heracl. B 1, ἔπη καὶ ἔργα.

19. Ibid. B 112, σοφίη (*scil.* ἐστί) ἀληθέα λέγειν καὶ ποιεῖν.

20. Ibid. B 73, οὐ δεῖ ὥσπερ καθεύδοντας ποιεῖν καὶ λέγειν.

21. Ibid. B 1.

22. See n. 14.

23. Ibid. B 2.

24. Ibid. B 113.

25. See *supra*, p. 95.

26. See ibid. B 29, B 104. Cf. also B 49.

27. See *supra*, p. 114.

28. Heracl. B 113.

29. See my essay 'Praise of Law: The Origin of Legal Philosophy and the Greeks' in *Interpretations of Legal Philosophy: Essays in Honor of Roscoe Pound* (N.Y., 1946), p. 359.

30. See *supra*, p. 36.

31. The Erinyes avenge every violation of what we should call the natural laws of life. Cf. Hom. *Iliad* xix. 418.

32. See *supra*, p. 31.

33. We had to make a similar statement about the meaning of Anaximander's *diké*. See *supra*, p. 36.

34. Diog. L. ix. 5 (Heracl. A 1): τὸ δὲ φερόμενον αὐτοῦ βιβλίον ἐστὶ μὲν ἀπὸ τοῦ συνέχοντος Περὶ φύσεως, διήρηται δὲ εἰς τρεῖς λόγους, εἴς τε τὸν περὶ τοῦ παντὸς καὶ πολιτικὸν καὶ θεολογικόν.

35. See *Paideia*, i², p. 183.

36. Diog. L. ix. 15 (Heracl. A 1) quotes among the commentators on Heraclitus the grammarian Diodotus, ὃς οὔ φησι περὶ φύσεως εἶναι τὸ σύγγραμμα, ἀλλὰ περὶ πολιτείας, τὰ δὲ περὶ φύσεως ἐν παραδείγματος εἴδει κεῖσθαι. The words 'to have a merely paradigmatic function' used in the text seem to me the best

translation of the Greek ἐν παραδείγματος εἴδει κεῖσθαι. This means that the cosmic parallels were used by Heraclitus as a mould for the philosophical interpretation of the life of man, in which he was primarily interested. The cosmos to him was the life of man writ large. That was certainly the way in which Heraclitus' predecessors had arrived at the idea of a cosmos. They had transferred the concept of social order to the world as a whole, where they had found it again. One may compare with Diodotus' view of Heraclitus' book the interpretation of Plato's *Republic* which I have offered in *Paideia*, ii: that this work of Plato's is not a treatise on civil government, as it is understood by most of its readers, but on the education of the human soul, and that the *politeia* is only the ideal framework of Plato's *paideia*.

37. Day and night, Heracl. B 57; life and death, B 62, B 77; wet and dry, warm and cold, B 126. See also B 65 and B 67 quoted in the text, p. 119. Cf. n. 43.

38. See the transition from the cosmic to the human sphere in B 67: day and night, winter and summer, war and peace, surfeit and hunger. On the interpretation of B 65 and B 67 and on the transition of the examples which Heraclitus gives in them from the cosmic sphere to human life and vice versa, see n. 43.

39. Heracl. B 24, B 25.

40. See ibid. B 53.

41. On the hymnodic element in the language of the pre-Socratic philosophers, see *supra*, p. 30. With Heraclitus' words πόλεμος πάντων μὲν πατήρ ἐστι, πάντων δὲ βασιλεύς, one might compare Anaximander's words (A 15) on the divine character of the *apeiron*: καὶ περιέχειν ἅπαντα καὶ πάντα κυβερνᾶν . . . καὶ τοῦτ' εἶναι τὸ θεῖον. Similar are the words in which Diogenes of Apollonia (B 5) predicates the divinity of his cosmic principle, the Air: καί μοι δοκεῖ τὸ τὴν νόησιν ἔχον εἶναι ὁ ἀὴρ καλούμενος ὑπὸ τῶν ἀνθρώπων καὶ ὑπὸ τούτου πάντας κυβερνᾶσθαι καὶ πάντων κρατεῖν, and in the next line, καὶ ἐπὶ πᾶν ἀφῖχθαι καὶ πάντα διατιθέναι καὶ ἐν παντὶ ἐνεῖναι. These parallels prove the divine rank of Heraclitus' Polemos. So Philodemus, *De piet.* 14, 26 (p. 81, Gomperz) interpreted Heraclitus' words. He stated: καὶ τὸν πόλεμον καὶ τὸν Δία τὸν αὐτὸν εἶναι, καθάπερ καὶ τὸν Ἡράκλειτον λέγειν. The divine character of Heraclitus' Polemos is confirmed by the fact that elsewhere he gives it predicates which connect or identify it with other aspects of his supreme principle, e.g. the fundamental concept of the 'common' (ξυνόν). Wisdom and reason are that which is common to all (see *supra*, p. 114). Frg. B 80 applies the predicate 'common' to War: εἰδέναι δὲ χρὴ τὸν πόλεμον ἐόντα ξυνόν, καὶ δίκην ἔριν, καὶ γινόμενα πάντα κατ' ἔριν καὶ χρεών. (The last word is corrupt and has not yet been aptly emended.) The comparison of War with a lawsuit (*dikē*), their common nature being strife, proves that in the last analysis Heraclitus' conception of the world goes back to Anaximander's interpretation of the process of becoming and passing-away as a lawsuit (*dikē*). See *supra*, p. 34. The words πόλεμον ἐόντα ξυνόν vary Homer's phrase (*Iliad* xviii. 309) ξυνὸς Ἐνυάλιος. So Homer 'knew the truth', and though Heraclitus' theory of opposites hardly originated from discussions about Homer (as Gigon thinks, op. cit., p. 117), the poet was quoted as witness for the theory, just as he was attacked whenever he seemed to disagree with the truth (see n. 46).

42. Heracl. B 114. See *supra*, p. 116. Of this divine νόμος Heraclitus says, similarly as of war (B 53), that it 'rules as far as it wants and is sufficient to all things and lords it over all'. These verbs are all predicates which befit only divine omnipotence. 'War' in this context, therefore, no longer means war but the world-governing principle of the (harmony of) conflicting opposites.

43. Ibid. B 65. Here the opposites are called χρησμοσύνη and κόρος. In B 67 they are κόρος and λιμός. Scholars have suspected that these are only variants of one and the same fragment, but apparently Heraclitus used to repeat and inculcate his principles, as is clear from other instances (cf. B 32 with B 41 and see Reinhardt, op. cit., p. 62, n. 1). This was due to the character of his prophetic language, and well expresses his attitude as a teacher of the 'sleeping'. The words κόρος and λιμός seem to point only to the human experience of hunger and surfeit, but the variant χρησμοσύνη and κόρος in B 65 shows that it is a principle of wider application. On the interpretation of both fragments see Gigon, op. cit., p. 49 (see n. 10). Gigon rightly understands the words as referring to a principle of cosmic universality. Also, the 'war and peace' which precede 'hunger and surfeit' (B 67) clearly have the same cosmic character, though man experiences them first in human life. There he comes to understand them first of all from within.

44. On Heracl. B 51 see Gigon, op. cit., p. 23.

45. Heracl. B 8. Gigon, who on the evidence of B 51 denies that Heraclitus' theory of harmony has anything to do with musical harmony (see op. cit., p. 23), must of course regard B 8 as suspect (pp. 25, 117) because its words about the καλλίστη ἁρμονία obviously refer to musical harmony as a product of strife (*eris*), the tension of the chords. But was not this coincidence of 'strife' and 'harmony' naturally the classical example for Heraclitus, which he then expanded into a symbol of cosmic universality? It was the same principle of strife and tension, according to him, that created the lyre and the bow, instruments of the arts of both peace and war.

46. Arist. *Eth. Eud.* viii. 1, 1235ª25 (Heracl. A 22).

47. Gigon, op. cit., p. 117, questions the authenticity of the opposites ἄρρεν: θῆλυ, which Aristotle expressly ascribes to Heraclitus (*Eth. Eud.* viii. 1, 1235ª 26–7). Gigon's argument is not made quite clear. He only says (p. 117): 'im Rahmen der bisher dargestellten heraklitischen Lehre lässt sich gerade ἄρρεν: θῆλυ kaum unterbringen.' Aristotle, *De gen. an.* i. 18, 724ᵇ9, also gives the mating of male and female as an example of γένεσις ἐξ ἐναντίων.

48. Heracl. B 60.

49. See K. Reinhardt, *Parmenides*, pp. 169 ff., who, following Schleiermacher and others, has proved with irrefutable arguments against Zeller that Heraclitus did not anticipate the Stoic theory of the ἐκπύρωσις of the world.

50. Anaximander (A 9) taught that things came into existence by a process of ἀπόκρισις of the *apeiron*; Anaximenes (A 5) said that they originated through πύκνωσις and μάνωσις of the primal substance, Air.

51. Thus it can in fact be stated that Heraclitus had no elaborate cosmology in the sense of the Milesian school, as Reinhardt remarks, op. cit., p. 173. Theophrastus, in the excerpt of Diogenes Laertius (ix. 8), obviously knows only what he takes from B 90 (πυρὸς ἀμοιβὴν τὰ πάντα). Thus fire was the στοιχεῖον of Heraclitus; that he derived τὰ γινόμενα from this principle by πύκνωσις and ἀραίωσις must be Theophrastus' own interpretation, and he adds resignedly: σαφῶς δὲ οὐδὲν ἐκτίθεται. But this can be explained easily if we keep in mind that Heraclitus' entire thought was directed towards the unity of things.

52. Heracl. B 10, B 50.

53. Ibid. B 51, B 59, B 60.

54. See K. Reinhardt. op. cit., pp. 64 ff. He has thus reversed the traditional

view of the historical relationship of Heraclitus and Parmenides: that Parmenides criticized Heraclitus. But even though I agree with Reinhardt that
Parmenides, B 6 is not directed against Heraclitus (see *supra*, p. 101), it does
not follow that the relationship of both thinkers must be reversed, and that
Heraclitus' theory of the unity of opposites is an attempt at reconciling Parmenides with the facts of common experience and the views of the earlier
philosophers of nature.

55. See Gigon, op. cit., pp. 135 ff. and throughout his book. Gigon sees Heraclitus as a synthetic mind influenced by heterogeneous historical traditions
and ideas. The theology of Heraclitus appears to him as a 'strange element' in
his philosophy, which 'looks very odd beside his cosmology'. Accordingly he
looks for an influence coming from without in order to explain the existence
of this element in Heraclitus' thought. He finds its source in Xenophanes, the
thinker who can be called the theologian *par excellence* among the pre-Socratics.
But although Heraclitus has some features in common with Xenophanes—
e.g. his rejection of all anthropomorphic analogies in his conception of God
—their theology is essentially different, and has not only different roots but an
entirely different spirit. We cannot say that Heraclitus is a late representative
of Ionian natural philosophy who implanted a Xenophanic theology as soul
into this body; rather, his theological ideas grew, just as his conception of
cosmic life, from the Milesian ἱστορίη, thereby transforming it into a philosophy
which became in the first place world-interpretation. As we have tried to
show in this book, the theological element existed from the beginning in
Ionian natural philosophy. The true root of Heraclitus' idea of God is Anaximander's *diké*, much more than the all-seeing supreme God of heaven we find in
Xenophanes. Heraclitus sees the nature of what he calls God revealing itself
in the workings of this *diké* in the cosmos, the strife and the harmony of the
basic opposites that constitute the life of the world. This is an entirely
original logical conception of Being. Xenophanes arrives at his concept of the
highest God in a quite different way by denying those traditional predicates
of the gods which seem to him 'not to fit' (πρέπειν) the nature of the Divine.
The author of the *silloi* starts from moral and cosmological criticism of the
conventional view of the gods. It is true, the new cosmic view of the universe
which he had learned from the Milesian philosophers of nature contributed to
Xenophanes' idea of divine dignity and power; only an all-embracing God of
heaven, controlling the universe by His mere thought, without moving hither
and thither, was able to fulfill the requirements of Xenophanes' sense of the
'fitting'. But it cannot be said that his concept of God's power and workings
in the world was born out of a new logical vision of the nature of human and
cosmic life, as is true of Heraclitus. On the other hand, in Heraclitus' thought
the problem of the nature of the Divine seems to have occupied a larger space
and more prominent position than in the cosmology of the Milesians, so that
later ancient interpreters could either distinguish a theological, a political, and
a cosmological part in his philosophy or could take his cosmology not at all
seriously (see nn. 34 and 36).

56. See Heracl. B 14 and B 15, where he attacks the rites of the worship of
Dionysus. But his attitude towards the religion of the people in general is
rather to reinterpret its concepts, in his philosophic sense, from his new centre.
He *legt nicht aus* but *legt unter* (Goethe, *Faust*), which is often the way of the
mystic. So he reinterprets Zeus (B 32) and the 'hope' (ἐλπίς) of the mystery-
religion of his time (B 27). Similarly the Erinyes are reinterpreted in a new
cosmic sense (B 34); the cryptic language of Apollo's oracle at Delphi becomes

in Heraclitus' thought a symbol of the language of nature (B 93), and so does the prophetic figure of the Sibyl (B 92). He reinterprets the myth of the heroes, who after their death became guardians of the living (B 63).

57. Xenoph. B 2, 19 ff. See *supra*, p. 49.

58. Heracl. B 78: ἦθος γὰρ ἀνθρώπειον μὲν οὐκ ἔχει γνώμας, θεῖον δὲ ἔχει. Diels, Gigon, and others translate γνώμας by 'insight', and I have kept this in the text; but the word needs interpretation. In Theognis 60, γνῶμαι are 'norms' or 'standards'; cf. ibid. 693: surfeit has ruined many silly men, for it is hard to know the measure when good fortune is present. γνώμη is just this γνῶναι μέτρον; therefore (ibid. 1171) it is called the best gift which the gods can give a man because 'it has the (knowledge of the) limits of everything'. These words are obviously a mere paraphrase of Solon's frg. 16 (Diehl), where he says that it is hardest to see the invisible measure of γνωμοσύνη, which has the limits (πείρατα) of everything. In *Paideia*, i², p. 452, n. 73, I have used these parallels to show that Clement of Alexandria must be wrong in referring the γνωμοσύνη in Solon's lines to God. Solon must be talking of a human quality, but one which is very rare. One could add Theognis 895: γνώμης οὐδὲν ἄμεινον ἀνὴρ ἔχει αὐτὸς ἐν αὐτῷ οὐδ' ἀγνωμοσύνης, Κύρν', ὀδυνηρότερον. But Heraclitus does say what Clement makes Solon say: that human nature does not possess γνώμη at all, and that only divine nature truly has it. Even a grown-up man is νήπιος compared with God (B 79). The divine σοφόν is in fact πάντων κεχωρισμένον (B 108) and therefore called ἐν τὸ σοφόν (B 32 and B 41). If γνώμη is to know the measure (μέτρον), it is easier from this to understand why Heraclitus speaks so much of measure with regard to the things divine: the sun will not exceed its measures (B 94); the cosmos is πῦρ ἁπτόμενον μέτρα καὶ ἀποσβεννύμενον μέτρα (B 30). See the phrase μετρέεται εἰς τὸν αὐτὸν λόγον (B 31), used with regard to θάλασσα and its transformations. Likewise, the permanent mutual exchange (ἀνταμοιβή) of fire and 'all things' (B 90) presupposes the idea of a measure to which it is subject.

59. See n. 56.

60. It can hardly be said that in calling and not calling his God by the name Zeus, Heraclitus 'made a concession to popular religion' (Gigon, op. cit., p. 140).

61. Anaximander A 15. See *supra*, pp. 29, 31. Cf. Gigon's remarks on the text of Heracl. B 41; but whether we read ὀτέη ἐκυβέρνησε (Diels) or ᾗ κυβερνᾶται (Bywater) makes little difference. On the divine γνώμη see *supra*, n. 58. πάντα διὰ πάντων is a religious formula which occurs in similar forms many times.

62. τὰ δὲ πάντα οἰακίζει Κεραυνός (Heracl. B 64). οἰακίζειν is the activity of the pilot (from οἴαξ); it is like κυβερνᾶν, οἴακα νωμᾶν, &c., used frequently in a figurative sense of the activity of the wise ruler or king. The fire or (in the mythological language) the 'thunderbolt' in B 64 takes the place of the divine ruler.

63. It should be remembered that in the experience of the Greeks law was mostly the work of one man, the lawgiver, who is a sort of embodiment of the highest human wisdom. Plato in his *Laws* (645 b) derives the wisdom of the lawgiver from the λόγος, which he calls divine. If we keep this in mind, it is easier to understand Heraclitus' thought in saying that νόμος καὶ βουλῇ πείθεσθαι ἑνός (B 33). It does not mean tyranny in the sense of Prometheus, who calls Zeus (Aesch. *Prom.* 186) τραχὺς καὶ παρ' ἑαυτῷ τὸ δίκαιον ἔχων.

CHAPTER VIII

EMPEDOCLES

1. Lucr. *De rerum nat.* i. 716 f.

2. Eduard Zeller, *Philosophie der Griechen*, i, p. 1001 (6th ed.).

3. See Hermann Diels, 'Über die Gedichte des Empedokles', *Ber. Berl. Ak.* 1898, pp. 396 ff.; Jean Bidez, *La biographie d'Empédocle* (Ghent, 1894).

4. Ettore Bignone, *Empedocle* (Turin, 1916). See the first chapter of his book, 'Considerazioni generali'.

5. Empedocles is regarded as a specific representative of Sicilian culture by Plato (see *Soph.* 242 d), who speaks of his poem and philosophy as 'the Muses of Sicily'. Similarly Lucretius, loc. cit., celebrates him as the greatest product of the rich Sicilian soil (cf. i. 726–30).

6. See *supra*, p. 55.

7. See Pindar, *Ol.* ii. 62 f. (Cf. *supra*, p. 86.)

8. On the Orphic gold plates found in south Italian graves (Petelia, Thurii), see *supra*, p. 65.

9. Arist. *Poet.* i. 1447^{b}19.

10. The same Aristotle, in his book *On Poets*, called Empedocles 'Homeric' because of his language, and praised the abundance of his metaphors and other poetical devices (frg. 70, Rose). He called him the inventor of rhetoric (frg. 65).

11. See *supra*, p. 55.

12. Emp. B 3 (formerly 4).

13. Ibid. B 3 (4), 5. I have therefore translated εὐσεβίη 'awe' or 'reverence' rather than 'holiness' (Burnet), see n. 20.

14. Ibid. B 3 (4), 4: ὧν θέμις ἐστὶν ἐφημερίοισιν ἀκούειν.

15. Parm. B 1, 16 f.

16. Ibid. B 8.

17. Ibid. B 7, 2 ff. (formerly B 1, 34 ff.).

18. Ibid. B 1, 27.

19. See *supra*, pp. 19–20.

20. The words (Emp. B 3 (4), 1) 'But, O ye gods, turn aside from me the madness of these men' must be referred to some bolder kind of speculation. Burnet, op. cit., p. 227, convincingly suggests that he meant Parmenides. Cf. Emp. B 3 (4), 5, πέμπε παρ' Εὐσεβίης ἐλάουσ' εὐήνιον ἅρμα, where he describes his own attitude as 'reverence'. What this εὐσεβίη is is shown clearly by the preceding line (quoted in n. 14). There Empedocles asks the Muse to bestow on him of her wisdom 'as much as is becoming for ephemeral man to hear'. In other words, this reverence manifests itself in its conscious self-limitation. It is contrasted with the madness of those who boasted 'to know the whole truth'. Cf. Emp. B 2, 6.

21. Emp. B 3 (4), 6–8.

22. Goethe, *Vermächtnis.* vv. 19–21 (*Sämtliche Werke*, Bd. 2 (*Jubiläums-Ausgabe*), p. 245).

23. Emp. B 3 (4), 9 f. Empedocles wants us to trust our senses, though only so far as they give us clear instructions.

24. See the polemic of the preceding lines, ibid. B 3 (4), 1–8.

25. Ibid. B 3 (4), 10–13.

26. Parm. B 7, 4–B 8, 1 (formerly B 1, 34–6).

27. Ibid. B 8, 12 ff.

28. Emp. B 8, B 9.

29. Cf. Arist. *Phys.* i. 4, 187ᵃ20 (Anaximander A 16).

30. See Simpl. *Phys.* 24, 26 ff., and 149, 32 (Anaximenes A 5).

31. Arist. *Metaph.* A 3, 984ᵃ8 ff. (Emp. A 28). Cf. also the following testimonia in Diels's *Vorsokratiker* i⁵.

32. Emp. B 11.

33. Ibid. B 12: ἔκ τε γὰρ οὐδάμ' ἐόντος ἀμήχανόν ἐστι γενέσθαι καί τ' ἐὸν ἐξαπολέσθαι ἀνήνυστον καὶ ἄπυστον. The whole thought of these lines is Parmenidean. The words ἀνήνυστον and ἄπυστον are taken from Parm. B 2 (formerly 4), 7 (where it is written ἀνυστόν) and B 8, 21.

34. Emp. B 6. What Aristotle later called the elements (στοιχεῖα) of Empedocles, he himself called 'the roots of all things' (ῥιζώματα πάντων).

35. The first step in this direction had been taken by the post-Hesiodic theogonies of the sixth century, with their increasing tendency to substitute allegoric deities, which clearly stand for physical principles, for the older Olympian and pre-Olympian gods of Hesiod's *Theogony*; see *supra*, pp. 55–72.

36. Emp. B 17, 13, calls them 'always existent' and 'unmoved in the cycle' (cf. B 26, 12). They are becoming and passing away in so far as they unite to bring things into existence and part in dissolving them again; but in so far as they never cease changing they are eternal and remain unmoved in the cycle. The subject of this whole paragraph can be supplied from the solemn repetition of the first lines, B 17, 1–2, in B 17, 16–17 (in B 17, 18 Empedocles expressly names fire, water, earth, and air). The neuter and masculine forms are used *promiscue* throughout the passage: 6, ἀλλάσσοντα; 7, συνερχόμενα; 8, φορεύμενα, &c. (*scil.* the elements); but 13 (cf. also B 26, 12), ταύτῃ δ' αἰὲν ἔασιν ἀκίνητοι (!) κατὰ κύκλον (*scil.* θεοί). Yet elements and gods are the same for Empedocles. Needless to say that he uses ἐόν and ἀκίνητον deliberately as categories of Parmenidean thought (cf. Parm. B 8, 26). Simplicius (*Phys.* 1124–5) understands the word ἀκίνητοι (Emp. B 17, 13 and 26, 12) as referring to the eternal sameness of the change (μεταβολή) and not to the elements themselves, but cf. also Emp. 35, 14: the formerly immortal elements become mortal when they come together and form the things of nature.

37. See Parm. B 8, 6, ὁμοῦ πᾶν, ἕν, συνεχές; B 8, 38, οὖλον; B 8, 42 f., τετελεσμένον, πάντοθεν ἴσον.

38. Emp. B 17, 7–8, 19–20; B 18–B 22, B 26. Instead of Φιλίη she is called also Φιλότης or Στοργή. Another word for Φιλίη is Γηθοσύνη. The word Νεῖκος is varied by Ἔρις, Κότος. See n. 39.

39. See Ἀφροδίτη, Emp. B 17, 24; B 22, 5; B 66; B 71, 23; B 86–B 87. She is called Κύπρις B 73; B 75; B 95; B 98, 3. The gods of the Greeks took a special pride in the many names (πολυωνυμία) by which they were invoked. Therefore Empedocles gives his elementary gods more than one name.

40. See *supra*, p. 15. Both Love and Hate in Empedocles are figures taken

from Hesiod's *Theogony* (224-5), where they are called Φιλότης and Ἔρις. But both are strongly individualized.

41. Empedocles' conception of Aphrodite inspired the famous hymn to Venus in the proem of the first book of Lucretius' *De rerum natura* (1-43). There Venus appears no longer as the goddess generally worshipped under this name but as the omnipotent creative force that permeates nature and animates all its beings. She is contrasted in Empedoclean manner with Mars, the god of war and strife, and she is the cause of peace and concord throughout the world (cf. i. 31 f.). Empedocles' conception of this divine force of nature, which he gives the name of Aphrodite and which possesses the qualities of Hesiod's cosmogonic Eros, seems to have been inspired by older Greek poets. The Hesiodic Eros had kept alive in philosophical as well as Orphic cosmogonic poems. In Aesch. *Danaides*, frg. 44, Nauck (Ath. xiii. 600 b), Aphrodite appeared for the first time instead of Eros, and in a long speech revealed the power of love (i.e. herself) as the all-pervading natural force which we meet some decades later in Empedocles. By choosing Aphrodite as his deity of creation, Empedocles not only rationalized the myth but also deified nature and made the mystery of life triumph over the realm of 'lifeless' matter.

42. See Emp. B 17; B 20, 2-5; B 22; B 26, where Aristotle (*Phys.* viii. 1, 250^{b}28 and 252^{a}8) supplies Philia and Neikos as subject of κρατέουσι, not the elements, as does Diels. See also Simplicius (*Phys.* 1183, 25), whom Diels wrongly quotes in favour of his own view (4th ed., p. 236). Kranz, in the fifth edition of Diels's *Vorsokratiker*, would like to refer the words to both, as he does in B 17, 27 (where Diels also refers Empedocles' words to the four elements only). See n. 48.

43. Emp. B 17, 21. He is speaking here of Love, but the same is true of Hate.

44. Ibid. B 17, 27-9.

45. Ibid. B 20.

46. Ibid. B 22.

47. Ibid. B 23. The 'long-lived gods' occur in B 23, 8, as well as in B 21, 12.

48. Ibid. B 17, 27. In the preceding lines, it is true, the plural of the neuter (δίχα τῶν and ἐν τοῖσιν, B 17, 19-20) refers to the four element-gods, and the mention of φιλότης compels the author to speak of her in the feminine. But then he comprises the four element-gods and the couple Neikos and Philia in B 17, 27, by speaking of ταῦτα πάντα. (Kranz, in the fifth edition of Diels's *Vorsokratiker*, now refers ταῦτα to both the elements and to Love and Hate, whereas Diels understood the four elements only.)

49. Emp. B 27.

50. Ibid. B 27, 4, Σφαῖρος κυκλοτερής.

51. Parm. B 8, 43, εὐκύκλου σφαίρης ἐναλίγκιον ὄγκῳ.

52. Emp. B 27, 3. Harmonia is taken from Hes. *Theog.* 975, where she is the daughter of Aphrodite. In Empedocles she has the individual gods of the four elements and the gods of Love and Hate firmly in her control. This is an obvious imitation of Parmenides' Diké (also called Ananké or Moira), who holds coming-to-be and passing-away firmly in bondage (see Parm. B 8, 30, 37, and 13, with our interpretation, *supra*, p. 227) and so prevents Being from being altered. Compared with this absolutist conception of Being, Empedocles' harmony of the element-gods under the rule of Sphairos is pluralist and democratic. (Cf. B 17, 27, where it is stated that they are 'all equal'; see *supra*, p. 140.)

53. Emp. B 28, ἀλλ' ὅ γε πάντοθεν ἴσος ⟨ἐοῖ⟩ καὶ πάμπαν ἀπείρων. Cf. Parm. B 8, 44, and especially B 8, 49, οἱ γὰρ πάντοθεν ἴσον. Hence P. Maas supplies ἐοῖ in the lacuna in Emp. B 28 (ἔην, Diels).

54. In making his Being (ἐόν) infinite like the *apeiron* of Anaximander, Empedocles may be following the younger Eleatic school, for Melissus of Samos had reinterpreted the finite Being of Parmenides in the same way. He wrote probably a few years before Empedocles composed his poem *On Nature*.

55. Simpl. *Phys.* 1124, 1, expressly states that Empedocles (B 31) called Sphairos a god.

56. Emp. B 27, 4 (cf. B 28, 2), Σφαῖρος κυκλοτερὴς μονίῃ περιηγέϊ γαίων. Empedocles' stereotyped phrase μονίῃ περιηγέϊ γαίων, which stresses the divine personality of the Sphairos, is a deliberate imitation of similar phrases in Homer, such as κύδεϊ γαίων.

57. See Simpl. *Phys.* 1183, 28 (Eudemus, frg. 71, Spengel): Εὔδημος δὲ τὴν ἀκινησίαν ἐν τῇ τῆς Φιλίας ἐπικρατείᾳ κατὰ τὸν Σφαῖρον ἐκδέχεται.

58. Tyrtaeus, frg. 1, 15 Diehl. Burnet, *Early Greek Philosophy*, 4th ed., p. 210, n. 3, had denied the possibility that the word μονίη could mean 'rest' and understood it with Diels as 'solitude'.

59. Xenophanes (B 26) says of his god, αἰεὶ δ' ἐν ταὐτῷ μίμνει κινούμενος οὐδέν, | οὐδὲ μετέρχεσθαί μιν ἐπιπρέπει ἄλλοτε ἄλλῃ. Cf. Parm. B 8, 29, on true Being: ταὐτόν τ' ἐν ταὐτῷ τε μένον καθ' ἑαυτό τε κεῖται | χοὕτως ἔμπεδον αὖθι μένει.

60. See *supra*, n. 36.

61. See Hippol. *Ref.* vii. 29, p. 247, 34; Simpl. *Phys.* 1124, 1.

62. Emp. B 29. Cf. Xenoph. B 23, 2, οὔτε δέμας θνητοῖσιν ὁμοίιος οὔτε νόημα. For the predicate of the Sphairos πάντοθεν ἴσος ἑαυτῷ (see also n. 53), we again find the model in Parmenides B 8, 49, οἱ γὰρ πάντοθεν ἴσον, where the οἱ equals ἑαυτῷ (Burnet, op. cit., p. 176, 49, wrongly takes it to be the relative pronoun, not the reflexive). Cf. also Parm. B 8, 57, ἑωυτῷ πάντοσε τωὐτόν.

63. Emp. B 30.

64. Ibid. B 35.

65. Heracl. B 53. See *supra*, p. 118

66. See the description of Strife in Emp. B 17, 8, and B 26, 6, Νείκεος ἔχθει; B 17, 19, Νεῖκος οὐλόμενον; B 115, 14, Νείκεϊ μαινομένῳ; B 20, 4, κακῇσι . . . Ἐρίδεσσι. Cf. B 22, 8: Strife keeps things separate from and unfamiliar with each other καὶ μάλα λυγρά. λυγρός is in Homer the usual epithet of 'ruin' (ὄλεθρος).

67. See ibid. B 115, 9–11.

68. On Strife see ibid. B 115, 4 and 14; on the realm of Love see B 128, 3.

69. Ibid. B 35, 1.

70. Ibid. B 112.

71. Empedocles' medical theories are discussed by M. Wellmann, *Die Fragmente der Sikelischen Ärzte* (Berlin, 1901), pp. 15, 21, 23, 35 f., 45, 49, 69 f., 104 f. See the tradition on Empedocles as a physician in Emp. A 1, § 58, 60 f., 69; A 2–A 3. Cf. also Hipp. *De vet. med.* 20 on his influence on contemporary medicine.

72. On Empedocles' political career see the reports by Aristotle (frg. 66, Rose) in Diog. L. viii. 63, and by the historian Timaeus, ibid. 64 f. (Emp. A 1).

73. Emp. B 112, 4. Timaeus referred to this passage when he remarked (in books xi and xii) on the striking contrast between his political faith in equality and his exaggerated opinion of himself in his poems. See Diog. L. viii. 66, Emp. A 1.

74. Ibid. B 113.

75. Ibid. B 114.

76. Ibid. B 114, 2–3. The concept of πίστις came to him from Parmenides' poem (B 1, 30; B 8, 50). Cf. Empedocles' poem *On Nature* B 3 (4), 10 and 13; B 4 (5), 1–2; B 71, 1.

77. They are perceptible only to the mind, not to the eyes; see ibid. B 17, 21.

78. Ibid. B 115.

79. Hes. *Works and Days*, 121 f. But Hesiod's demons are the former generation of blessed men who lived on earth in the Golden Age.

80. Emp. B 136.

81. Sext. Emp. ix. 127.

82. Xenoph. B 7.

83. Emp. B 137.

84. Ibid. B 126.

85. Ibid. B 127.

86. Ibid. B 115, 13–14.

87. Ibid. B 115, 6–8.

88. Ibid. B 117.

89. Ibid. B 109, 10, says that everything possesses consciousness and shares in thinking.

90. Ibid. B 119.

91. Ibid. B 118. The earth, not the underworld, is probably to be understood by the words ἄτης λειμών, ibid. B 121, 4. See Erwin Rohde, *Psyche*, i (7th and 8th ed.), p. 178, no. 1, as against Ernst Maass, *Orpheus* (Munich, 1895), p. 113.

92. Emp. B 120.

93. Ibid. B 115, 9–12.

94. Ibid. B 121, 1.

95. Verg. *Aeneid* vi. 273 f.

96. In epic tradition the journey to Hades was undertaken not only by Odysseus (*Od.* xi), but also by Hercules and by Theseus and Pirithous. The old epic poem called the *Nostoi* contained a *Nekyia* too. See E. Rohde, *Psyche*, i, p. 302, n. 2. Later centuries possessed an Orphic poem under the title Κατάβασις εἰς Ἅιδου, but it is unlikely that it was of pre-Empedoclean origin. It seems to have been composed during the Hellenistic age. Eduard Norden in the *Einleitung* to his *Vergils Aeneis Buch VI* has proved that Virgil followed an epic poem of this sort as model for his κατάβασις of Aeneas.

97. Emp. B 122. There exists another fragment containing a similar list of couples of deified physical and spiritual entities in B 123. It enriches the picture of the theogonic character of Empedocles' poetry and thought.

98. Ibid. B 115, 14.

99. Ibid. B 124.

100. Ibid. B 128.

101. Ibid. B 128.

102. Ibid. B 130.

103. Ibid. B 129.

104. See the rule forbidding the eating of beans, ibid. B 141.

105. Ibid. B 2. On man's limited experience see also B 39, 3.

106. Ibid. B 129. 6.

107. Ibid. B 115, 13 f. Cf. B 124.

108. See *supra*, p. 71, for what we have said on the position of allegorizing theogonic poetry after the time of Hesiod, and its relationship to Ionian natural philosophy.

Chapter IX

THE TELEOLOGICAL THINKERS: ANAXAGORAS AND DIOGENES

1. Diog. L. ii. 7 (Anaxag. A 1).

2. This consciousness of his form of life (βίος) is expressed in another anecdote, Diog. L. ii. 10. When asked what he was born for, Anaxagoras answered: 'For the contemplation (θεωρία) of sun, moon, and heaven.' But this story is also told of Pythagoras.

3. Plat. *Apol.* 26 d (Anaxag. A 35).

4. See Plin. *N.H.* ii. 149; Plut. *Lys.* 12 (Plutarch takes his information from Daïmachus' Περὶ εὐσεβείας), and other later ancient authors quoted by Diels (Anaxag. A 11–A 12).

5. On the sun as a glowing stone, see Diog. L. ii. 8 (Anaxag. A 1); on the meteoric stone of Aegospotami, see the passages quoted in n. 4.

6. On this empirical trend, see T. Gomperz, *Greek Thinkers*, i, pp. 307–15; *Paideia*, iii, p. 17; Hugo Berger, *Geschichte der wissenschaftlichen Erdkunde der Griechen* (Leipzig, 1903), p. 51.

7. On the constructive spirit of early Greek ἱστορίη, see *Paideia*, i², p. 157.

8. The classical representatives of this methodical attitude in Greek medicine are the Hippocratic authors of *On Ancient Medicine* and of the first three books of the 'Επιδημίαι. See *Paideia*, iii, pp. 17–19, and T. Gomperz, op. cit. i, pp. 310 ff.

9. Anaxagoras' methodical principle is formulated in B 21 a: ὄψις γὰρ τῶν ἀδήλων τὰ φαινόμενα. Accordingly, his theory of *homoeomeries* is based not on mere speculation but on the observation of certain phenomena. We get a hint as to the methodical point of departure of Anaxagoras' physics in B 10. There it is stated that he wondered how out of the same sperm the most diverse parts of an organic body (such as hair, nails, veins, arteries, sinews, and bones) could develop if these substances were not all contained in the sperm from the beginning. Of course, there were other observations taken from colours or from mechanics by which Anaxagoras tried to support his conclusion. But that he started from the problem of the nourishment and growth of organic bodies

is confirmed by Simpl. *ad Arist. Phys.* iii. 4, 203ᵃ19 ff. (Anaxag. A 45). Simplicius says that Anaxagoras was influenced by the consideration of the phenomena of τροφή. Cf. also Anaxag. A 46.

10. See 'Hippocrates', *On Ancient Medicine*, 20.

11. See *supra*, p. 106.

12. See Emped. B 8, Anaxag. B 17. Both agree that the words for becoming and passing-away ought not to be used in their strict sense, for what happens in reality is only a process of mixing and unmixing of certain basic elements. This idea obviously influenced Euripides' chorus in the lost drama *Chrysippus* (frg. 839 Nauck), θνῄσκει δ' οὐδὲν τῶν γιγνομένων κτλ. See also Anaxag. A 43.

13. Alcmaeon B 4. He uses the term κρᾶσις, as does Parm. B 16, 1. Empedocles often speaks of κρᾶσις but also of μίξις. Anaxagoras seems to prefer μίξις and μίγνυσθαι. The sharp distinction of both words which we find later in Stoic philosophy does not seem to have existed yet in the authors of the fifth century.

14. In the Hippocratic writings the notion of mixture holds a dominant position, and from there it invaded all fields of Greek thought: the theory of education, the State, the soul, etc.

15. On this influence in general, see my *Paideia*, iii, pp. 5 ff.

16. 'Hippocrates', *On the Sacred Disease*, c. 1. This traditional use of the words ἱερὴ νοῦσος must have become a problem for physicians trained in the school of Ionian natural philosophy, for in it the synonymous word 'divine' (θεῖον) had acquired a different meaning ('natural causality'), which we have traced throughout this book. See the sarcastic characterization of the magicians and quacks who pretended to possess certain religious rites for the treatment of the 'sacred disease', op. cit., c. 2.

17. Herod. iii. 33. The illness of Cambyses, according to Herodotus, develops gradually: although he has had this epileptic disposition from early youth, its fits are connected with the crimes which he perpetrates, and follow his evil deeds like a divine Nemesis; see iii. 30, after the killing of the Egyptian Apisbull, where Herodotus expressly states that the *post hoc* was a *propter hoc*. On the other hand, in iii. 33 Herodotus seems to hold the more modern view that the pathological disposition of his body was the condition of a similar weakness of Cambyses' mind.

18. On Hesiod's idea of divine retribution, see my 'Solons Eunomie' (*Ber. Berl. Ak.*, 1926), p. 77 f. However, it is not easy to distinguish sharply between the theological and the physical aspects of Herodotus' explanation of Cambyses' illness; see n. 17. Even the Ionian philosophers of nature interpreted causality in nature, including the nature of the human body, as a kind of natural retribution. See my *Paideia*, i², pp. 161, 182. On the Hippocratic writings, cf. *Paideia*, iii, pp. 6 ff. Herodotus himself often gives the concept of νέμεσις, τίσις, &c., this wider application, which makes nemesis a kind of natural causation and compensation. On this problem in general, see K. Pagel, *Die Bedeutung des aitiologischen Momentes bei Herodot* (Berlin diss., 1927), and the criticism of F. Hellmann in *Herodots Kroisos-Logos* (*Neue philol. Untersuch.*, ed. W. Jaeger, vol. ix, 1934), p. 7.

19. 'Hippocrates', *On the Sacred Disease*, c. 21. Cf. c. 1. It is true, also, that the Hippocratic writers often speak of illness in terms of a disturbance of the divine equilibrium of the forces of nature, but they do not see a τιμωρίη in the illness. Rather, they use the terms τιμωρεῖν or βοηθεῖν in connexion with

the medical cure of an illness by which the physician tries to restore a disturbed balance. See *Paideia*, iii, p. 6, with n. 11. The notions of sin and punishment are entirely absent from this conception of a δίκη and τίσις in nature.

20. See *supra*, pp. 29, 31, &c.

21. See *supra*, p. 157, with n. 12. Cf. Arist. *Phys.* i. 4, 187ª26 ff. (Anaxag. A 52).

22. Anaxag. B 1.

23. On the separating-out (ἀποκρίνεσθαι), see ibid. B 2, B 4, B 7, B 9, B 12, B 16.

24. Ibid. B 12 (last sentence).

25. See n. 9.

26. See ibid. B 10.

27. The fact as such was observed by Plato, *Phaedo* 97 b, and Arist. *Metaph.* A 3, 984ᵇ15 (Anaxag. A 47, A 58).

28. See *supra*, p. 130.

29. Anaxag. B 11.

30. See *supra*, p. 159.

31. Ibid. B 12, *fin.*; cf. B 11: ἐν παντὶ παντὸς μοῖρα ἔνεστι πλὴν νοῦ, ἔστιν οἷσι δὲ καὶ νοῦς ἔνι.

32. Ibid. B 12, *init.*: τὰ μὲν ἄλλα παντὸς μοῖραν μετέχει, νοῦς δὲ ... μέμεικται οὐδενὶ χρήματι, ἀλλὰ μόνος αὐτὸς ἐπ' ἑωυτοῦ ἐστιν. Evidently the idea contained in B 11 that νοῦς exists in some things (see n. 31) does not contradict this statement. Even in them the νοῦς is not 'mixed'. This Anaxagoras concludes from the very fact that νοῦς is to be found only in some things. All other things are mixed with everything else.

33. Ibid. B 12.

34. Diels translated ἄπειρον by *unendlich*. K. Deichgraeber, *Philologus*, lxxxviii, p. 348, rejects this interpretation because he thinks it does not strictly fit the antithesis. If 'the other things' are all mixed with one another, the Nous must be unmixed. Deichgraeber understands ἄπειρον in this unusual figurative sense (= πεῖραν ἔχον οὐδενός). He compares the sophist Antiphon (B 10), who says of God: οὐδενὸς δεῖται οὐδὲ προσδέχεται οὐδενός τι, ἀλλ' ἄπειρος καὶ ἀδέητος. There the antithesis is a similar one, and the new interpretation appears quite plausible at first sight. Anaxagoras obviously wanted to attribute to his Nous a predicate which in the theological speculation of other pre-Socratics belonged only to God. Deichgraeber points this out very convincingly. The question is only whether this is not an argument that could also be used in favour of ἄπειρος = infinite. Quite apart from the fact that Anaxagoras himself uses the word exclusively in this sense in other passages (see A 43, A 45, A 50, B 1, B 2, B 4), it had always been used so in connexion with the divine principle of the universe by his philosophical predecessors (see *supra*, pp. 28 ff.). Aristotle discusses this predicate in the sense of 'infinite' in his theology (*Metaph.* Λ 7, 1073ª5 ff.), and he evidently does so not because he approves of it himself but because the tradition of Greek philosophical theology offered him this category as one of the fundamental predicates of the Divine, like ἀπαθές, ἀναλλοίωτον, &c. Furthermore, Deichgraeber's argument that if ἄπειρον were equivalent to 'infinite' it would not give us the required logical antithesis to the preceding words (τὰ μὲν ἄλλα παντὸς μοῖραν μετέχει), and that therefore ἄπειρον must mean 'unmixed, unadulterated', is vulnerable, because the

following words καὶ αὐτοκρατές do not convey this idea of the unmixed either, which is added only by the third predicate καὶ μέμεικται οὐδενὶ χρήματι. It is neither possible nor necessary to make all three predicates say the same thing, that the Nous is unmixed, nor should we expect such tautological language in a theological predication like this. The analogy of other passages of the same kind would be rather in favour of an enumeration of different predicates of God, among which, in Anaxagoras' Nous-theology, the predicate 'unmixed' naturally would obtain a prominent place—the third and last. The combination of ἄπειρος and ἀδέητος as predicates of God in the parallel passage from Antiphon quoted by Deichgraeber (see *supra*) allows the same interpretation. The predicate ἀδέητος, on which Antiphon places the main emphasis, follows directly from God's infiniteness, for only he who comprises in his own nature everything that exists is not in need of anything else.

35. See Deichgraeber's article quoted in n. 34.

36. See *supra*, p. 31.

37. See the examples quoted *supra*, pp. 31, 49, 96, 115, 138, 166.

38. On the stylistic form of the theology of the pre-Socratic thinkers, see *supra*, p. 202, and the observations of Deichgraeber, loc. cit.

39. See *supra*, p. 47.

40. But on Anaximenes see *supra*, p. 36. He seems to have chosen air as his first principle on both physical and theological considerations.

41. Emp. B 134.

42. Heracl. B 108.

43. This was the conception of the supreme principle of the universe which the Ionian philosophers of nature had in mind from the beginning, and which was derived from the godlike nature of that rational principle. Applied to Anaxagoras' Nous, this conception must have seemed to gain new life and a more definite shape.

44. Anaxag. B 12: καὶ ἂν ἐκώλυεν αὐτὸν τὰ συμμεμειγμένα, ὥστε μηδενὸς χρήματος κρατεῖν ὁμοίως ὡς καὶ μόνον ἐόντα ἐφ' ἑαυτοῦ. ἔστι γὰρ λεπτότατόν τε πάντων χρημάτων καὶ καθαρώτατον, καὶ γνώμην γε περὶ παντὸς πᾶσαν ἴσχει καὶ ἰσχύει μέγιστον· καὶ ὅσα γε ψυχὴν ἔχει καὶ τὰ μείζω καὶ τὰ ἐλάσσω, πάντων νοῦς κρατεῖ.

45. Ibid. B 12: καὶ τῆς περιχωρήσιος τῆς συμπάσης νοῦς ἐκράτησεν, ὥστε περιχωρῆσαι τὴν ἀρχήν. On the comparison with modern astronomers, see T. Gomperz, *Greek Thinkers*, i, pp. 217 ff.

46. On the intelligence of the Nous, see Anaxag. B 12: καὶ γνώμην γε περὶ παντὸς πᾶσαν ἴσχει καὶ ἰσχύει μέγιστον (scil. νοῦς); on its effect on the life of the cosmos, cf. the second half of B 12. For the planning of the Nous, see especially the words πάντα ἔγνω νοῦς.

47. On Xenophon's *Memorabilia* and Diogenes of Apollonia, see *infra*, p. 244.

48. See *supra*, n. 27.

49. Anaxag. B 12 (towards the end).

50. Cf. the similar consideration in Xen. *Mem.* i. 4, 8 and 17.

51. On the concept of the 'aim' of life (τέλος) and its origin from Socrates' ethical inquiries on the nature of the good (ἀγαθόν), see my *Paideia*, ii, pp. 68 ff., 120.

52. This is criticized by Plato's Socrates in *Phaedo*, 97 b, Arist. *Metaph.* A 4, 985ᵃ18, and Eudemus, frg. 21, Spengel; see Anaxag. A 47.

53. Certain features of Diogenes' philosophy of nature, especially his natural theology, which proclaimed his cosmic principle Air as the god who rules the universe, were parodied by Aristophanic comedy, as modern scholars have been able to demonstrate; see H. Diels in *Ber. Berl. Ak.*, 1891. See also the comic allusion to Diogenes' theology in Philemon frg. 91, Kock. There the god Air makes his personal appearance and proves his divine nature by his omnipresence.

54. We find a similar trend towards philosophical speculation in some of the greatest exact scientists of our age, such as Max Planck, Albert Einstein, Otto Schroedinger, Svante Arrhenius, and others.

55. Diog. B 2.

56. Ibid. A 5, A 7, A 8, A 9. Cf. B 5.

57. Ibid. B 3.

58. Ibid. B 3: οὐ γὰρ ἄν, φησίν, οἷόν τε ἦν οὕτω δεδάσθαι ἄνευ νοήσιος, ὥστε πάντων μέτρα ἔχειν. The criteria of the presence of a creative mind in the universe are measure and perfection (μέτρα ἔχειν and διακεῖσθαι κάλλιστα).

59. Diog. B 5. Notice, as in Anaxagoras' Nous-theology, the stylistic form of Diogenes' statement about his first principle:

καὶ ὑπὸ τούτου
πάντας καὶ κυβερνᾶσθαι
καὶ πάντων κρατεῖν·
αὐτὸ γάρ μοι τοῦτο θεὸς δοκεῖ εἶναι
καὶ ἐπὶ πᾶν ἀφῖχθαι
καὶ πάντα διατιθέναι
καὶ ἐν παντὶ ἐνεῖναι.
καὶ ἔστιν οὐδὲ ἕν ὅ τι μὴ μετέχει τούτου

The form of the arrangement of the divine predicates (a δίκωλον and a τρίκωλον), all beginning with forms of the word πᾶς, is the *typos* of a hymn. The predicates of Diogenes' God follow the pattern of earlier pre-Socratic thinkers; see *supra*, pp. 203 ff., where I have given a comparative analysis of this form of theological thought. See Deichgraeber, loc. cit., p. 354. Cf. Euripides' imitation of this theology in Hecuba's prayer to the Air, *Troad.* 884: 'Thou, earth's support, enthroned on the earth, whoever thou mayst be, hard to discover, Zeus, be thou nature's law or the mind of man, I pray to thee : for by a noiseless course thou guidest human fate in righteousness.' The godhead invoked cryptically in the first line is Air. Euripides takes this *theologoumenon* from Diogenes, his contemporary, who lived in Athens. What Hecuba's words add to the theology of Diogenes is the effort of the poet to give this cosmic deity two more qualities which are required in a god to whom mortals can pray : that he must have a conscious mind, and that he must represent a supreme law in accordance with which he rules the world in righteousness.

Diog. C 2 and C 3 show two more traces of the influence of Diogenes' Air-theology on contemporary Greek literature. They are the more interesting because they are found not in poetic works but in a strictly scientific context, in the 'Hippocratic' treatises *On Breaths*, 3 (vi. 94, Littré) and *On Flesh*, 2 (viii. 584, Littré). The former of these passages praises Air as the cause of the life of the body and as a great power in nature. As gods used to have the honour of more than one name, so this god is called Breath in the body of organic creatures and Air in the universe. He is predicated as μέγιστος ἐν τοῖς πᾶσι τῶν πάντων δυνάστης (notice the imitation of Diogenes), and his omnipresence is praised as in Philemon's comedy (see *supra*, n. 53). 'Hippocrates', *On Flesh*, c. 2, transfers this kind of predication from the Air to the Warm (θερμόν): 'And it seems to me that what we call the Warm is immortal and thinks everything and sees and hears and knows everything, that which is and that which will be.' The author of this interesting book has a clear mind and is a serious scientific personality. This turn from pure physical observation to theological thought in the words quoted above proves only how closely connected these two aspects of pre-Socratic philosophy appeared to him.

60. Diog. B 7.

61. Ibid. B 8.

62. Simpl. *Phys.* 151, 20 ff. (Diog. A 4).

63. Arist. *Hist. an.* iii. 2, 511^{b}30 (Diog. B 6).

64. Diog. B 5. There are many forms (τρόποι) of the air and of the mind (νόησις). Therefore the air is called πολύτροπος several times. In the same way, Hippocratic medicine speaks of the many τρόποι of illness.

65. See *supra*, p. 140.

66. It is the original pantheistic trend of the early Greek monists that revives in Diogenes' view of the world. Later it revived once more in Stoic philosophy, which seems to be indebted to Diogenes.

67. Anaxag. B 12.

68. See Xen. *Mem.* i. 4 and iv. 3.

69. See *supra*, n. 27.

70. Ibid. i. 4 (conversation of Socrates with Aristodemus). On Aristodemus' deism, see ibid. i. 4, 11.

71. Ibid. i. 4, 5–8.

72. Cf. ibid. i. 4, 6 ff., with Arist. *De part. an.* ii. 15, 658^{b}14 (cf. also 661^{b}7). Xenophon and Aristotle have some of their arguments in common, others occur only in one of these two; but all belong to the same source and have the same stamp. On the problem of the origin of Socrates' arguments in this chapter of Xenophon's *Memorabilia*, see W. Theiler, *Zur Geschichte der teleologischen Naturbetrachtung bis auf Aristoteles* (Zürich, 1925), p. 18 f. (on Aristotle and Xenophon, see p. 24 f.). Theiler quotes the older literature, p. 18. Cf. F. Duemmler, *Akademika* (Giessen, 1889), p. 96 f., who was the first to see that Diogenes must be the source of Xenophon, and especially S. O. Dickerman, *De argumentis quibusdam apud Xenophontem Platonem Aristotelem obviis e structura hominis et animalium petitis* (diss., Halle, 1909).

73. See W. Theiler, op. cit., p. 38, and Dickerman, op. cit., p. 36 f., on parallels in Xen. *Mem.* i. 4 and Euripides, *Suppl.* 201–13. On Diogenes in Attic comedy (Aristophanes, Philemon), see Theiler, op. cit., p. 50.

74. See the literature quoted in n. 72.

75. Xen. *Mem.* i. 4, 2 and 11. Cf. iv. 3, 2; 12; 15–18. On Xenophon's adaptation of his philosophical source to his own religious needs and ideas, see Theiler, op. cit., p. 49 f.

76. Xen. *Mem.* i. 4, 6. Xenophon's Socrates calls all these provisions of nature for the security and preservation of man's life the product not of blind accident (τύχη) but of conscious planning (γνώμη), i.e. of art (τέχνη). He speaks of nature as a δημιουργός and of her activity as δημιουργεῖν. It is perfectly

believable that this term had been used by previous philosophers who, like Diogenes, interpreted nature in this teleological way. See Theiler, op. cit., p. 52.

77. The eye is like the sun's disc, according to Arist. *Thesm.* 14, and the ears are like funnels, *Thesm.* 18. In *The Clouds* he lends Socrates some features taken from Diogenes, as we have seen *supra*, n. 53. The nose is compared to a wall (τεῖχος) dividing the face into two halves by Cic. *De nat. deor.* ii. 143, in a passage full of the same comparisons of parts of human nature with technical tools or inventions. It occurs also in Xen. *Symp.* v. 5 ff. Aristotle (see n. 72) has several other analogies of this sort in common with Xenophon. He has taken them all from his and Xenophon's common source, Diogenes. We find a similar analogy of the tongue with a sponge quoted expressly from Diogenes, Aët. iv. 18, 2 (Diels, *Doxographi*, p. 406); see Diog. A 22.

78. Xen. *Mem.* iv. 3, 3–9.

79. Diog. B 3.

80. In Xen. *Mem.* i. 4, 5 ff., the argument from the purposeful construction of human nature is the basis of Socrates' reflections on the gods. But in book iv. 3, 3–9, the cosmological and meteorological argument is put into the foreground. Nevertheless, Socrates adds to it, iv. 3, 11 ff., other reasons taken from the structure of human nature, beginning with the nature and function of the senses (as in i. 4, 5), though this part of the demonstration is only given in rough outline in book iv (it is evident that Xenophon has cut his source at this point, perhaps because he did not want to repeat what he had already taken from it and used in book i. 4, 5 ff.).

81. See *supra*, p. 43.

82. Ibid. iv. 3, 13. This argument for the existence of God from his works (ἔργα) became the main proof of the Stoics. It is found likewise, of course, in the Old Testament.

83. One may say with Erich Frank, *Philosophical Understanding and Religious Truth* (N.Y., 1945), p. 33 (see also p. 49), that for the Greeks the problem of God's existence did not have the same importance which it assumed later within the Christian world, when God was conceived as transcendent, and that the primary concern of the Greek philosophers was rather with the *natura deorum*. But this is true most of all in the early period, which took the existence of the Divine in the universe for granted and turned immediately to the problem of what it was like and how it could be approached by reason. Xenophon shows that at the time of the Sophists the existence of the gods was often regarded as doubtful, or at least incapable of proof in any direct way, and therefore had to be proved from what was obviously the work of some higher creative intelligence.

84. Xen. *Mem.* iv. 3, 14. In Diogenes' cosmology the soul of the universe, Air, builds its own body, so to speak. This is possible through a process of gradually differentiated alterations (ἑτεροιώσεις) of the primal substance; see Diog. B 5.

85. Xen. *Mem.* i. 4, 9.

86. See *supra*, p. 21.

87. Ibid. i. 4, 8.

88. Ibid. i. 4, 9. Cf. the same argument, iv. 3, 14.

89. Plat. *Phileb.* 28 c.

90. On Diogenes' close relationship to Anaxagoras, see Simpl. *Phys.* 25, 1 (Diog.
A 5; Theophr. *Phys. opin.* frg. 2). Diogenes' cosmology presupposes Anaxagoras' theory of Mind as the principle which has ordered the universe (διεκόσμησε πάντα). This is particularly evident in Diog. B 5, where he introduces
his Air-theory. Obviously taking for granted that Anaxagoras is right in
postulating as the first cause of the world a divine Mind, Diogenes says:
'And it seems to me that the thinking principle (τὸ τὴν νόησιν ἔχον) is the so-
called air and that it is this which steers all things and rules all things.' In
other words, air is the material principle which seems to Diogenes best to
explain the existence of an all-powerful Mind in the world at the beginning of
the cosmogonic process. The same is stated again in the last sentence of B 5.
He points out first that according to the various forms (τρόποι) of modification
(ἑτεροίωσις) of the primal substance (air) which have produced variegated
kinds of creatures, they all have different degrees of νόησις (consciousness?);
but at the end of B 5 Diogenes reasserts that nevertheless they all live and see
and hear and possess all other forms of νόησις from one and the same principle
(i.e. air). So the identity of Nous and Air is maintained throughout the long
demonstration as Diogenes' original idea. Accordingly, death is defined in
B 4 as the state in which breathing and thinking (νόησις) have ceased. Perhaps
it was Anaxagoras himself who suggested this identification to Diogenes,
because, according to Anaxag. B 1 and B 2, air and ether were the elements
which prevailed in the primordial mixture of everything with everything, and
it was this mass of air and ether which the activity of the Nous first separated
out of the mass in the cosmogonic process.

91. Theophr. *De sens.* 42 (Diels, *Doxographi*, p. 510, Diog. A 19) tells us that
Diogenes distinguished the 'inner air' (ὁ ἐντὸς ἀήρ) in man from the air without.
The 'inner air', by virtue of which man has sense-perception (= soul), he called
'a small part of God' (μικρὸν μόριον θεοῦ), i.e. of the cosmic air. This peculiar
view enables us to understand the argument in Xen. *Mem.* i. 4, 8. There
Socrates proves his thesis (which is really the theory of Diogenes), that mind
exists not only in man but also in the universe, by showing that all other parts
of man's nature (such as fire, water, air, and earth) are to be found in the
cosmos, too, and in infinitely larger proportions than in the human body.
Therefore it would be arrogant for man to assume that mind alone existed
only in him and that he could monopolize it. This must have been a famous
argument in the philosophical discussion of the question whether mind exists
in the macrocosm as a creative principle. That Xenophon is here making his
Socrates pronounce doctrines of pre-Socratic origin is proved by the identical
argument in Plat. *Phileb.* 29 a, as has been shown convincingly by modern
scholars (see Theiler, op. cit., p. 21). In the *Philebus* Socrates expressly names
some earlier philosophers of nature (οἱ πρόσθεν ἡμῶν) as his source for this
argument to which he subscribes, and which he contrasts with the opposite
view that this world was produced by mere chance (τύχη). Both Xenophon's
and Plato's proofs of the existence of a divine creative mind are based on
Diogenes' argument that the human mind is 'only a small part of God', just as
the human body contains only a small part of the physical elements which
exist in the universe. This correlation of man and God, and the emphasis on
the smallness of the parts which man possesses compared with nature at large,
runs through Xenophon's and Plato's argument like a golden thread. Even
the details of their expression agree amazingly; see Socrates' ironic question
(Xen. *Mem.* i. 4, 8): 'If of all the other elements man's nature contains only
a small part compared with the great mass of them contained in the rest of
the world, do you think that he has somehow picked up his mind by a lucky

chance (εὐτυχῶς πως συναρπάσαι), and that there is no mind anywhere else?'
Similarly Plat. *Phileb.* 30 a writes: 'Does not our body have a soul? Whence
did it get that soul unless the body of the universe were animated, too, having
the same (soul) as the body of man and one even more perfect?' This is
Diogenes' view of the human soul as 'being only a small part of God'.

CHAPTER X

THEORIES OF THE NATURE AND ORIGIN OF RELIGION

1. On the origin of the concept of 'the Divine' (τὸ θεῖον), see *supra*, p. 31.

2. See the numerous passages discussed *supra*, p. 242, n. 37.

3. See p. 29.

4. See pp. 161, 166.

5. See *supra*, pp. 45, 50, 125.

6. Heracl. B 32.

7. On the spiral as the most fitting symbol of the historical development of
   Greek philosophical thought and its position in the life of Greek religion and
   society, see my 1943 Aquinas Lecture, *Humanism and Theology*, p. 54.

8. On the hymnic form of predication about 'the Divine' in the statements of
   the early thinkers, see *supra*, pp. 29 ff., and *passim*.

9. It is this opposition to the popular religion of the Greeks which predestined
   their philosophical theology later to become the natural ally of the Christian
   Church Fathers. See St. Augustine's statement *supra*, p. 3. But the religious
   ideas of the Greek philosophers never became a new popular religion themselves
   as did Christianity. They were not religion in the collective sense of the term.
   At the utmost they were the common religious creed of a philosophical sect
   in Hellenistic times. That is why the philosophical term 'sect' (αἵρεσις) was
   never applied to the Christian Church as a whole, but only to groups of dis-
   senters.

10. The nature of the universe (φύσις τοῦ παντός) was the object of the earliest
    philosophy of the Ionians. The nature of man (φύσις τοῦ ἀνθρώπου) is a part
    of that universal nature. It was made the centre of their pedagogical and
    sociological theories by the sophists and some of their contemporaries in the
    field of natural philosophy, such as Empedocles and Diogenes of Apollonia.

11. On the relationship of Hippocratic medicine to Greek natural philosophy,
    see my *Paideia*, iii, pp. 4–8, 15 f. The term φύσις τοῦ ἀνθρώπου occurs often in
    Greek medical literature, and in the Hippocratic school it was made the
    subject of separate books, such as the treatise of Hippocrates' son-in-law
    Polybus Περὶ φύσιος ἀνθρώπου.

12. On Heraclitus as the first philosophical 'anthropologist', see *Paideia*, i²,
    pp. 183 and 294, and *supra*, p. 117.

13. On the Sophists' 'educational trinity' of *physis*, *mathesis*, and *askesis*, see
    Paideia i², p. 312.

14. The connexion of Protagoras' educational theories with his views of State
    and society is made perfectly clear by Plato in the *Protagoras* 320 d–326 e,
    where he introduces the great Sophist as speaker on the subject of the

possibility of educating man. See *Paideia*, i², pp. 308–11. Plato must have felt justified in representing him thus, because the Sophist himself had stated his view of education in close connexion with his sociological theory. The latter was expounded in Protagoras' lost book Περὶ τῆς ἐν ἀρχῇ καταστάσιος. There it was presented in the same historical and genetic form as in the myth of Protagoras in Plato's dialogue. Protagoras' speech in the *Protagoras* refers continually to the conditions of primitive human society and the origin of civilization. That makes it highly probable that Plato used Protagoras' treatise on this subject as his source, and that it touched the educational problem in some form or other. Another book in which Protagoras treated the problems of State and society was his *Antilogies*; cf. Diog. L. iii. 37 (Protag. B 5).

15. Plat. *Protag.* 322 a.

16. See *supra*, p. 189.

17. Xen. *Mem.* i. 4, 2 ff. See *supra*, pp. 167 ff.

18. See Willi Theiler, *Geschichte der teleologischen Naturbetrachtung bis auf Aristoteles* (Zürich, 1925), pp. 36–54.

19. Xen. *Mem.* i. 4, 15.

20. Aesch. *Prom.* 457 ff. and 484 ff.

21. Xen. *Mem.* i. 4, 16.

22. Ibid. § 16.

23. Cf. Cic. *De nat. deor.* iii. 4, 9. On this problem see my article 'Authority and Freedom in Greek Thought' in the *Harvard Tercentenary Publication*.

24. Xen. *Mem.* i. 4, 16: τὰ πολυχρονιώτατα καὶ σοφώτατα τῶν ἀνθρώπων, πόλεις καὶ ἔθνη, θεοσεβέστατά ἐστι. Besides Xenophon's reference to religious tradition as the most reliable source of wisdom, there are other traces of a similar attitude in the period of Greek enlightenment. It finds its most impressive form in the words of the seer Tiresias in Euripides' *Bacchae* 200 ff.:

οὐδὲν σοφιζόμεσθα τοῖσι δαίμοσι,
πατρίας παραδοχὰς ἅς θ' ὁμήλικας χρόνῳ
κεκτήμεθ', οὐδεὶς αὐτὰ καταβαλεῖ λόγος.

The words for 'tradition' are here πάτριαι παραδοχαί. They are opposed to the rational criticism called λόγος. The defiant phrase οὐδεὶς αὐτὰ καταβαλεῖ λόγος plays on the boastful title of Protagoras' irreligious book, the Καταβάλλοντες λόγοι (Protag. B 1). καταβάλλειν is a metaphor taken from the wrestler who 'throws down' his opponent.

25. This is the philosophical conviction underlying the new respect for religious tradition which we found manifest in Socrates' words in Xenophon's *Memorabilia* and in Tiresias' defence of religion in Euripides' *Bacchae* (see n. 24). If I am right in my interpretation of Protagoras' pragmatism with regard to the problem of religious certainty (see this chapter, p. 189), the polemic of the new believers in God against Protagoras' Καταβάλλοντες λόγοι (see n. 24) is not quite fair, because the same man who had forged his logical arguments to destroy all rational certainty about the nature of the gods had in his philosophical positivism given them a strong weapon with which to defend their faith. See Protagoras' myth in Plat. *Protag.* 322 a (*supra*, p. 176).

26. The word ἐμφύειν, 'implant', is used by Xenophon several times with regard to the endowment of human nature in the fourth chapter of book i of the *Memorabilia* (§§ 7 and 16). There are other words such as διδόναι, προστιθέναι, συναρμόττειν, &c., which equally suggest the creative activity of a divine δημιουργός and his πρόνοια.

27. See the physiological arguments in Xen. *Mem.* i. 4, 5 ff., and iv. 3, 11 ff.

28. Ibid. iv. 3, 16.

29. Tiresias in Eurip. *Bacchae* 272 ff. wants to prove that Dionysus is a true god. He says that there are two divine gifts of special importance to mankind: bread and wine. Demeter and Dionysus are worshipped by mortals as the givers of these two blessings. Their adoration, therefore, appears as an act of gratitude; thus they are perfect examples of Prodicus' theory of the origin of religion. Euripides must actually have taken the argument from him. The Stoic Lucilius Balbus in Cic. *De nat. deor.* ii. 23, 59, quotes Prodicus extensively (though without giving his name) in a passage which is concerned with the origin of the idea of the gods in general, among them Ceres and Liber. In the same book the Stoic Cleanthes is said to have distinguished four reasons for the rise of the idea of gods in the mind of man, one of which is gratitude for the gifts of nature. It is taken from Prodicus' theory (*De nat. deor.* ii. 5, 13).

30. Philod. *De piet.* c. 9, 7, p. 75 G. Cic. *De nat. deor.* i. 37, 118 (Prodicus B 5). According to Philodemus, loc. cit., the Stoic Persaeus, too, had accepted Prodicus' theory of religion.

31. Sext. *Adv. math.* ix. 18 (Prod. B 5). See Eurip. *Bacchae* 272 ff. on the deity of Demeter and Dionysus (cf. n. 29). On the word νομισθῆναι in the context of Sextus' report, see *supra*, p. 226, nn. 36 and 46.

32. Sext., op. cit., ix. 52 (Prod. B 5).

33. Themist. *Or.* 30, p. 422 Dindorf (Prod. B 5).

34. See nn. 29, 30.

35. Democritus' theory of the gods, like that of Prodicus (see n. 29), was accepted by the Stoic Cleanthes. According to Cic. *De nat. deor.* ii. 5, 13, Cleanthes incorporated it in his own theory as the third of his *quattuor causae* of man's belief in the existence of gods. As in the case of Prodicus, Cleanthes in Cicero does not give the name of Democritus as an authority for this opinion. But the Democritean origin of the fear-theory will be sufficiently evident from our following discussion.

36. On Democritus' explanation of dream-visions as εἴδωλα, see Plut. *Quaest. conv.* viii. 10, 2, p. 734 F (Democr. A 77). The fact that he also explained the visions of gods and demons which men experience as εἴδωλα is reported by the author of Hermipp. *De astrol.* 122 (p. 26, 13, Kroll–Viereck) and by Clem. Alex. *Strom.* v. 88 (ii. 383, 25 St.) (Democr. A 78–9). Lucretius v. 1169 ff. likewise emphasizes dream-visions as a source of primitive man's belief in the existence of gods. His source, Epicurus, obviously followed Democritus' theory of the origin of religion.

37. Sext. *Adv. math.* ix. 19 (Democr. B 166).

38. Sext. loc. cit.: εἶναι δὲ ταῦτα μεγάλα τε καὶ ὑπερφυῆ καὶ δύσφθαρτα μέν, οὐκ ἄφθαρτα δέ.

39. Ibid.: ἔνθεν καὶ εὔχετο εὐλόγχων τυχεῖν εἰδώλων. The phrase εὐλόγχων τυχεῖν εἰδώλων seems to reproduce Democritus' original words.

40. Stob. ii (*Ecl. eth.*) 52, 40, Wachsmuth (Democr. B 297). This passage, if a genuine fragment of Democritus' work Περὶ εὐθυμίης, is the earliest one in which the noun 'conscience' (συνείδησις) appears in Greek tradition.

41. Lucretius iii. 978 ff. has preserved for us Democritus' theory that a bad conscience causes man's fear of punishment after death, just as he follows

Democritus in deriving the origin of the idea of gods from dream-visions (see n. 36). The claim of Epicurus' philosophy to free man from fear of the gods and fear of punishment after death was really suggested to him by Democritus' theory about the gods. But whereas Epicurus only takes away the threat of belief in an after-life, Democritus gives this thought an educational and moral turn.

42. Stob. iv. 5, 46 (Democr. B 264).

43. Sext. ix. 24 (Democr. A 75). Lucretius (v. 1183), who with his master Epicurus follows Democritus in this respect also, combines the motive of fear, with which natural phenomena inspired primitive man, with the theory of 'images' (*praeterea caeli rationes*).

44. Philod. *De piet.* 5 a, p. 69 G (Democr. A 75).

45. See n. 38.

46. Plat. *Protag.* 322 a.

47. Clem. Alex. *Protr.* 68 (i. 52, 16 St.); *Strom.* v. 103 (ii. 394, 21 St.); Democr. B 30.

48. See *supra*, p. 242, n. 37.

49. *Pap. Oxyrh.* xi. 1364, Hunt. See the text of the papyrus in Diels's *Vorsokratiker*, ii⁶, pp. 346 ff., frg. A, col. 1, 1–33. Cf. 1, 6.

50. See my *Paideia*, i², pp. 324–5; cf. also the preceding pages.

51. *Pap. Oxyrh.* 1364, frg. A, col. 1, 6, Diels.

52. Ibid. frg. A, col. 4, 3: τὰ μὲν ὑπὸ τῶν νόμων κείμενα δεσμὰ τῆς φύσεώς ἐστι, τὰ δ' ὑπὸ τῆς φύσεως ἐλεύθερα. Col. 2, 26 ff.: τὰ πολλὰ τῶν κατὰ νόμον δικαίων πολεμίως τῇ φύσει κεῖται. Cf. the examples given by Antiphon, ibid., frg. A, col. 4, 31, col. 5, 17.

53. Ibid., frg. A, col. 4, 8 ff.; col. 5, 17 ff.

54. Ibid., frg. A, col. 1, 12; col. 2, 23.

55. *Paideia*, i², pp. 327 ff., ii, pp. 204 ff.

56. Plat. *Rep.* 359 d.

57. See *supra*, p. 182, and n. 42 of this chapter.

58. This is the definition of Justice which Callicles gives in Plato's *Gorgias* and Thrasymachus in the *Republic*, book i. Cf. *Paideia*, i², p. 321, ii, p. 203.

59. The classic example of conflict between religious and State law is Sophocles' *Antigone*. What underlies it is the new experience of that generation, which is that of the Sophists, that even law can be arbitrary, because it is made by man. Religion still appears in the *Antigone* as an unshakable and eternal norm.

60. The long fragment of Critias' *Sisyphus* is preserved by Sextus, ix. 54 (Critias B 25).

61. On respect for the law as one of the foundations of Greek civilization, see my article 'Praise of Law: the Origin of Legal Philosophy and the Greeks' in *Interpretations of Legal Philosophy*: *Essays in Honor of Roscoe Pound* (N.Y. Oxford University Press, 1947), pp. 352–75.

62. Plat. *Gorgias* 482 e, 483 b–c. Cf. *Paideia*, ii, pp. 138 ff.

63. The most impressive representation of the divine sanction of law and the legal institutions of the modern democratic State of Athens is to be found in Aeschylus' *Eumenides*.

64. See *supra*, p. 183.

65. See *supra*, pp. 179–82. Critias' lawgiver combines the theory of fear (Democritus) and that of the gifts of nature (Prodicus) as the origin of the human belief in gods.

66. When Critias' lawgiver located his gods in heaven, because from heaven there appear to mortals all sorts of terrifying phenomena of nature, such as lightning, thunder, &c., he clearly took this feature from Democritus (A 75). Democritus also made his λόγιοι attribute the highest wisdom to their God in the same manner as Critias (Democr. B 30). Democritus also knew, as did Critias, that one of the functions of God in religion was to be the omniscient witness of all human deeds; this is proved by his derivation of the belief in punishment after death from man's bad conscience (Democr. B 297). On the other hand, Democritus' λόγιοι were not lawgivers but wise men, and it was Critias who stressed the practical and political use of religion as a means to rule the people. He made God's function as a witness of human deeds the very fulcrum of his theory. This theory has appealed to later statesmen: Polybius attributes to the Roman senate the same role which Critias gives to his early lawgiver, and religion (δεισιδαιμονία) appears to the Hellenistic historian as one of the most important vehicles of Roman statecraft.

67. Critias' theory of religion, if correct, would be an important example of Vaihinger's *Philosophie des Als ob*. This is particularly clear from such phrases as v. 16 of B 25, ἐντεῦθεν οὖν τὸ θεῖον εἰσηγήσατο, or the last verses quoted by Sextus from the *Sisyphus*:

οὕτω δὲ πρῶτον οἴομαι πεῖσαί τινα
θνητοὺς νομίζειν δαιμόνων εἶναι γένος.

That Critias' idea of God had for him the character of a conscious fiction is proved by vv. 24 ff., τούσδε τοὺς λόγους λέγων | διδαγμάτων ἥδιστον εἰσηγήσατο | [notice the repetition of this word from v. 16], ψευδεῖ καλύψας τὴν ἀλήθειαν λόγῳ. Critias' own nephew, Plato, transcended this social theory of religion, which must have interested him greatly, in the following generation. He did not think of God as a subjective fiction made by a clever lawgiver to keep the masses under the control of law, but by determining 'God' as the idea of good itself Plato demonstrated in his *Republic* that He was in reality the all-powerful force that kept the life of every community together. He thereby replaced fiction by reality and truth. See the end of this chapter and n. 76.

68. Sextus, *Adv. math.* ix. 18 (Prod. B 5), says that according to Prodicus primitive men accepted the belief in gods (ἐνόμισαν) because they deified the useful gifts of nature. The word νομισθῆναι is repeated when he cites Demeter and Dionysus as examples for this opinion. Cf. also Philod. *De piet.* c. 9, 7, p. 75 G (Prod. B 5), νενομίσθαι καὶ τετιμῆσθαι. Cicero, *De nat. deor.* i. 37, 118, who follows the same source as Philodemus, translates the phrase taken from Prodicus by *habitos esse deos*, but this is obviously not enough; cf. the famous words of the accusation of Socrates, Σωκράτης ἀδικεῖ οὓς ... ἡ πόλις νομίζει θεοὺς οὐ νομίζων. It is this element in νομίζω which Philodemus in his Hellenistic Greek wanted to express in paraphrasing it by νενομίσθαι καὶ τετιμῆσθαι.

69. Parmenides says (e.g. B 6, 8) that by the *communis opinio* of men the identity and non-identity of Being and Not-being has been accepted (νενόμισται), even though the opposite of this view is true. This is νόμος as opposed to φύσις, ἀλήθεια; and νενόμισται means 'it has been accepted as convention'.

70. Euseb. *P.E.* xiv. 3, 7; Diog. L. ix. 51 (Protag. B 4).

71. See Diels *ad* Protag. B 4.

72. Similarly Xenophanes (B 23) speaks of the oneness of the highest God and of his form (δέμας), which differs from that of man. Parmenides likens his Being to a well-rounded sphere (B 8. 43). Herodotus (ii. 53) says of Homer and Hesiod, whom he wants to represent as the fathers of all Greek theology, that they taught the Greeks about the names and honours and the forms (εἴδεα) of their gods. The Stoics taught that their cosmic deity was of spherical form. The Stoic Lucilius Balbus, in Cic. *De nat. deor.* ii. 1, 3, distinguishes the problem of the form of the gods (*quales sint*) from the more fundamental question of whether they exist or not (*esse deos*). On the form of the deity see *De nat. deor.* ii. 17, 45 ff., especially ii. 18, 47. These examples prove that the words in Protag. B 4, περὶ θεῶν οὐκ ἔχω εἰδέναι οὔθ' ὡς εἰσὶν . . . οὔθ' ὁποῖοί τινες ἰδέαν, are the only appropriate form of reference to the actual theological speculations of his predecessors, the Ionian philosophers of nature.

73. Protag. B 1.

74. With Protagoras' words (B 4) οὐκ ἔχω εἰδέναι compare Xenoph. B 34:

> καὶ τὸ μὲν οὖν σαφὲς οὔτις ἀνὴρ γένετ' (Plut., ἴδεν Sext.) οὐδέ τις ἔσται
> εἰδὼς ἀμφὶ θεῶν τε καὶ ἄσσα λέγω περὶ πάντων.
> εἰ γὰρ καὶ τὰ μάλιστα τύχοι τετελεσμένον εἰπών,
> αὐτὸς ὅμως οὐκ οἶδε· δόκος δ' ἐπὶ πᾶσι τέτυκται.

Cf. the similar evaluation of philosophical speculation on τὰ ἀφανέα and μετέωρα in 'Hippocrates', *De vet. med.*, c. 1, p. 572, Littré.

75. On the pragmatism of Protagoras, see my *Humanism and Theology*, p. 39.

76. See my treatment of Plato's new approach to the problem of God in *Paideia*, ii and iii (cf. also n. 67 of this chapter). Later philosophers mostly saw Plato's theological achievement in line with the cosmological theology of the pre-Socratic and Hellenistic philosophers of nature, and therefore stressed the importance of Plato's *Timaeus*. But Plato's new point of departure with regard to the problem is the Socratic dialectic of *areté* and its relation to society and State, as it appears in the sixth book of the *Republic*.

INDEXES

I

II

GREEK WORDS AND PHRASES

PRINTED IN GREAT BRITAIN
AT THE UNIVERSITY PRESS, OXFORD
BY VIVIAN RIDLER
PRINTER TO THE UNIVERSITY